APPLAUSE!

SUPPORTING THE BRECKENRIDGE MUSIC FESTIVAL

Live. Love. Laugh. Eat!

ENTERTAINING!

SUMMIT STYLE

*[handwritten inscription: To Allen
The Allen Family keys
Happy Cooking to Breck
& more visits to Breck
Janney & Russ
March 2011
(See pp 111 & 212)]*

The proceeds generated from the sale of *Entertaining! Summit Style!* will support the Breckenridge Music Festival, a 501 (C) (3), nonprofit organization.

ISBN #978-0-692-00575-0

To obtain additional copies of
ENTERTAINING! SUMMIT STYLE!
Use the order form at the back of the book.

First printing: 5,000 copies
printed in China.

Published by McGraphix Creative, Ltd.
201 North Ridge, St., Breckenridge, CO 80424
mcgraphixcreative.com

Welcome to life at high altitude!

If you ask long time residents why they live in Summit County, they NOTE the active life style, powerful mountains, tranquil scenery and down-to-earth people. Newcomers invariably say, "I came for the winter, but stayed for the summer." The Summit County community has a flavor and character of its own, which we hope you discover as you read this cookbook. We introduce you to a selection of our fine restaurants and talented chefs. We organize recipes into seasonal events that pepper our lives. Sidebars tell the story.

This cookbook is the volunteer effort of countless supporters of the Breckenridge Music Festival. Over 200 recipes were selected from more than a thousand submittals, each recipe tested and retested by scores of tasters. The ubiquitous "tasting party" defined the summer of 2009.

The cookbook is designed to help you create your menu, with a range of simple to elegant recipes. Each event has several choices, or you have the option to start from scratch by using the detailed index. We hope you feel the spirit of Summit County living as you use this cookbook; that you can feel the warm hospitality, energy, creativity and history of the people who live here.

In Summit County, we live life to the fullest. And we love to entertain. Welcome to our world!

The Applause! Cookbook Committee
Applause!, the volunteer fund raising committee
of the Breckenridge Music Festival

COOKBOOK COMMITTEE

CHAIR, Nancy Sawvell

CO-CHAIR
Maggie Ducayet

RESTAURANT LIAISON CO-CHAIRS
Sue Nelson
Mickey Sullivan

PHOTOGRAPHY CHAIR
Gene Sosville

EDITORIAL/ SIDEBAR CHAIR
Laura Dziedzic

SALES CHAIR
Nancy Karklins

MARKETING ADVISOR
Rob Matzke

RECIPE COLLECTION CHAIR
Terri Eaton

RECIPE TESTING CHAIR
Jo Ann Hess

TASTING LUNCHEONS CHAIR
Linda Ebright

TREASURERS
Linda Hague
Janet Ulrey

A word from the Maestro

For The Breckenridge Music Festival Cookbook 2010 — Maestro Gerhardt Zimmermann

Whoever tells a lie cannot be pure in heart—and only the pure in heart can make good soup.

— Ludwig van Beethoven

Ah! Food and Music (and a little drink). What a wonderful combination. Imagine eating a 14 course meal while listening to all nine of Ludwig's symphonies.

Actually, cooking and putting together an orchestra are not all that dissimilar. In both, you need a basic ingredient—in the main dinner dish it could be beef, chicken or fish. Or perhaps just pasta. For the orchestra that main ingredient or foundation would be the string section. After the all important decision of the main ingredient, we need to decide on the sauce: white sauce, flute; red sauce, oboe; cream sauce, clarinet; verde sauce, bassoon.

You thicken the sauce with butter - lots of butter: Piano

Vegetables anyone?
Broccoli - Accordion or Ukulele (I don't like broccoli)
Guacamole - Trumpets
Beans (any kind) - French Horns
Cauliflower - Trombones
Butternut Squash - Tuba

And finally, the herbs and spices. Here we need to use our imagination.

Basil -	Campanili (bells)
Cayenne pepper -	Xylophone
Chile pepper -	Snare Drum
Cilantro -	Ratchet (Don't care for this one either)
Nutmeg -	Bass Drum
Chives -	Triangle
Onion -	Tambourine
Rosemary -	Harp

GOOD EATING - HAPPY LISTENING

Breckenridge Music Festival

Featuring Year-Round Music In the Key of Excellence

The Breckenridge Music Festival has provided classical orchestral and chamber music performances to Summit County since 1980. The Festival has expanded its presence with additional performance series and education events. The festival's offerings include the Champagne Series, chamber concerts in private homes, Blue River Series, a non-classical series of performances of many genres and a Winter Series of concerts to provide year-round performances.

Key to the summer festival is the Breckenridge Music Festival Orchestra, a chamber orchestra of forty-five to fifty professional players, in residence for five weeks in July and August. Orchestra members are drawn from major symphonies and university faculties across the nation. The orchestra is under the artistic direction of principal conductor, Gerhardt Zimmermann. Orchestra members join guest artists as the featured performers in chamber music as well as orchestral concerts.

The festival's success is largely due to a supportive board, the fund-raising committee, Applause!, our generous donors and the community.

2010 BRECKENRIDGE MUSIC FESTIVAL, ADMINISTRATIVE STAFF:

Gerhardt Zimmermann,
    Musical Director and Conductor
Marcia Kaufmann,
    Executive Director
Rick F. Hansen,
    Director of Marketing and Administration,
    Blue River Series Manager
Mike Koscso,
    Orchestra Personnel Manager and Librarian

2010 BRECKENRIDGE MUSIC FESTIVAL ADVISORY COUNCIL:

Janis Bunchman
Sherrie Calderini
Jan Coles
Doris Koneman
Suzanne Lanuza
Nancy Macey
Randy Nations, MD
Anne Stonington
Richard Thomas
Shirley Thomas
Charles Tyler

2010 BRECKENRIDGE MUSIC FESTIVAL BOARD:

Mary Grace McAlister, President
Wally Ducayet, Treasurer
Rick Oshlo, Secretary
Genia Gallagher, VP, Applause!
Annette McGrew, VP, Performance
Jon Sawvell, VP, Fundraising
Allison Saxe, VP, Marketing
Dick Sosville, VP, Corporate Development
Hans Wurster, VP, Blue River Series
Linda Hague, Assistant Treasurer
Debbie Kullby, Chair, Champagne Series
Karen Hynds, Assistant Chair, Education and Exploritas/Elderhostel
Andy Lewis, Chair, Board Development and Nominating
Sally Lewis, Chair, Special Events
Stuart List, Chair, Community Development
Charlie Simpson, Chair, Administrative Services
Carol Simpson, Chair, Support Activities
Jack Thomas, Chair, Fundraising and Special Programs
Janet Ulrey, Chair, Applause! Gala
Mary Jane Wurster, Chair, Education and Exploritas/Elderhostel

Applause! is the fund-raising committee of the Breckenridge Music Festival, raising support dollars through special events since its creation in 1990. Applause! membership is open to all.

Throughout the year, Applause! Bon Appétit events are enjoyed by newcomers and long-time residents alike. An annual summer Gala raises additional funds for the Festival. Applause! events are designed to highlight the Festival's programs and activities, while building community in Summit County.

2010 APPLAUSE BOARD

Sharon Buzzell	Linda Ebright	Sandy Kuschnerus	Nancy Sawvell
Sherrie Calderini	Eileen Finkel	Sally Lewis	Gene Sosville
Pat DeCarli	Genia Gallagher, Chairman	Mary Grace McAlister	Sandy Terrill
Diana Dettmering	Judy Green	Annette McGrew	Pat Thomas
Marilyn Dobbs	Linda Hague	Sandi Perlstein	Janet Ulrey
Terri Eaton	Debbie Kullby	Crista Povar	Joyce Yob

Sponsors

*The production of **Entertaining! Summit Style!** would not have been possible without the financial contributions of our sponsors. We wish to offer our heartfelt thanks for their gifts.*

PLATINUM

Maggie and Wally Ducayet
Mary Grace and Hardy McAlister
Nancy and Jon Sawvell

Mary Jane and Hans Wurster
Joyce and Joe Yob

GOLD

Sue and Jim Aiken
Sally and Andy Lewis
Kathleen and John Schnobrich

Sue and Gary Stimac
Carre and John Warner

SILVER

Linda and Mike Anderson	Laura and Jerry Dziedzic	Pam and Jack O'Neil	Pat and Jack Thomas
Shirley and Jerry Becker	Sharon and Gary Fitzgerald	B J and Chuck Ordner	Debby and Jeff Underwood
Paige Beville and Jim Manwaring	Judy and Fred Green	Allison Saxe	Susan and Bryan Whitcomb
Maria and Tom Blong	Monique Haverhorn	Rebecca and Daniel Scheer	
Christine and Bob Dickemper	Mary and Dick Heend	Gene and Dick Sosville	

BRONZE

Kelly and Trip Butler	Linda and Rick Hague	Mary Lou Johns and John Rynes	Linda Kay and Pete Peterson
Diana and Don Dettmering	Laurel and Joe Harris	Caroline and Jim Nixon	Rebecca and Peter Podore
Judy and John Goebel	Debrah and Rob Irvine	Sharon and Steve Parry	Nancy and Chris Wackman
Becky and Mike Koscso			

Table of Contents

Select and create your own custom menus for these unique events to entertain with ease: Summit Style!

Opening Night

Heavy hors d'oeuvres and party specialties provide an elegant pre-concert repast.

Champagne Punch
Gold Rush Slush

Mango-Avocado Salsa with Crostini
Mini Reubens
Riverwalk Potatoes
Feta Custard in Phyllo
Seasonal Crudités with Mayonnaise Verte

Wasabi Crusted Seared Tuna
Maestro's Shrimp
Grilled Chicken Satay
Symphony Tenderloin Canapés

Amaretto Bundt Cake
Fudge Extraordinaire
Peaches and Raspberries in Puff Pastry

OPENING NIGHT

Excitement builds in July for "Opening Night" of The Breckenridge Music Festival. Orchestra musicians prepare to delight summer audiences. Some rejoin friends, others are newcomers. Wind sections work to catch their breath at 9600 feet! The volunteer fundraising group, Applause!, presents the festive Patrons Party and Opening Night Party. Everyone is gearing up for the start of a new season.

Champagne Punch

Punches always make stunning presentations at cocktail parties.

½ cup confectioners' sugar
3 ounces curaçao liqueur
3 ounces brandy
3 ounces lemon juice
2 (750 ml.) bottles champagne, chilled
1-2 quarts club soda

1. The day before the event, choose a floral shaped Bundt pan or other attractive mold and fill with water. For added flair, place slices of oranges and lemons in the water. Freeze overnight.
2. Allow mold to defrost just long enough to loosen the ice from its mold.
3. Combine sugar, curaçao, brandy and lemon juice in a large punch bowl.
4. At serving time, float ice block on top of punch, add champagne and soda to taste.

Yield: 15 servings

Gold Rush Slush

Make this punch ahead and store in the freezer until happy hour.

1 (6-ounce) can lemonade concentrate, thawed
1 (6-ounce) can orange juice concentrate, thawed
1 cup strong tea (brewed with 6 tea bags)
1 cup sugar
7 cups water
2 cups bourbon
Lemon lime soda or ginger ale
Sprigs of mint for garnish

1. In a gallon container, mix concentrates together.
2. Brew tea and while hot, stir in sugar to dissolve. Add to concentrates.
3. Add water and bourbon and mix well.
4. Put in freezer and freeze until solid, about 24 hours.
5. To serve, fill a tall glass halfway with slush and top off with lemon lime soda or ginger ale.
6. Garnish with mint.

Yield: 15 servings

Mango-Avocado Salsa with Crostini

Crostini or "little toasts" can be served with a variety of toppings.

CROSTINI:
1 baguette
½ cup extra virgin olive oil
Salt and freshly ground black pepper, to taste

TOPPING:
1 large mango, peeled, pitted and diced (⅓-inch dice)
3 tablespoons minced sweet onion
3 tablespoons finely diced green bell pepper (¼-inch dice)
3 tablespoons finely diced red bell pepper (¼-inch dice)
1½ tablespoons white wine vinegar
1 tablespoon minced fresh cilantro
1 tablespoon extra virgin olive oil
1 teaspoon minced chives
1 avocado, halved, pitted, scooped out and diced (⅓-inch dice)

THE BEGINNING

Many people live out their dreams in Summit County, where the Breckenridge Music Festival has deep roots. Dr. Kenny Evans and his wife, Dona, aspired to create a summer music festival. They succeeded in 1980 with a delightful ten day music event. Since then, the Festival has grown into a year round program at the heart of the robust Summit County experience.

CROSTINI:
1. Preheat oven to 400 degrees.
2. Slice baguette diagonally as thinly as possible.
3. Lightly brush olive oil on both sides of bread and arrange in a single layer on a baking sheet. Season lightly with salt and pepper.
4. Bake until crusty and golden and still soft within, about 10-12 minutes. Turn once halfway through cooking. Store in airtight container until ready to use.

TOPPING:
1. Combine mango, onion, green and red bell peppers, vinegar, cilantro, olive oil and chives. Cover and chill for 30 minutes.
2. Just before serving, prepare avocado and toss with topping.
3. Top each crostini with a mound of topping and serve immediately.

Yield: about 32 crostini

Mini Reubens

A cocktail version of a popular sandwich that is easy to fix.

36 slices cocktail rye bread
¾ cup Thousand Island dressing
1 (8-ounce) can sauerkraut, drained and rinsed

¼ pound thinly sliced corned beef
1 (6-ounce) package Swiss cheese slices, cut into 2-inch squares

1. Preheat oven to 375 degrees.
2. Arrange bread slices on baking sheet and toast one side of bread in oven, about 5 minutes.
3. Spread a teaspoon of dressing on toasted side of each slice.
4. Add a small amount of sauerkraut and corned beef to each slice.
5. Top slices with 1 square of Swiss cheese.
6. Bake for 8-10 minutes or until cheese is melted and edges are lightly browned.

Yield: 12 servings

ABOUT THE FESTIVAL

The Breckenridge Music Festival offers treats for every musical taste. In summer, the highly acclaimed Orchestra is led by Maestro Gerhardt Zimmermann. The largely classical repertoire is sprinkled with jazz, pops, blues, Broadway, opera, song and dance. And through all seasons, the Blue River Series presents a range of genres, such as jazz, country, blues, folk and rock'n'roll.

Riverwalk Potatoes

A finger food that can be topped with either expensive or inexpensive garnishes.

40 bite-size red-skinned potatoes, or 20
   slightly larger ones
½ teaspoon kosher salt
1 (7½-ounce) container of crème fraîche

GARNISHES:
1 (2-ounce) small jar caviar, or 1 cup of
   either chopped parsley, grated cheddar
   cheese or crumbled crispy bacon

1. Bring salted water to a boil and add potatoes. Boil 10-12 minutes, or until skins can be pierced easily with a fork.
2. Remove from water and using a melon baller, make a well in the top of each potato. If using larger ones, cut them in half and hollow out the center.
3. Stir the crème fraîche to make smooth. Place in a plastic sealed bag and cut corner of bag to form a makeshift pastry bag. Pipe crème fraîche into potato shells.
4. Top each serving with choice of garnish.

Yield: 40 servings

Feta Custard in Phyllo

If pressed for time, use a quality olive tapenade straight from your pantry.

2 packages mini phyllo shells (1¾"size)
1 (4-ounce) package crumbled feta cheese
1 (3-ounce) package cream cheese,
   softened
1 egg
2 teaspoons lemon juice
1 teaspoon all-purpose flour

OLIVE TOPPING:
⅓ cup chopped pitted kalamata olives
½ teaspoon dried oregano
½ teaspoon extra virgin olive oil
¼ teaspoon balsamic vinegar
1 garlic clove, minced
Dash ground cumin
Dash crushed red pepper (or to taste)
Snipped fresh oregano

SHELLS:
1. Preheat oven to 325 degrees.
2. Place phyllo shells on large baking sheet.

CUSTARD FILLING:
1. Using an electric mixer, blend feta, cream cheese, egg, lemon juice and flour until nearly smooth.
2. Spoon 1 rounded teaspoon of filling in each shell.
3. Bake 17-20 minutes or until shells are lightly browned and crisp; filling will be set and have a dull finish.

OLIVE TOPPING:
1. Stir together olives, oregano, olive oil, balsamic vinegar, garlic, cumin and red pepper.
2. Spoon olive topping over custard.
3. Garnish with fresh oregano and serve immediately.

Yield: 30 servings

Seasonal Crudités with Mayonnaise Verte

This dip can be served with any number of seasonal crudités.

1 cup packed flat-leaf parsley leaves
¼ cup extra virgin olive oil
2 tablespoons fresh lemon juice
1-2 teaspoons Dijon-style mustard, or to taste
1 cup mayonnaise
Salt and freshly ground black pepper

1. Purée parsley, olive oil, lemon juice and mustard in a blender or food processor until smooth.
2. Stir purée into mayonnaise and season with salt and pepper to taste.
3. Refrigerate until ready to serve.

Yield: 1½ cups

MORE THAN JUST A FESTIVAL

Throughout the year, musical performances are offered at various venues, such as Colorado Mountain College and Father Dyer Church. The Breckenridge Music Festival provides educational programs for patrons and for students in our local schools.

Wasabi Crusted Seared Tuna

Even non-sushi lovers will gobble this up.

¾ cup crushed wasabi peas
1 pound sushi grade ahi tuna loin, rinsed and patted dry
Kosher salt and freshly ground black pepper to taste
1 tablespoon grapeseed oil

TAMARI DIPPING SAUCE:
2 tablespoons mirin or sake
2 tablespoons tamari soy sauce
2 tablespoons rice vinegar
Chopped fresh chives for garnish
Chopped cilantro for garnish
Flat rice crackers

1. Using a food processor, pulse the wasabi peas until finely chopped and spread on a flat plate.
2. Cut tuna into 3-4 pieces. Season both sides with salt and pepper.
3. Press the chopped peas on both sides of the tuna.
4. Heat oil on high heat in a nonstick skillet and then sear tuna pieces 30 seconds on each side, keeping the interior rare.
5. Transfer to plate and chill. Cover when cold.
6. Combine sauce ingredients in a small bowl and set aside.
7. To serve, place crackers on a plate. Using a sharp knife, slice tuna crosswise into thin slices. Top each cracker with a slice of tuna and drizzle sauce on the tuna.
8. Garnish with chives and cilantro. Serve immediately.

Yield: 12 servings

"I think I should have no other mortal wants, if I could always have plenty of music. It seems to infuse strength into my limbs and ideas into my brain. Life seems to go on without effort, when I am filled with music."

George Eliot (English novelist, 1819-1880)

Maestro's Shrimp

Grand enough for a maestro and your guests.

3 garlic cloves, minced

⅓ cup extra virgin olive oil

¼ cup tomato sauce

2 tablespoons red wine vinegar

2 tablespoons chopped fresh basil

½ teaspoon salt

¼ teaspoon cayenne pepper

2 pounds fresh shrimp, peeled and
    deveined, tail on

Fresh basil for garnish

1. In a large bowl, stir together garlic, olive oil, tomato sauce and vinegar. Add basil, salt and cayenne pepper and whisk well to combine.
2. Add shrimp to the marinade and stir until evenly coated.
3. Cover and refrigerate for 30 minutes to 1 hour, stirring shrimp once or twice.
4. Preheat broiler and lightly oil a rimmed baking sheet.
5. Remove shrimp from marinade and layer on sheet. Discard marinade.
6. Broil shrimp for 2-3 minutes per side or until opaque.
7. Serve in a warm bowl garnished with fresh basil.

Yield: 8 servings

Grilled Chicken Satay

Try tamari for a richer more balanced flavor.

PEANUT MARINADE AND
DIPPING SAUCE:

½ cup chunky peanut butter

½ cup peanut oil

¼ cup rice wine vinegar

¼ cup tamari or soy sauce

¼ cup fresh lemon juice

3 garlic cloves, finely chopped

8 sprigs cilantro, finely chopped

3 teaspoons crushed red pepper

2 teaspoons peeled and finely chopped
    fresh ginger

CHICKEN:

1½ pounds chicken tender strips

20-25 (8-inch) wooden skewers

1. In a blender, combine marinade ingredients and purée until smooth. May need to thin with water.
2. Reserve ¾ cup of marinade for dipping sauce.
3. Place remaining marinade in a large re-sealable plastic bag. Add chicken and mix to coat.
4. Marinate 3-4 hours, refrigerated, turning and mixing several times.
5. Remove chicken 30 minutes prior to grilling. Soak the wooden skewers in water for 30 minutes.
6. Preheat grill to medium heat.
7. Thread one chicken tender strip onto each skewer.
8. Grill, uncovered, over medium heat for 8-10 minutes, turning to grill all sides evenly.
9. Garnish skewers with extra chopped cilantro and reserved marinade for dipping.

Yield: 12 servings.

Symphony Tenderloin Canapés

This is a finger food of great elegance.

TENDERLOIN:

1 (2 pound) beef tenderloin, center cut, tied, room temperature
Salt and freshly ground black pepper
1 tablespoon extra virgin olive oil
1 loaf French bread, sliced into ¼-inch diagonal pieces.

SAUCE:

5-6 tablespoons minced shallots
½ cup brandy
1½ cups low sodium beef broth
2 tablespoons milk
1 teaspoon cornstarch
2½ tablespoons stone ground mustard
1 tablespoon lemon juice
2 teaspoons chopped fresh tarragon or
    1 teaspoon dried tarragon
Salt and freshly ground black pepper

TENDERLOIN:

1. Preheat oven to 425 degrees. Place oven rack in upper middle position.
2. Pat tenderloin dry and season with salt and pepper.
3. Heat oil in a frying pan over medium high heat until smoking and sear meat on all sides for about 10 minutes. Place seared meat in a roasting pan and put in oven.
4. Roast until internal temperature registers 125 degrees.
5. Remove from oven and transfer to a carving board; cover with foil and let rest for 15-20 minutes.
6. Slice into ¼-inch pieces.

SAUCE:

1. Using the same pan, sauté shallots until soft. Add more oil if needed.
2. Remove pan from heat, stir in brandy scraping up the browned bits.
3. Add beef broth, bring to a simmer and reduce to 1 cup. Pour any accumulated beef juices into sauce.
4. Whisk milk and cornstarch together; whisk into sauce. Once sauce is thickened, remove from heat and stir in mustard, lemon juice, tarragon and season with salt and freshly ground pepper to taste.

ASSEMBLY:

1. Spread sauce on each bread slice and top with meat.

Yield: 20-24 servings

CHAMPAGNE SERIES

The Champagne Series takes chamber music into the warm home setting of Summit County residents. It brings musicians and music lovers together for an intimate evening of food, music and conversation. The home vibrates with sounds of the festival. The musicians and audience are so close that each share the other's experience and together create a magical musical moment.

VARIOUS VENUES

The Breckenridge Music Festival began in humble settings, proving the love of fine music trumps creature comfort. The Bergenhof at Peak 8 and Father Dyer Church served as the first venues. Then in 1988, with the program expanding, an event tent was erected in downtown Breckenridge. The performances here produced a rugged outdoorsy experience.

Amaretto Bundt Cake

A rich slice of Italy.

CAKE:
½ cup chopped pecans
2 (7-ounce) packages almond paste (often comes in tubes)
1 deluxe yellow cake mix; (follow high altitude directions)
1 small package instant vanilla pudding mix
2 tablespoons all-purpose flour, (for high altitude)
4 large eggs
⅓ cup canola oil
½ cup Amaretto liqueur
½ cup water, plus 2 tablespoons, (for high altitude)

GLAZE:
½ cup (1 stick) butter, melted
½ cup sugar
¼ cup Amaretto liqueur
¼ cup water

1. Preheat oven to 350 degrees.
2. Lightly grease Bundt cake pan.
3. Sprinkle pecans evenly over the bottom.
4. Pulse almond paste in food processor until crumbled.
5. Combine cake mix, pudding mix and flour in a large mixing bowl. Add almond paste.
6. Add eggs, oil, Amaretto and water. Beat with a mixer for 4 minutes at medium speed or until well blended.
7. Pour batter into pan and bake for 50-60 minutes. Cool for 20 minutes in pan.
8. In a medium saucepan, combine melted butter, sugar, Amaretto and water. Bring to a boil on high heat for 2 minutes. Stir once.
9. Using a wooden skewer, poke holes over entire top of cake. Pour glaze over cake in the pan. Let stand several hours. Invert onto cake plate.

NOTE: This recipe is adjusted for high altitude baking. At sea level, omit 2 tablespoons of flour and additional 2 tablespoons of water.

Yield: 8 generous servings.

Fudge Extraordinaire

Satisfies the most wicked sweet tooth.

1 (12-ounce) package semi-sweet chocolate
   morsels, chopped
6 (1-ounce) square bittersweet chocolate, grated
1 (14-ounce) can sweetened condensed milk

2 teaspoons vanilla
½ cup shredded coconut
½ cup chopped walnuts
2 (1-ounce) squares white chocolate

1. Line an 8-inch by 8-inch baking dish with foil; be sure to cover the sides as well. Coat foil with cooking spray.
2. Combine semi-sweet and bittersweet chocolates with condensed milk in a large saucepan over medium-low heat. Cook until chocolate melts and mixture is smooth, stirring frequently to prevent scorching. Be careful not to overcook.
3. Remove saucepan from heat and stir in vanilla, coconut and walnuts.
4. Spread mixture into prepared baking dish, smoothing the top.
5. Melt white chocolate in microwave. Drizzle the melted chocolate over the top of the fudge. Refrigerate until firm, about 2 hours.
6. Invert fudge onto work surface, peel off the foil and turn over. Cut into squares with a sharp knife.

Yield: 16 servings

In 1993, a state of the art, higher capacity event tent was constructed at the current Riverwalk location. In 2008, a roof, walls and other remodeling transformed the tent into the acoustically excellent hall we enjoy today.

Peaches and Raspberries in Puff Pastry

Sweet, fragrant peaches make a wonderful dessert.

FILLING:
8 large peaches
½ cup sugar
2 tablespoons cornstarch
1 cup water
1 teaspoon cinnamon
1 tablespoon lemon juice
1 pint raspberries

PASTRY:
1 sheet frozen puff pastry, thawed
1 egg
1 tablespoon water

GARNISHES:
Whipped cream and/or sprigs of mint

FILLING:
1. Bring a large pot of water to a boil; remove from heat. Place peaches in water for 1 minute. Remove and peel. Slice and set aside.
2. Mix sugar and cornstarch in a large saucepan. Gradually stir in water and whisk until cornstarch is dissolved. Over medium heat, bring to a boil and cook for one minute. Remove pan from heat.
3. Add sliced peaches, cinnamon, lemon juice and raspberries.

PASTRY:
1. Preheat oven to 400 degrees.
2. On a lightly floured surface, roll out the pastry sheet into a 12-inch by 12-inch square. Cut sixteen 3-inch squares and place into muffin tins, forming cups.
3. Fill each cup with peach/raspberry filling.
4. Beat egg and water together. Brush the edges of the pastry cups.
5. Bake for 10-12 minutes or until pastries are golden brown. Remove and cool in pan for 10 minutes. Serve with a dollop of whipped cream and/or a sprig of mint.

Yield: 16 servings

Wildflower Hike

Choose from simple snacks to hearty sandwiches, and keep in mind the importance of nutrition when hiking.

Sunflower Seed Granola

Blue Cheese Spread
Cheese Wafers

Melon Medley

Best Friends' Biscuits

Summit Gorp

Chicken Lettuce Wraps
Pesto and Spinach Wraps

PEAK PERFORMERS:
The Imperial Sandwich
The Copper Mountain Stromboli
The Outback Sandwich

High Country Trail Bars
Molasses Sugar Cookies
Lemon Pound Cake

PICNIC

The exertion of a summer hike is the perfect excuse to indulge in good food with friends and family. Pause to feast your eyes on the natural beauty of lakes, waterfalls and mountain vistas. Settle down in a colorful meadow or on a rocky ledge. Enjoy the repast and share the moment before heading back down to the trail.

Sunflower Seed Granola

Peanut butter and honey are a great combination for this snack.

¾ cup shelled sunflower seeds
1½ cups oats
¼ cup ground flaxseed
½ cup dried cranberries
½ cup slivered almonds
⅓ cup honey or agave nectar

½ cup shredded coconut (unsweetened preferred)
3 tablespoons natural peanut butter or almond butter
½ teaspoon salt
½ teaspoon vanilla

1. Preheat oven to 250 degrees.
2. Combine all ingredients in a large bowl and mix until evenly blended.
3. Spread mixture into large rimmed cookie sheet and bake for 40 minutes, stirring after 20 minutes. Remove from oven and allow to cool. Store in a re-sealable plastic bag.

Yield: 5 one cup servings

Blue Cheese Spread

Enjoy this spread on either crackers or slices of apple while you absorb the scenery surrounding you.

1 (8-ounce) package cream cheese, softened
2 tablespoons apple jelly

½ cup crumbled blue cheese
½ cup dried cranberries
½ cup chopped pecans

1. Blend cream cheese, jelly and blue cheese.
2. Stir in cranberries and pecans. Store in a plastic container and chill until ready to transport.

Yield: 2½ cups

Cheese Wafers

A crisp wafer that is easy to make.

½ cup all-purpose flour
½ teaspoon salt
Dash cayenne pepper

1½ cups crisp rice cereal
½ cup (1 stick) butter, softened
2 cups shredded sharp cheddar cheese

1. Preheat oven to 350 degrees.
2. Stir together flour, salt, pepper and cereal. Set aside.
3. In a large bowl, beat butter and cheese until light and fluffy.
4. Add cereal mixture and stir until combined.
5. Drop a rounded measuring teaspoon onto ungreased baking sheet. Flatten slightly with fork dipped in flour.
6. Bake 15 minutes or until lightly browned around edges.
7. Remove immediately from baking sheet and cool on wire racks.
8. Store in airtight container.

Yield: 36-42 wafers

Melon Medley

Colorado's world famous Rocky Ford melons are available at farmers' markets and local grocers.

GINGER SYRUP:
3 cups water
2 cups sugar
2 cups thinly sliced, unpeeled fresh ginger

FRUIT:
4 cups of your choice of Rocky Ford
    cantaloupe, honey dew or watermelon,
    seeded and cut in chunks
Sprigs of fresh mint

1. Bring water, sugar and ginger to a boil in a 2-quart saucepan. Stir until sugar is dissolved.
2. Simmer 10 minutes, stirring occasionally. Remove from heat and let steep 15 minutes.
3. Pour ginger syrup through a sieve into a bowl, discarding ginger.
4. Chill, covered, at least 2 hours. Syrup will keep up to 2 weeks in refrigerator.
5. Toss ¼-½ cup syrup with chunks of melons. Add more to taste. Add fresh mint if desired.
6. Store in a plastic bag, seal tightly. Chill and transport in backpack next to chilled
    drinks or ice pack. Bring toothpicks to eat these juicy treats.

Yield: 8 servings

Best Friends' Biscuits

Dogs get hungry too; do not forget some treats for your fellow trailblazer.

¾ cup hot water
⅓ cup butter, softened
½ cup powdered milk

1 big pinch salt
1 egg, beaten
3 cups whole wheat flour

1. Preheat oven to 325 degrees.
2. In a large bowl, pour hot water over butter. Stir in powdered milk, salt and egg.
3. Add flour ½ cup at a time. Knead to form stiff dough.
4. On a lightly floured surface, roll dough to ½-inch thickness. Cut with a cookie cutter
    (perhaps a dog bone shape) and place on baking sheet.
5. Bake for 50 minutes. Biscuits will harden as they cool.

Yield: 24 biscuits

"I think dogs are the most amazing creatures;
They give unconditional love. For me they
are the role model for being alive."

Gilda Radner (Comedienne, actress, 1946-1989)

Summit Gorp

Commonly known as trail mix, this snack is considered by many to be the best hiking food.

2 cups candy coated chocolate pieces
2 cups favorite cereal
2 cups chocolate morsels, either
    semi-sweet or white chocolate
2 cups raisins or other dried fruit

2 cups peanuts
2 cups cashews, almonds and/or walnuts
2 cups miniature marshmallows
2 cups granola clusters

1. Combine your choice of goodies in a large bowl.
2. Pack in small re-sealable plastic bags for individual servings.

Yield: 16 one cup servings

VIVID WILDFLOWER COLORS

We can thank Mother Nature's unique chemical, anthocyanin, for the vivid flowers that burst into bloom across our mountain meadows and slopes. This chemical works like a natural antifreeze in high elevation plants so they can photosynthesize in marginal conditions.

Chicken Lettuce Wraps

A light and refreshing lunch to enjoy at the summit.

LETTUCE WRAPS:
1 head of iceberg or Romaine lettuce

SAUCE:
1 tablespoon soy sauce
2 tablespoons oyster sauce
1 teaspoon sugar

WRAP FILLING:
1 tablespoon sesame oil
1 teaspoon minced fresh ginger
1 garlic clove, minced
2 green onions, diced
1 red bell pepper, diced
1 pound chicken breast, boneless, skinless, diced
1 teaspoon cornstarch
2 tablespoons water
1 cup chopped salted cashews

1. Wash and separate lettuce leaves. Put in a re-sealable plastic bag and refrigerate until crisp.
2. Combine sauce ingredients. Set aside.
3. Heat sesame oil in a large skillet or wok on high heat.
4. Sauté ginger, garlic, onions and bell pepper until fragrant.
5. Add chicken and cook until golden. Add sauce mixture; stir.
6. Combine cornstarch with water and add to pan.
7. Stir in cashews. Place chicken on a platter with chilled lettuce on the side. Guests should fill leaves with about 1 heaping tablespoon of filling and fold together.

NOTE: To enjoy on a hike: Cool filling and store in a plastic container; refrigerate until cold. Pack lettuce leaves and filling separately and place in backpack next to chilled drinks; prepare wraps when ready to eat.

Yield: 8 servings

Pesto and Spinach Wraps

Be creative with wraps; try deli meats or leftover grilled chicken.

1 package large spinach tortillas
1 (8-ounce) container whipped cream cheese
1 (8-ounce) container pesto with basil

1 (6-ounce) bag baby spinach
1 (12-ounce) jar "fire" roasted red peppers, cut into thin strips
½ pound deli meats, sliced thinly

1. On each tortilla, spread 1-2 tablespoons cream cheese.
2. Spread thin layer of pesto over cream cheese layer.
3. Cover with overlapping layer of baby spinach in concentric circles.
4. Place strips of the roasted red peppers on top of the spinach (about 12 strips per tortilla). Cover with deli meats.
5. Roll up tightly and wrap in plastic wrap. Refrigerate for 6-24 hours.
6. Unwrap tortillas. Cut in half or into rounds and rewrap for individual servings. Refrigerate until ready to transport.

Yield: 6 servings

Peak Performers

These sandwiches are quick to make and easy to carry. Combinations are unlimited. Choose fabulous breads, meats and cheeses from the local delis and top with either fresh veggies or check the pantry; roasted peppers, artichoke hearts or chopped olives create a "Dagwood" that will surely please the hungry hiker.

THE IMPERIAL SANDWICH

8 ounces cream cheese or ricotta

4 ounces crumbled blue cheese

2 tablespoons chopped walnuts

1 Bartlett pear, sliced

Lemon juice or raspberry vinegar

12 slices multigrain bread or 6 whole wheat rolls, split

1. Mix together cheeses and add walnuts.
2. Spread on bread slice and top with slices of pear. Sprinkle with lemon juice or vinegar. Top with bread slice. Wrap in plastic wrap.

Yield: 6 servings

PLACES TO HIKE

Wildflowers are a mountain treasure in summer when Summit County is blessed with astounding color. Blooming season peaks in early July, but early flora are found at lower elevations like Cataract Lake and the family friendly Lily Pad Hike. Later in summer, move above tree line to spots like Shrine Pass, Loveland Pass, Mosquito Gulch and Black Powder Pass.

THE COPPER MOUNTAIN STROMBOLI

1 (13.8-ounce) tube of refrigerated pizza dough

6 ounces deli ham, thinly sliced

6 green onions, sliced

6 bacon strips, cooked until crisp, crumbled

1½ cups (6 ounces) shredded Provolone cheese

1. Preheat oven to 350 degrees.
2. Unroll dough on a greased baking sheet. Place ham on dough to within ½-inch of edge, sprinkle evenly with onions, bacon and cheese. Roll up jelly roll style, starting with the long side. Pinch seams to seal and tuck ends under. Place seam side down on baking sheet.
3. With a sharp knife, cut several slits ¼-inch deep on top of loaf. Bake for 26-30 minutes or until golden brown. Cool slightly before cutting into 1 inch slices. Serve warm or at room temperature. Wrap in plastic wrap.

Yield: 4-6 servings

THE OUTBACK SANDWICH

2 tablespoons sour cream

1 teaspoon minced fresh thyme

Freshly ground black pepper to taste

Crusty sourdough bread

½ pound deli smoked turkey

Radicchio leaves

1 red onion, sliced thinly

1. Mix sour cream, thyme and pepper. Spread on slice of bread.
2. Top with turkey, radicchio and onion. Finish with another slice of turkey and bread. Wrap in plastic wrap.

Yield: 4 servings

POISONOUS FLOWERS

Please don't eat the flowers! A field full of blosoms may look good enough to eat, but beware. While you can nourish your soul gazing at these clusters of color, don't try adding them to your salad. Some poisonous species are Death Camus, False Hellebore, aka Indian Corn Lily, and Monkshood.

High Country Trail Bars

A sweet and nutty treat that is quick to make; also great on ice cream.

3 cups old-fashioned oats	1 cup packed brown sugar
1 (11½-ounce) can lightly salted mixed nuts	1½ teaspoons cinnamon
½ cup raisins, dried cranberries or dried cherries	6 tablespoons light corn syrup
	2 tablespoons dark molasses
6 tablespoons butter	1 teaspoon kosher salt

1. Prepare a 13-inch by 9-inch baking pan with a lining of plastic wrap. Leave extra wrap over edges to grab.
2. In a large skillet over medium-high heat, toast oats and nuts, stirring constantly. Watch closely and toast until golden brown, about 8-9 minutes. Remove from heat; transfer to a bowl and stir in raisins.
3. Allow skillet to cool; using a paper towel, wipe out the pan. Add the remaining ingredients to skillet and cook, stirring frequently, over medium-heat until mixture bubbles, about 3 minutes. Pour hot mixture over toasted oats; stir well.
4. In baking pan, press mixture evenly to fill pan. Refrigerate until set. Use plastic edges and remove mixture from pan and break into servings.

Yield: 8-10 servings

Molasses Sugar Cookies

Cookies are a treat after hiking all day.

¾ cup shortening	2¼ cups all-purpose flour, sifted
1 cup sugar	½ teaspoon cloves
¼ cup molasses	½ teaspoon ginger
1 large egg	1 teaspoon cinnamon
1 teaspoon baking soda (use 2 teaspoons at sea level)	½ teaspoon salt
	Sugar for rolling

1. Melt shortening in a 3-quart saucepan over low heat. Remove from heat and let cool slightly (keep as liquid).
2. Add sugar, molasses and egg and beat well.
3. Sift together dry ingredients. Stir into molasses mixture; will form a large ball. Cover and chill in refrigerator for 30 minutes.
4. Preheat oven to 350 degrees.
5. Remove cookie dough from refrigerator and form into 1-inch balls. Roll in granulated sugar.
6. Place balls on greased cookie sheet 2 inches apart. Bake cookies 7-10 minutes until flattened and browned slightly; watch carefully.

NOTE: This recipe has been adjusted for high altitude baking. Use 2 teaspoons of baking soda for sea level baking.

Yield: 3 dozen

Lemon Pound Cake

A moist and delicious cake that can be served with ice cream at home.

CAKE:

1 cup (2 sticks) butter, at room temperature

2 cups granulated sugar, minus 2 tablespoons
    (at sea level, use 2 cups)

5 extra large eggs, at room temperature
    (at sea level, use 4)

⅓ cup lemon zest (6-8 large lemons)

3 cups all-purpose flour, plus 3 tablespoons
    (at sea level, use 3 cups)

¼ teaspoon baking powder (at sea level, use ½
    teaspoon)

¼ teaspoon baking soda (at sea level, use ½
    teaspoon)

1 teaspoon kosher salt

¼ cup freshly squeezed lemon juice

¾ cup buttermilk plus 2 tablespoons
    (at sea level, use ¾ cup)

1 teaspoon vanilla

LEMON SYRUP:

½ cup granulated sugar

½ cup freshly squeezed lemon juice

LEMON GLAZE:

2 cups confectioners' sugar

3½ tablespoons freshly squeezed
    lemon juice

CAKE:

1. Preheat oven to 350 degrees. Grease and flour two 8½ -inch by 4¼-inch by
    2½-inch loaf pans. Line bottoms with parchment paper.

2. Cream butter and sugar until light and fluffy, about 5 minutes.

3. At medium speed, add eggs, one at a time; add lemon zest.

4. Sift together flour, baking powder, baking soda and salt in a large bowl.

5. In another large bowl, combine lemon juice, buttermilk and vanilla.

6. Add flour mixture and buttermilk mixture alternately to the batter, beginning and
    ending with flour.

7. Divide batter between pans, smooth tops and bake for 45-60 minutes, until tester
    comes out clean. Remove from oven.

8. Cool for 10 minutes. Remove cakes from pans and set on rack.

LEMON SYRUP:

1. Combine ingredients in a small saucepan and cook over low heat until sugar dissolves.

2. Make holes over top of cakes with a small skewer. Slowly spoon lemon syrup over cake
    tops. Allow to cool completely.

GLAZE:

1. Combine ingredients in a bowl and whisk until smooth.

2. Pour over cake tops and allow to drizzle down the sides.

Yield: 2 cakes

HIKE INFO

Find descriptions and directions for hikes at www.summitcountyexplorer.com or in Mary Ellen Gilliland's book, *The Summit County Hiker.*

To learn more about wildflowers, Colorado Mountain College runs a wonderful series of Wildflower Hiking classes starting in June and July.

Fabulous Fourth

Take your pick from these summer favorites for a festive family gathering.

FIRECRACKER FIFTY FEAST
Guamosas
Spicy Avocado Dip

Pasta with Fresh Tomatoes and Brie
Asian Spiced Chicken with Warm Slaw

Fruit Pizza

BREAKFAST BEFORE THE RACE AND PARADE
Biker's Granola
Red, White and Blue Overnight Toast
Independence Strata

FOURTH OF JULY FAMILY GATHERING
Patriotic Punch
Stuffed Sweet Chile Peppers
Spinach Dip

Olive Peasant Bread
Watermelon Salad
Fresh Corn Pudding

Potato Salad

Barbeque Baby Back Ribs
Firecracker Salmon

Peaches in Rum Sauce
Kahlúa Chocolate Sauce
Deep Dish Apple Pie

IMAGINE: BOISTEROUS CELEBRATIONS

Boisterous celebrations in Summit County are nothing new. In the early 1900s, Johnny Deming launched a tradition that tickled him and rankled fellow Frisco residents. "At 4 am on the 4th of July, he detonated a huge dynamite blast on Frisco's Piston Hill, rattling windows, waking babies, and jarring the entire population awake." *SUMMIT* by Mary Ellen Gilliland

Guamosas

Serve this sweet tropical fruit drink for cocktails or a brunch.

1 (750 ml.) bottle champagne or Prosecco, chilled
2 (11½-ounce) cans guava juice, chilled

1. Fill a champagne flute half full of champagne. Add juice to desired level.
2. Garnish.

Yield: 8 servings

Spicy Avocado Dip

Sambal oelek is a Southeast Asian condiment that adds a new slant to an old favorite.

2 ripe avocados, halved, pitted, scooped out; 1 diced and 1 mashed (reserve 1 pit)
1 medium-size sweet onion, finely diced
1 medium tomato, seeded and diced
¼ cup sliced green onions, green part only
3 tablespoons sake, rice vinegar, white wine or vermouth
2 tablespoons lime juice
2 tablespoons minced fresh ginger
1 tablespoon chopped fresh cilantro
1 tablespoon extra virgin olive oil
1 tablespoon sambal oelek
Salt and freshly ground black pepper to taste

1. Combine all ingredients in a bowl. Stir gently.
2. Serve immediately or cover and refrigerate after placing the reserved pit in bowl.

Yield: 3-4 cups

Pasta with Fresh Tomatoes and Brie

A vegetarian pasta that is a perfect pre-race dinner.

4 large ripe tomatoes, chopped
1 pound Brie cheese, rind removed, cubed into ½-inch squares
1 cup shredded fresh basil
3 garlic cloves, minced
1 cup extra virgin olive oil
½ teaspoon garlic salt
½ teaspoon freshly ground black pepper
1 pound dry pasta, such as linguine
1 tablespoon extra virgin olive oil
1 teaspoon salt
Parmesan cheese, freshly grated

1. Combine first 7 ingredients in a large serving bowl. Cover and allow to marinate at room temperature, for at least 2 hours.
2. Bring 6 quarts of water to boil in a large pot. Add olive oil and salt. Add pasta and cook until tender but still firm, about 8 to 10 minutes.
3. Drain pasta and immediately toss with sauce. Serve with grated Parmesan cheese and French bread.

Yield: 4-6 servings

Asian Spiced Chicken with Warm Slaw

Save time by buying prepackaged coleslaw.

16 boneless, skinless chicken thighs

MARINADE:
1 cup sherry
1 cup hoisin sauce
2 teaspoons Chinese five spice powder

SLAW DRESSING:
4 tablespoons soy sauce
2 tablespoons cider vinegar
4 teaspoons sesame oil
4 teaspoons minced fresh ginger
½ cup creamy peanut butter
4 teaspoons Thai roasted red chili paste (may substitute chili sauce)
1 teaspoon sambal oelek or Chinese chili garlic sauce

SLAW:
2 tablespoons vegetable oil
4 cups shredded carrots
12 cups shredded cabbage (¼-inch slices)
Cilantro sprigs
Honey roasted peanuts

CHICKEN AND MARINADE:
1. Mix the sherry, hoisin sauce and Chinese five spice powder in a gallon re-sealable plastic bag; add the chicken thighs and marinate 8 hours in the refrigerator.
2. Preheat the oven to 400 degrees with rack in the middle position.
3. Place thighs and marinade in a foil lined glass baking dish. Bake for 30 minutes.

SLAW DRESSING:
1. Whisk all dressing ingredients in a small bowl.

SLAW:
1. Heat oil in a large skillet or wok on moderately high heat.
2. Add the carrots and stir-fry for 2 minutes.
3. Add the cabbage, stirring constantly, continue cooking until crisp-tender; about 4 more minutes.
4. Remove from the heat and toss with the slaw dressing.

TO SERVE:
1. Divide the slaw into equal amounts on 8 plates
2. Place 2 chicken thighs on each plate.
3. Drizzle remaining sauce from the baking pan over the thighs.
4. Garnish with cilantro and honey roasted peanuts.

Yield: 8 servings, easily halved

FIRECRACKER FIFTY

Headed for backcountry, 750 mountain bikers kick off the Independence Day parade for friendly crowds on Main Street, Breckenridge. Cyclists test their mettle on a 50 mile route that follows old narrow gauge railroad and mining pathways, climbing a total of 12,000 vertical feet. Organizers boast that the feat combines "grunty little climbs, long lung busters and rippin' descents."

EATING FOR EXERCISE

High-intensity exercise demands mostly carbohydrate calories because they quickly reach the bloodstream and, from there, feed laboring muscles.

Fruit Pizza

Make this kid-friendly pizza the night before.

2 rolls of ready to serve sugar cookie dough
1 (10-12 ounce) package of vanilla baking chips
¼ cup whipping cream
1 (8-ounce) package cream cheese, softened

Fruits for topping: blueberries, blackberries, sliced strawberries and kiwis
¾ cup apricot preserves
2 tablespoons water

1. Preheat oven to 350 degrees.
2. Roll cookie dough to fit a large cookie sheet. Place in oven and bake 10-12 minutes, until golden brown. Remove from oven and cool.
3. Microwave chips and whipping cream until melted; usually 1½ minutes. Stir well.
4. Combine cream cheese and melted chips; beat with mixer until smooth.
5. Spread cream cheese mixture on cookie crust and arrange cut fruit on top of cream cheese.
6. Mix apricot preserves and water in a bowl; spread over fruit.
7. Chill overnight and cut into portions.

Yield: 12-16 servings

Biker's Granola

Serve over yogurt for a kick start on the race.

4 cups regular oats
½ cup toasted or honey crunch wheat germ
½ cup sliced almonds
¼ cup nonfat dry milk
¼ cup shelled sunflower seeds
2 tablespoons sesame seeds
1½ teaspoons cinnamon
¼ teaspoon salt

½ cup honey
¼ cup orange juice
2 teaspoons canola oil
1 teaspoon vanilla
1 cup chopped mixed dry fruit
1 cup golden raisins
½ cup dried cranberries

1. Preheat oven to 350 degrees.
2. Combine dry ingredients in a large bowl.
3. Combine honey and orange juice in small saucepan over medium heat and cook 4 minutes until warm. Add oil and vanilla and stir well.
4. Pour over dry ingredients and stir well.
5. Spread oat mixture onto a jelly roll baking pan coated with non-stick cooking spray. Bake at 350 degrees for 15 minutes and then stir.
6. Bake an additional 10 minutes until a little crisp. Cool in pan.
7. Place baked mixture in large bowl and stir in dried fruits.
8. Store in airtight container. Serve over yogurt.

Yield: 7-8 cups

Red, White and Blue Overnight Toast

This French toast recipe can easily be halved for a smaller group.

16 slices French bread, ¾ to
    1 inch thick
10 eggs, beaten
1 cup milk
2 cups orange juice
⅔ cup sugar
1 teaspoon vanilla

½ teaspoon cinnamon or nutmeg
½ cup dried cherries
½ cup (1 stick) butter, melted
½ cup sliced almonds
Sliced strawberries, blueberries and
    confectioners' sugar for garnish
Maple syrup to taste

1. The night before serving, arrange bread slices in a single layer in two 13-inch by 9-inch baking dishes.
2. Whisk eggs in a large bowl to blend. Gradually whisk in milk. Blend in orange juice, sugar, vanilla and cinnamon or nutmeg. Add dried cherries.
3. Pour mixture over bread slices in pan. Let soak 10 minutes. Turn slices over and cover with plastic wrap. Refrigerate overnight.
4. In morning, preheat oven to 400 degrees. Remove pan from refrigerator and pour melted butter evenly on top. Sprinkle with almonds.
5. Bake 45 minutes or until golden.
6. Serve with fresh berries and dust with confectioners' sugar.

Yield: 8, 2 slice servings

Independence Strata

Prepare the night before.

10 large eggs
½ cup all-purpose flour
½ teaspoon salt
1 teaspoon baking soda
1 pint small curd cottage cheese

1 pound grated Monterey Jack cheese
½ cup (1 stick) butter, melted
2 (4-ounce) cans diced green chiles
Fresh salsa and cilantro for garnish

1. Combine all ingredients and mix well. Place in lightly buttered 13-inch by 9-inch pan or 2 pie pans. Cover and refrigerate overnight.
2. Preheat oven to 350 degrees.
3. Bake for 45 minutes or until set. Serve immediately with garnishes.

Yield: 10 servings

CELEBRATIONS

Summit County loves to celebrate and the Fourth of July is the perfect occasion. Family and friends fill streets in all the towns to enjoy parades, free concerts, art shows, games, contests, dancing, food and fun. The day closes grandly with events like thunderous fireworks over Lake Dillon or a patriotic concert at the Riverwalk in Breckenridge.

SUMMIT SUMMER PUNCH

Combine:

Brilliant blue skies

Bursts of sunshine

Cool, starry nights

Carpets of wildflowers

And dense forest trails

Allow to simmer, add zest

Serve on the rocks

Patriotic Punch

A refreshing punch for your family and friends to celebrate the holiday.

½ gallon cranberry juice, chilled
1 quart orange juice, chilled
½ cup lemon juice

½ cup light corn syrup
1 quart club soda, chilled
Vodka to taste

1. Mix first 4 ingredients.
2. When ready to serve, add club soda and vodka to taste.

Yield: 15-20 servings

Stuffed Sweet Chile Peppers

Use a variety of fillings such as other cheeses, hummus or mushroom paté.

1 package small, multi-colored sweet
   chile peppers
1 (4-ounce) package goat cheese,
   room temperature
2 tablespoons sun-dried tomato
   pesto

1 teaspoon dried basil or 2
   teaspoons chopped fresh
1 tablespoon balsamic vinegar
1½ tablespoons extra virgin olive oil

1. Cut each pepper in half, lengthwise, remove seeds.
2. Add peppers to a pot of boiling water and blanch for 2 minutes.
3. Remove peppers from water, drain and cool.
4. Mix goat cheese, pesto, basil, vinegar and olive oil.
5. Stuff each pepper with the cheese mixture.

Yield: 8 servings

Spinach Dip

Use "hot" or "mild" diced tomatoes depending on your taste.

1 (10-ounce) package frozen chopped
   spinach, thawed and drained
1 (8-ounce) package cream cheese,
   softened

1 (10-ounce) can diced tomatoes with
   green chiles
3 cups shredded Colby Jack cheese
1 tablespoon lemon pepper
½ cup minced onion

1. Using paper towels, squeeze the spinach dry.
2. Combine the spinach and cream cheese; mix well.
3. Add tomatoes with green chiles, cheese, lemon pepper and onion and mix well.
    Can be made ahead to this point, covered and refrigerated. Bring to room temperature
    before baking.
4. Preheat oven to 350 degrees. Prepare a 9-inch square baking dish with cooking spray
    and spoon dip into dish.
5. Bake for 20 – 30 minutes or until bubbly.

Yield: 15 servings

Olive Peasant Bread

This bread freezes well.

½ package (1⅛ teaspoons) active dry yeast, adjusted for high altitude
1 cup warm tap water (105-110 degrees)
1 large egg
1 tablespoon salted butter, softened
1 teaspoon dried basil
1 teaspoon dried oregano

1 teaspoon garlic salt
1 tablespoon sugar
3½ - 4 cups all-purpose flour
1¼ cups coarsely chopped olives (mixed black, green and kalamata)
1 cup freshly grated Parmesan cheese, divided
1 large egg, beaten

DOUGH AT ALTITUDE

For yeast dough, punch down the dough twice to improve flavor and texture. Keep an eye on how quickly the dough rises. Allow the dough to double and no more.

1. In a large bowl combine yeast and water; stir until dissolved.
2. Stir in egg and butter. Add basil, oregano, garlic salt, sugar, 3½ cups flour, olives and ¾ cup of the grated Parmesan cheese and stir until well mixed.
3. Turn dough onto a floured surface and knead until smooth and elastic, 10-12 minutes adding additional flour if too sticky.
4. Shape into a ball and place in a lightly greased bowl. Turn ball once to grease surface of bread. Cover and let rise in a warm place until doubled, about 1½ hours.
5. Punch dough down, form into a 10-12 inch round loaf. Place on a greased 13-inch pizza pan or cookie sheet. Do not cover. Put in a warm place to let the dough double again, about 30 minutes.
6. Preheat oven to 350 degrees.
7. Slit top of dough 3-4 times, brush with beaten egg and sprinkle on the remaining ¼ cup of Parmesan cheese.
8. Bake for about 35 minutes, until golden brown. Remove from pan and cool slightly before cutting.

NOTE: This recipe is adjusted for high altitude baking. Use 1 package of yeast (2¼ teaspoons) for sea level baking.

Yield: 1 large loaf, 8-16 servings

Watermelon Salad

Ice cold watermelon and feta cheese make a surprising combination.

½ medium watermelon, seeded and cut into chunks, chilled
½ cup chopped fresh mint leaves
¼ cup crumbled feta cheese

4 cups baby greens (arugula or watercress)
3 tablespoons extra virgin olive oil
1 tablespoon balsamic vinegar

1. In a salad bowl, combine watermelon, mint, feta cheese and greens and toss together.
2. Whisk oil and vinegar to combine.
3. Pour dressing over watermelon mixture and toss gently.

Yield: 8 servings

HOW TO PREPARE CORN

Boil: Drop cleaned corn into a large pot of boiling water just long enough to warm it, about 1-2 minutes.

Microwave: Trim both ends of the husk and pull off the toughest outer leaves. Wrap in wet paper towels. Microwave at full power for about 5 minutes. Half way through the cooking time turn the corn. Let cool slightly before husking.

Grill: Brush cleaned corn with melted butter on all sides. Place on grill, turning and basting with butter until the kernels are brown but not charred, about 5 minutes.

Fresh Corn Pudding

With the abundance of fresh corn, this dish is a must for the Fourth.

6 ears corn, husks and silk removed
1½ teaspoons sugar
½ teaspoon salt
¼ teaspoon nutmeg
½ teaspoon cayenne pepper

⅛ teaspoon white pepper
3 large eggs, lightly beaten
2 teaspoons cornstarch
2 cups half-and-half
2 teaspoons butter, melted

1. Preheat oven to 325 degrees.
2. Cut kernels from corn cobs.
3. In a medium bowl, combine kernels, sugar, salt, nutmeg, cayenne pepper and white pepper. Add eggs and mix well.
4. Whisk cornstarch and half-and-half; add melted butter and mix well.
5. Combine half-and-half mixture with corn mixture and pour into an 8-inch square baking dish.
6. Bake for 60 minutes or until set.

Yield: 6-8 servings

Potato Salad

A delicious salad for your next family gathering.

1 pound fingerling potatoes (use a variety)
3 whole garlic cloves
3 sprigs fresh thyme
3 hard-cooked eggs, minced
¼ cup niçoise olives, pitted and chopped
   (may use kalamata olives)
2 tablespoons flat leaf parsley, chopped

¼ cup capers, drained
¼ cup sherry vinegar
¼ cup whole grain mustard
¼ cup extra virgin olive oil
1 shallot, minced
1 tablespoon sea salt
Salt and freshly ground black pepper

1. Preheat oven to 425 degrees.
2. Prick potatoes with a fork and place in a greased roasting pan along with the garlic and thyme. Roast 45 minutes or until fork tender.
3. Remove from oven and discard the thyme. Refrigerate for 2 hours.
4. Half or quarter potatoes in a large mixing bowl. Add eggs, olives, parsley and capers and toss gently.
5. Combine vinegar, mustard, olive oil and minced shallot in a small bowl and whisk thoroughly.
6. Toss the dressing with the potato salad gently.
7. Add salt and pepper to taste.

Yield: 4 servings

Barbeque Baby Back Ribs

A dish that is everyone's favorite.

3 racks baby back pork ribs, membranes on back removed

RUB:
3 tablespoons kosher salt
3 tablespoons freshly ground
    black pepper
1½ teaspoons paprika
3 tablespoons chili powder
3 teaspoons brown sugar
1½ teaspoons garlic powder
1½ teaspoons ground cumin

SAUCE:
2 cups ketchup
2 cups white vinegar
2 (12 ounce) bottles of beer
6 tablespoons of sugar
6 tablespoons Worcestershire sauce
4 teaspoons kosher salt
4 teaspoons hot pepper sauce
2 teaspoons dry mustard
2 teaspoons black pepper
4 bay leaves
2 teaspoons vanilla
2 whole onions, peeled
2 tablespoons cornstarch or arrowroot
½ cup water

1. Combine rub ingredients.
2. Rub mixture on bone and meat sides of ribs.
3. Place ribs bone side down in large rimmed pan, making sure the ribs are in a single layer.
4. Cover with foil and place in refrigerator overnight.
5. Preheat oven to 275 degrees.
6. Place covered ribs in oven and bake for 1½ hours.
7. While ribs are cooking, make sauce. Combine ketchup, vinegar, beer, sugar, Worcestershire sauce, salt, hot pepper sauce, dry mustard, pepper, bay leaves and vanilla. Place in a heavy saucepan; add whole onions and simmer for 1 hour.
8. Whisk cornstarch or arrowroot and water. Add to the sauce and cook on low heat until sauce thickens. Remove bay leaves.
9. Remove ribs from oven and brush sauce over top of meat. Turn ribs so meat side is down. Brush sauce on bone side, return to oven, uncovered, and continue baking for another hour.
10. Preheat grill to medium-low heat.
11. Place ribs bone side down and grill approximately 20 minutes, watching that ribs do not char. Brush sauce frequently on ribs during grilling, turning once.
12. Place onions on grill during these 20 minutes. Slice for serving with ribs.
13. Remove ribs from grill, cut ribs apart and serve with remaining sauce.

Yield: 9-12 appetizer servings, 6 entrée servings

BARBEQUE GALORE

There's barbeque at street parties and on back decks for the Fourth of July, but the festival competitions during the summer are "one smokin' good time". Barbeque lovers can eat all day at the Colorado BBQ Challenge in June in downtown Frisco and head to Dillon in August for BBQ in the Summit competition.

PALISADE PEACHES

Colorado farmers have grown peaches since the 1880s. The western slope is world famous for peach orchards. Eat your peaches market fresh, ripe and juicy or dried and chewy, or made into jams, salsas, cobblers, pies, muffins and cake. A truly versatile delight!

Firecracker Salmon

A marinade that works with grilled flank steak and other seafood such as shrimp and scallops.

12 (4-6 ounces each) salmon fillets
¾ cup peanut oil
6 tablespoons soy sauce
6 tablespoons balsamic vinegar
6 tablespoons chopped green onions
4½ teaspoons brown sugar

3 garlic cloves, minced
2¼ teaspoons grated fresh ginger
3 teaspoons crushed red pepper
 (more or less to taste)
1½ teaspoons sesame oil
⅜ teaspoon salt

1. Place salmon fillets in a glass dish.
2. Whisk together remaining ingredients for marinade. Reserve ¾ cup for grilling and pour the rest over salmon.
3. Cover with plastic wrap and place in refrigerator for 4-6 hours.
4. Prepare grill to medium heat. Remove salmon from marinade, scraping green onion, garlic and ginger from top.
5. Place salmon on well-oiled grill with skin side up. Grill for 5 minutes.
6. Turn salmon over and spoon reserved marinade on top of fillets. Continue to grill 5 more minutes; total cooking time is 10 minutes or when center of each fillet flakes when tested with fork.

Yield: 12 servings

Peaches in Rum Sauce

Substitute bananas for your own version of "Bananas Foster".

⅓ cup unsalted butter
8 tablespoons light brown sugar
1 teaspoon cinnamon
8 peaches, peeled and cut into wedges
2⅓ teaspoons vanilla
2⅓ tablespoons dark rum
Vanilla or peach ice cream

1. Melt butter in a large heavy skillet over medium heat.
2. Add sugar and cinnamon and cook, stirring often until sugar begins to dissolve (mixture may clump together).
3. Add peaches and vanilla. Sauté until tender, stirring occasionally, about 4 minutes.
4. Remove skillet from heat and stir in rum.
5. Return skillet to heat and cook until sauce thickens, stirring frequently, about 2 minutes.
6. Spoon peaches and sauce over ice cream.

Yield: 8 servings

Kahlúa Chocolate Sauce

A quick and impressive topping for a luscious ice cream sundae.

½ cup heavy whipping cream
8 ounces bittersweet chocolate morsels
2 tablespoons Kahlúa or coffee liqueur
1 teaspoon vanilla

1. Heat whipping cream in a heavy saucepan until bubbles form. Do not scald.
2. Remove from heat; stir in chips, liqueur and vanilla. Mix well.
3. Serve over your favorite ice cream.

Yield: 1 cup

Deep Dish Apple Pie

What is more American than a delicious apple pie?

PASTRY FOR 2-CRUST, 10 INCH PIE:
3 cups all-purpose flour, sifted
1 teaspoon salt
1¼ cup shortening
1 large egg
1 teaspoon vinegar
6-8 tablespoons water, as needed
1 egg beaten with 1 tablespoon
    water for egg wash
Sugar to sprinkle

APPLE FILLING:
4 pounds Granny Smith apples, peeled,
    quartered and cored
Zest of 1 lemon
Zest of 1 orange
2 tablespoons lemon juice
1 tablespoon orange juice
½ cup sugar
¼ cup all-purpose flour
1 teaspoon kosher salt
¾ teaspoon ground cinnamon
½ teaspoon ground nutmeg
⅛ teaspoon ground allspice
1 tablespoon butter

ACTIVE SUMMER IN THE SUMMIT

Summer is an active time for Summit County. Off season, ski areas shift to mountain biking and horseback rides. In addition, there is a County-wide Recpath for walking, jogging, biking or in-line skating. For a beautiful day on the water, take a sailboat on Lake Dillon and enjoy the solitude.

1. In a large bowl, combine flour, salt and shortening; using a pastry blender cut until crumbly (size of small peas).
2. In a small bowl, whisk egg, vinegar and 6 tablespoons water.
3. Add egg mixture to dough and stir together adding water if too dry; take care to not stir too much or dough will be tough.
4. Form into 2 balls and refrigerate for 15 minutes.
5. Place waxed paper on counter and sprinkle with flour. Place one of the balls onto paper and roll out pie dough to a 12-inch circle. Drape crust over pie pan to extend about ½-inch over rim. Repeat for top crust.
6. Preheat oven to 450 degrees.
7. Combine filling ingredients except butter and toss gently. Fill crust and dot with butter. Top with second crust and seal edges. Brush entire top crust with egg wash and sprinkle with 1 teaspoon sugar. Make several slits to vent. Cover crust with either foil strips or a pie crust protector.
8. Bake for 10 minutes. Reduce temperature to 350 degrees and continue baking for 35 minutes, or until apples are tender. Remove edge protector and allow to brown.

Yield: 6-8 servings

relish
colorado inspired cuisine

Relish

Proprietor and Chef Matt Fackler

Fruits de Mer

Grilled Western Slope Tomato Basil Soup

Almond Crusted Colorado Farm Raised Striped Bass
Organic Pattypan Squash
Fingerling Potatoes
Lemon Chive Butter Sauce

Colorado Lamb Meatloaf
Spring Morel Gravy
Porcini Mountain Gorgonzola Mac-n-Cheese

Relish, located on South Main Street in Breckenridge, opened in the summer of 2008 and is known for American style dining with a little Colorado flavor.

Fruits de Mer

½ pound lobster meat

1 pound crab-claw, lump, Dungeness

1½ pounds squid, cooked (as the squid cooks, it releases liquid), remove squid from liquid, add Pernod and reduce to ½ cup

2 teaspoons Pernod liqueur

1 cup each roasted red, green and yellow bell peppers, cut into matchstick strips

¾ cup sundried tomato, cut into matchstick strips

½ red onion, cut into matchstick strips

2 tablespoons fresh parsley

¾ cup chopped Marcona almonds

½ tablespoon roasted garlic

½ tablespoon Old Bay Seasoning

Salt and freshly ground black pepper

½ cup mayonnaise

4 tablespoons mustard

Lemon juice to taste

1. Mix together and refrigerate. Enjoy on a roll or on a half avocado.

Yield: 4-6 servings

Grilled Western Slope Tomato Basil Soup

TOMATO PREP:

8 whole Colorado tomatoes

1 tablespoon olive oil

Salt and pepper

SOUP PREP:

2 tablespoons olive oil

1 sweet onion, small diced

1 carrot, small diced

2 stalks celery, small diced

2 tablespoons minced garlic

1 tablespoon tomato paste

½ cup white wine

2 quarts chicken or vegetable stock

½ cup fresh basil leaves

¼ cup fresh oregano leaves

1 cup heavy cream

Salt and pepper to taste

Sugar if necessary

1. Cut tomatoes in half and season with olive oil and salt and pepper. Grill tomatoes on medium high grill for 4 minutes a side; set aside when done.
2. While tomatoes are grilling, sauté onion, carrot and celery in oil over medium heat until translucent, approximately 12 minutes. Add in garlic, tomato paste and white wine and cook for 3 minutes.
3. Add grilled tomatoes and stock – bring to a boil – reduce heat to low. Simmer and continue cooking for 45 minutes or until all vegetables are extremely tender and mushy.
4. Add in herbs and cream and cook for 5 minutes.
5. Purée soup until smooth.
6. Season with salt and pepper and if necessary adjust acidity of soup with sugar.

Yield: 10 servings

Almond Crusted Colorado Farm Raised Striped Bass

CRUST:

1 cup slivered almonds, toasted

½ cup flour

6 striped bass filets, skin on and bones removed

Salt and pepper

1 teaspoon extra virgin olive oil

1. Combine almonds and flour in food processor and pulse until almonds are chopped and combined with flour.
2. Score skin on fish to prevent curling.
3. Season with salt and pepper and dredge in almond flour.
4. Sauté fish in olive oil on flesh side first for 4 minutes and 2 minutes on skin side.

Organic Pattypan Squash

5 pattypan squash (large) cut into quarters to make wedges

1 teaspoon extra virgin olive oil

1. Preheat oven to 400 degrees.
2. Sear squash on cut sides in olive oil until golden brown.
3. Finish in oven until just past al dente.

Fingerling Potatoes

30 fingerling potatoes

2-3 tablespoons extra virgin olive oil

Salt and pepper

1. Boil potatoes in salted water until you are able to barely pierce with a paring knife
2. Drain and let air cool.
3. Cut potatoes in half and sear in olive oil until golden brown

Relish is open, airy and full of light. The breathtaking views of the Breckenridge Ski Area, Riverwalk Center and the Ten Mile Range make the deck a perfect spot to enjoy happy hour or dinner, weather permitting.

Lemon Chive Butter Sauce

Juice of 2 lemons

½ cup white wine

1 teaspoon minced garlic

1 small shallot, minced

1½ cups (3 sticks) butter, cut into small cubes

½ cup chopped chives

1. Heat lemon juice, white wine, shallots and garlic and reduce until almost dry.
2. Fold in butter a few chunks at a time into sauce and continue cooking until sauce is combined.
3. Add chives and season with salt and pepper.

TO SERVE:

Arrange potatoes, squash and fish on serving plate. Lemon chive butter sauce may be served under the fish or as a topping.

Yield: 6 servings

Chef/Owner Matt Fackler treats you to Colorado inspired cuisine, blending his extensive culinary experience with regional influences to create a menu full of diverse flavors. Fackler is a graduate of the Culinary Institute of America in Hyde Park, New York, and practiced his trade in some of the most elite kitchens in Summit County before opening his own restaurant with his wife, Lisa.

Colorado Lamb Meatloaf

1-2 tablespoons olive oil
1 medium yellow onion, diced small
1 carrot, diced small
1 rib celery, diced small
1 tablespoon minced garlic
5 pounds ground lamb
½ tablespoon dry thyme
½ tablespoon dry oregano
½ tablespoon dry basil
½ tablespoon dry tarragon
5 eggs
1 cup milk
2½ cups bread crumbs

GLAZE:
1 cup ketchup
½ cup grain mustard
¼ cup honey
¼ cup white balsamic vinegar

1. Sauté onion, carrots and celery until translucent. Add garlic and cook 20 seconds, then cool.
2. Combine all ingredients in a tabletop mixer using the paddle attachment; mix on low for 2 minutes and on high for 30 seconds.
3. Form into 10 equal individual loaves.
4. Bake at 375 degrees for approximately 35 minutes (internal temp 160 on meat thermometer).
5. At minute 20, glaze with a mixture of ketchup, grain mustard, honey, and white balsamic vinegar.

Yield: 10 servings

Spring Morel Gravy

2 cups sliced morel mushrooms (any wild mushroom will do)
2 tablespoons butter
½ cup red wine
¼ cup sherry wine
2 teaspoons Worcestershire sauce
3 cups store-bought demi-glace (we make our own), available at specialty food stores
1 tablespoon honey
1 tablespoon fresh oregano

1. Sauté mushrooms in butter until ½ its original volume.
2. Add in wine, sherry, Worcestershire, and cook down by two-thirds original volume.
3. Add in demi-glace, honey and oregano. Cook to heavy gravy consistency.

Porcini Mountain Gorgonzola Mac-n-Cheese

1½ pounds small pasta shells or elbow macaroni

2 tablespoons diced shallot

1 tablespoon minced garlic

½ ounce olive oil

½ cup white wine

1 tablespoon porcini powder (available at specialty shops)

1 quart heavy cream

1½ cups mountain Gorgonzola

Salt and pepper to taste

2 ounces bread crumbs per ramekin or serving

1 ounce grated Asiago Romano cheese per ramekin or serving

1. Cook pasta in boiling water. Drain.
2. Sauté shallot and garlic in olive oil until translucent.
3. Add white wine and reduce by two-thirds its volume.
4. Add in porcini powder and heavy cream. Bring to a boil and reduce to 3 cups in volume.
5. Season with salt and pepper and fold in Gorgonzola; cook until melted.
6. Combine pasta with cream sauce in a large bowl, mix well.
7. Place mac-n-cheese in 10 ramekins or your favorite casserole dish, sprinkle with bread crumbs and Asiago Romano cheese.
8. Bake at 350 -375 degrees until golden brown and bubbly.

Yield: 10 servings

A full service bar and an exceptional selection of wines and beers can be found at Relish. Chef Fackler's eclectic, seasonally changing menu is sure to delight and provide a dining experience "that you will relish."

Market To Market

A menu that features fresh ingredients available at our local farmers' markets held weekly throughout the summer season in Summit County.

Fresh Peach Salsa
Marinated Broccoli and Curry Aioli

Savory Beets
Roasted Asparagus Salad
Green Beans with Tomatoes
Portobello Napoleons

Gazpacho Salad
Sweet Corn Salad

Blue Cheese Biscuits

Vegetable Gratin
Grilled Greek Lamb Chops
Cedar Plank Salmon
Cherry Sauce

Blueberry Cobbler
Individual Lemon Sponge Cakes
Minty Sun Tea

Fresh Peach Salsa

For the best salsa, be sure to use Colorado peaches fresh from the farmers' markets.

4 ripe Colorado peaches	3 tablespoons chopped fresh cilantro
1 cup rice vinegar	1 tablespoon finely chopped chipotle
¼ cup sugar	chiles in adobo

1. Cut peaches in half and remove pits. (Do NOT peel.) Cut peaches into thin wedges, then cut each wedge in half.
2. Put vinegar and sugar in sauté pan over medium heat and reduce by one-half. Add peaches and stir well.
3. Spread the mixture out on a baking sheet and chill in refrigerator. Once cool, add the cilantro and chopped chipotles and refrigerate.
4. Serve with crackers or as a side dish with spicy pork tenderloin.

Yield: 8 servings

Marinated Broccoli and Curry Aioli

Prepare this appetizer ahead of time.

1 large bunch fresh broccoli, about 2½ pounds	CURRY AIOLI:
	1 cup mayonnaise, (may use light mayonnaise)
MARINADE:	2¼ teaspoons curry powder
½ cup apple cider vinegar	½ tablespoon ketchup
¾ cup vegetable oil	⅛ teaspoon Worcestershire sauce
2 garlic cloves, chopped	
1 teaspoon sugar	
2 teaspoons dried dill	

1. Wash and cut florets from broccoli leaving 1½-inch stems. Split the large florets to make them bite-size.
2. Combine ingredients for marinade in a jar and shake well.
3. Put cut broccoli in a large re-sealable bag and add marinade. Close tightly and shake well. Refrigerate overnight.
4. Combine ingredients for aioli, cover and refrigerate.
5. To serve, drain the broccoli and serve with aioli as a dip.

Yield: 8-10 servings

Savory Beets

Made with farm-fresh beets, this is a great summer salad.

2 pounds golden or red beets

½ cup water

1 red onion, peeled, halved, thinly sliced
   vertically (root to tip)

1 tablespoon chopped fresh dill

2 tablespoons red wine vinegar

2 teaspoons extra virgin olive oil

2 tablespoons pine nuts, toasted

Salt and freshly ground black pepper,
   to taste

Crumbled goat cheese for garnish

1. Preheat oven to 450 degrees.
2. Leave root and 1 inch of stem on beets; scrub with a brush.
3. Place beets in a 13-inch by 9-inch baking dish; add ½ cup water to dish. Cover and bake for 1 hour or until tender.
4. Drain and rinse with cold water. Allow to cool.
5. Trim off beet roots; rub off skin (use thin plastic gloves to prevent staining hands). Cut each beet into 8 wedges.
6. Combine beets and onions in a large bowl.
7. In a separate small bowl, combine dill, vinegar and oil. Mix well.
8. Add pine nuts to dressing and drizzle over beets, stirring gently. Season to taste with salt and pepper. Cover until ready to serve; sprinkle goat cheese on top.

Yield: 8 servings

Roasted Asparagus Salad

For a casual family-style meal, arrange lettuce, asparagus and egg slices on a platter. Drizzle with dressing and top with cheese.

ASPARAGUS:

48 medium size asparagus (2 pounds),
   trimmed and peeled

1 tablespoon extra virgin olive oil

Salt and freshly ground black pepper
   to taste

DRESSING:

2 tablespoons extra virgin olive oil

2 tablespoons fresh lemon juice

Salt and freshly ground black pepper
   to taste

SALAD:

6 cups torn Boston lettuce (about
   2 small heads)

2 large hard-cooked eggs, each
   cut into 6 slices

¼ cup (1-ounce) shaved fresh pecorino
   cheese (or fresh Parmigiano-Reggiano
   cheese), use a vegetable peeler to shave
   cheese

1. Preheat oven to 450 degrees.
2. Toss asparagus with olive oil, salt and pepper.
3. Roast on baking sheet in oven for 8 minutes or until crisp-tender.
4. Whisk together dressing ingredients.
5. Arrange lettuce on 6 plates. Top each serving with 8 asparagus spears and 2 egg slices.
6. Drizzle 2 teaspoons of dressing over each serving and garnish evenly with shaved cheese.

Yield: 6 servings

FRESH FOOD

Enjoy the taste of summer with fresh and wholesome Colorado grown foods. Fruits and vegetables reach markets at their peak of flavor for a summer of healthy eating. The western slope Palisade farm country is particularly famous for produce, with peaches, apples, apricots, pears, plums, cherries and grapes. There's nothing like the quality and nutrition of truly fresh farm produce.

STEAMING VEGETABLES AT ALTITUDE

Increase cooking times for fresh and frozen vegetables. Add more liquid to prevent scorching; watch closely and keep records for future reference.

Green Beans with Tomatoes

Fresh green beans straight from the farm are superb.

1½ pounds green beans, trimmed	2 bay leaves
¼ cup extra virgin olive oil	½ teaspoon capers, rinsed
1 medium onion, chopped	1 tablespoon lemon juice
1 garlic clove, finely chopped	Salt and freshly ground black pepper,
2 Roma tomatoes, seeded and	to taste
coarsely chopped	½ cup slivered almonds, toasted

1. Cook beans in boiling salted water until tender, about 6-8 minutes. Drain and immerse in ice water for 1 minute. Remove from water and set aside.
2. Heat oil in a medium skillet and add onion and garlic. Sauté over medium heat, stirring frequently, until onions are transparent, about 5 minutes.
3. Add tomatoes, bay leaves, capers and lemon juice and cook on low for 5 more minutes. Remove from heat.
4. Season to taste with salt and pepper and stir gently.
5. Place green beans and vinaigrette in serving bowl, cover and let stand 2 hours prior to serving. Can be made up to 2 days ahead, covered and refrigerated. Return to room temperature to serve. Discard bay leaves.
6. Before serving, garnish with toasted almonds.

Yield: 8 servings

Portobello Napoleons

Mozzarella, tomato and basil make this dish delicious.

2 cups balsamic vinegar	6 (¼-inch thick) slices fresh Mozzarella
6 (3-inch) portobello mushrooms, cleaned	cheese, 2½ to 3 inch diameter
and stemmed	6 fresh basil leaves, additional chopped
1 tablespoon extra virgin olive oil	basil for garnish
Salt and freshly ground black pepper	¼ cup pine nuts, toasted
6 slices Roma tomato, 2½ to 3 inch	
diameter	

1. Pour vinegar into a saucepan and cook over high heat until reduced by half. Set aside to cool.
2. Preheat grill to medium-high heat.
3. Brush mushrooms with olive oil and sprinkle with salt and pepper.
4. Grill for 2-3 minutes on each side, or until tender. Remove from grill and set aside.
5. When ready to serve, top each mushroom with a slice of tomato, a slice of cheese and basil leaf.
6. Place under broiler for 2 minutes to soften cheese.
7. Remove from oven. Drizzle with balsamic glaze, sprinkle with pine nuts and add chopped basil for garnish.

Yield: 4-6 servings

Gazpacho Salad

Farm fresh tomatoes found at Summit County's farmers' markets are a special summer treat.

VINAIGRETTE:

3 tablespoons tomato juice

2 tablespoons red wine vinegar

1 tablespoon extra virgin olive oil

1 teaspoon Worcestershire sauce

¼ teaspoon salt

¼ to ½ teaspoon hot pepper sauce

⅛ teaspoon freshly ground black pepper

SALAD:

2 cups fresh tomatoes (1-pound), diced

1½ cups peeled, seeded and diced
  cucumber

½ cup diced green bell pepper

2 tablespoons minced shallots

2 tablespoons coarsely chopped fresh basil

1. Combine vinaigrette ingredients in a jar. Mix well and refrigerate until ready to serve.
2. Combine salad ingredients in a large bowl.
3. When ready to serve, toss salad gently with vinaigrette.

Yield: 4 servings

Sweet Corn Salad

A light summer dish that tastes delicious with salmon.

4 ears sweet corn

6 green onions, thinly sliced

4 teaspoons sherry or red wine vinegar

1 teaspoon Dijon-style mustard

1 teaspoon kosher salt

½ teaspoon freshly ground black pepper

4 tablespoons extra virgin olive oil

½ cup fresh basil leaves

1 cup quartered cherry tomatoes

Leaf lettuce

1. Husk and clean corn, removing silk.
2. In a large pot, cover corn with water. Place lid on pot and bring water to a boil. Turn off heat and allow corn to sit while preparing salad.
3. Whisk together green onions, vinegar, mustard, salt and pepper. Drizzle in olive oil and whisk until smooth.
4. Remove corn from pot and allow to cool. Slice kernels off the cob and add to vinaigrette.
5. Stack basil leaves in a pile and snip with cooking shears into fine pieces (this method keeps leaves crisp).
6. Add basil and tomatoes to vinaigrette and stir well to coat. Serve on leaf lettuce.

Yield: 8 servings

CORN

Olathe Sweet, the Colorado rage, comes from the western slope and is known for its tenderness and balanced sugar. It is fresh and sweet when it reaches Summit County markets. The succulent flavor comes from Colorado's warm summer days and cool summer nights. For eight weeks, it's a special summertime treat!

BACK IN THE SIXTIES

Back in the sixties, Summit County was an eclectic community in transition from the Old West to a resort. Mixing and mingling could get interesting. On a Saturday night, the Old Dillon Inn was the place for rock-n-roll and the Mint for country music. But the real show was often the fight breaking out among miners, cowboys and hippies.

Today, Summit County still remains an unpretentious place where people come from different backgrounds and experiences to share a common love for the lifestyle and beauty of the high country.

Blue Cheese Biscuits

Herbs can be substituted for the blue cheese for a variation.

2 cups all-purpose flour
2 teaspoons baking powder (for sea level, use 1 tablespoon)
2 teaspoons sugar
½ teaspoon salt

½ teaspoon cream of tartar
½ cup vegetable shortening
8 ounces crumbled blue cheese
1 large egg, slightly beaten
⅔ cup milk

1. Sift dry ingredients together.
2. Cut in shortening until mixture resembles coarse crumbs. Mix in blue cheese.
3. Combine egg and milk; add to flour mixture all at once. Stir until dough is sticking to fork. Gently knead the dough, about 20 strokes.
4. Roll to ¾-inch thickness. Dip cutter in flour and cut straight down, do not twist. Place on ungreased baking sheet and chill 1-3 hours.
5. Preheat oven to 450 degrees. Bake 10-14 minutes until golden brown.

NOTE: This recipe is adjusted for high altitude baking. At sea level, use 1 tablespoon of baking powder.

Yield: 24 biscuits

Vegetable Gratin

A pretty dish that doubles as a vegetarian entrée or a side.

1 medium baking potato, thinly sliced
1 medium sweet potato, thinly sliced
1 red bell pepper, diced
2 carrots, sliced
1 red onion, thinly sliced
2 medium zucchini, thinly sliced
1 large tomato, thinly sliced

½ cup Italian bread crumbs
½ cup grated Parmesan cheese
½ tablespoon chopped fresh rosemary
Salt and freshly ground black pepper to taste
Extra virgin olive oil for drizzling

1. Preheat oven to 400 degrees. Butter an 10-inch by 8-inch baking dish.
2. Place vegetables in 3 layers in prepared dish.
   Layer 1 – potato, sweet potato, red pepper, carrots. Drizzle with olive oil
   Layer 2 – red onion, zucchini. Drizzle with olive oil.
   Layer 3 – tomato
3. Bake in oven for 30 minutes until bubbly and cooked through.
4. In a small bowl, mix bread crumbs, Parmesan cheese, rosemary, salt and pepper.
5. Remove gratin from oven and spread crumbs over the tomato layer and drizzle with olive oil. Return to oven and bake an additional 20 minutes, or until top is golden brown.

Yield: 8-10 servings

Grilled Greek Lamb Chops

The tzatziki will keep in the refrigerator for about a week and is also terrific with chicken breasts or as a dip for pita wedges.

LAMB CHOPS:

2 tablespoons dried oregano

2 teaspoons dried spearmint leaves
    (preferable, but may use mint)

1 teaspoon garlic powder

1 teaspoon dried thyme leaves

1 teaspoon salt

Freshly ground black pepper, to taste

16 loin lamb chops

Juice of 2 lemons

TZATZIKI:

2 cups plain yogurt or Greek style yogurt

¾ cup shredded English cucumber

½ teaspoon salt

1 tablespoon chopped fresh mint

1 tablespoon chopped fresh dill

2 garlic cloves, minced

¼ teaspoon white pepper

1 tablespoon extra virgin olive oil,
    optional garnish

"Give a man a fish and you feed him for a day. Teach a man to fish and you feed him for a lifetime."

Chinese Proverb

LAMB CHOPS:

1. Combine dry ingredients and grind until powdery.
2. Sprinkle lamb chops with lemon juice, coat with rub on both sides and refrigerate for 1-2 hours.
3. Preheat grill to high heat.
4. Place lamb chops on grill and cook to desired temperature; medium rare is best for lamb. Continue to sprinkle with lemon juice while cooking.

TZATZIKI:

1. If using plain yogurt: Drain in a fine sieve, cover and place in refrigerator, at least 12 hours. Greek-style yogurt can be drained and used immediately.
2. Place shredded cucumber in a sieve inside a bowl and sprinkle with ½ teaspoon salt. Mix well and allow to drain for 15 minutes.
3. Place cucumber on paper towel and squeeze until nearly dry. Add to drained yogurt.
4. Add mint, dill, garlic and pepper to yogurt mixture. Mix well and refrigerate until ready to use. Serve with lamb chops. If desired, drizzle with olive oil.

Yield: 8 servings

Cedar Plank Salmon

A healthy entrée for an easy summer dinner.

1 cedar plank (14 inches by 6 inches),
    soaked in salted water for 2 hours

1 or 2 salmon filets (about 2 pounds total)

Salt and freshly ground black pepper,
    to taste

3 tablespoons Dijon-style mustard

2 tablespoons brown sugar

1. Remove skin and remaining bones. Rinse the salmon under cold water and pat dry.
2. Season the salmon with salt and pepper on both sides.
3. Spread the mustard on the non-skin side of the salmon. Sprinkle with brown sugar.
4. Preheat the grill to medium-high heat; place the plank on the grill for 3-4 minutes. Turn the plank over and place the fish on the plank with mustard side up. Grill until cooked through, about 15 to 20 minutes.

Yield: 4 servings

IMAGINE: SCHOOL MARM

"When a young school marm showed up in the county, she usually didn't get away," commented Karl Knorr, a rancher who married a school teacher in 1948. Since the early settlers, women have been scarce in Summit County. In the 1960s, a hundred years after the 1859 gold rush began; the ratio of men to women was 50 to 1. (*Summit Pioneers*)

Cherry Sauce

Cherries from the market are so delicious and when in season make a superb sauce to slather on grilled salmon or other grilled meat or to be used as dessert sauce.

3 cups pitted fresh sweet cherries
   or frozen cherries
½ cup water
½ cup dry white wine
¼ cup chopped onion
1 garlic clove, finely chopped

2 tablespoons honey
2 tablespoons lemon juice
1 teaspoon lemon zest
½ teaspoon salt
¼ teaspoon crushed red pepper
   (omit pepper for dessert)

1. Combine all ingredients in a large suacepan and bring to a boil over medium-high heat.
2. Simmer uncovered for 30-40 minutes or until mixture thickens.

Yield: 6 servings

Blueberry Cobbler

This dumpling topping can be used with other seasonal fruits.

FILLING:
6 cups fresh blueberries
⅓ cup sugar
2 tablespoons cornstarch
1 teaspoon lemon zest

TOPPING:
1⅓ cups all-purpose flour
2 tablespoons sugar
¾ teaspoon baking powder (for sea level, use 1½ teaspoons)
¼ teaspoon salt
¼ teaspoon baking soda (for sea level, use ½ teaspoon)
5 tablespoons chilled butter, cut into small pieces
1 cup fat-free sour cream
3 tablespoons reduced-fat milk
1 teaspoon sugar

1. Preheat oven to 350 degrees.
2. Combine blueberries, sugar, cornstarch and lemon zest in an 11-inch by 7-inch baking dish.
3. Using a food processor, combine flour, sugar, baking powder, salt and baking soda; process to mix.
4. Add butter and pulse until mixture resembles coarse meal.
5. Stir in sour cream to form soft dough.
6. Drop dough by spoonfuls onto blueberry filling to form dumplings.
7. Brush dumplings with milk; sprinkle with 1 teaspoon sugar.
8. Place dish on a baking sheet.
9. Bake for 50 minutes or until filling is bubbly and dumplings are lightly browned.

NOTE: This recipe is adjusted for high altitude baking. Use 1½ teaspoons baking powder and ½ teaspoon baking soda for sea level baking.

Yield: 10 servings

Individual Lemon Sponge Cakes

An attractive presentation with a luscious treat at the bottom.

2 tablespoons butter, melted

¾ cup sugar

4 tablespoons flour

⅛ teaspoon salt

3 egg yolks, well-beaten

1½ cups milk

Zest of 1 lemon

5 tablespoons fresh lemon juice

3 egg whites, whipped (at sea level also use 3)

½ teaspoon cream of tartar

Fresh berries (raspberries, blueberries or strawberries)

Confectioners' sugar for sprinkling (optional)

6 (1-cup) ramekins

1. Preheat oven to 350 degrees.
2. Cover outside of ramekins with foil to keep from absorbing water. Butter insides of ramekins.
3. Combine sugar, flour and salt in a large bowl.
4. In a small bowl, combine egg yolks and milk. Mix well and blend in lemon zest and lemon juice.
5. Add liquids to flour mixture and mix well.
7. Whip egg whites with cream of tartar to stiff peaks and fold into the batter.
8. Ladle into prepared ramekins and set into a 13-inch by 9-inch baking pan.
9. Place baking pan with ramekins in center of preheated oven. Fill baking pan half full with boiling water.
10. Bake for 30 minutes or until tops are nicely browned.
11. Remove ramekins and cool.
12. To serve, top with fresh seasonal berries and a sprinkling of confectioners' sugar, if desired.

Yield: 6 servings

SUMMER ART FESTIVALS

In early summer, Keystone mixes it up with the Blues and Art Show. Breckenridge, Frisco and Dillon offer art festivals throughout the summer featuring hundreds of artists highlighting mixed mediums.

Minty Sun Tea

With an average of 300 days of sunshine per year, there are many opportunities to brew sun tea.

1 gallon of water

15 fresh mint leaves

3 family-size tea bags

Sugar to taste

Mint sprigs

1 lemon, sliced

1 orange, sliced

1. Fill a gallon jar with cold water and add mint leaves.
2. Place tea bags in jar and add sugar to sweeten, if desired.
3. Put the lid on the jar loosely and place in sun for a few hours.
4. Remove tea bags and serve with mint sprigs and lemon and orange.

Yield: 1 gallon

Briar Rose Chophouse and Saloon

Proprietors
Chris Galceran, Ken Nelson and Todd Nelson

Briar Rose Chophouse Mac-n-Cheese

Giampietro's Red Bell Pepper Soup

Briar Rose Chophouse Buffalo Short Ribs

Mountain Berry Tiramisu

The Briar Rose has an old west feel with high-end flair and is located on Lincoln Avenue in historic Breckenridge. Brothers Ken and Todd Nelson partnered with Chris Galceran to create the inviting chophouse and saloon.

Briar Rose Chophouse Mac-n-Cheese

MAC-N-CHEESE SAUCE BASE:
4 tablespoons butter
¼ cup all-purpose flour
1 cup milk
1 cup vegetable stock
⅛ teaspoon dry mustard
⅛ teaspoon Worcestershire sauce
⅛ teaspoon hot pepper sauce
1 tablespoon salt
2 teaspoons fresh cracked pepper

1. Melt butter in saucepan, add flour; cook 2 minutes, stirring until smooth.
2. Add milk and vegetable stock; cook on medium heat until sauce is thick and bubbly.
3. Remove from heat and season with dry mustard, Worcestershire, hot pepper sauce, salt and pepper. Allow to cool before using.

MAC-N-CHEESE MIX:
24-ounce package large elbow macaroni
¾ pound sharp yellow cheddar, grated
½ pound Gruyère, grated
½ pound extra sharp white cheddar, grated
28 ounces Velveeta cheese cut into 1-inch cubes

1. Cook the elbow macaroni in boiling salted water until al dente, drain and rinse in cold water.
2. Combine all cheeses and elbow macaroni in a large bowl and mix thoroughly; add the sauce base and combine well.

MAC-N-CHEESE TOPPING:
About 1 cup panko bread crumbs
½ cup Parmesan cheese, grated

ASSEMBLY OF MAC-N-CHEESE
1. Combine topping ingredients.
2. Butter a large baking dish or 8-10 ramekins. Pack with macaroni and cheese mix leaving a ½-inch of space at the top and making sure cheese is evenly distributed, especially the cubes.
3. Top generously with bread crumb mix. Bake at 375 degrees for 20-30 minutes depending on the size and depth of your dish. It should be hot and bubbly with areas of golden brown. Let stand 5 minutes before serving.

Yield: 8 – 10 servings

Giampietro's Red Bell Pepper Soup

2 ounces olive oil

1 large yellow onion, peeled and sliced thin

6 red bell peppers, stemmed and seeded, chopped rough

Red chili flakes to taste

2 quarts chicken or vegetable stock

1 cup heavy cream

1 medium russet potato, peeled and sliced thin

Kosher salt to taste

1. Add oil to a large pot and sweat the onion and peppers together until the onions are translucent. Add the desired amount of red chili flakes at this time.
2. Add the stock to the onions and peppers until they are covered (about 1 inch), add the cream and bring to a simmer.
3. Add the potato to the soup and lightly season with salt. Bring the soup to a boil and then simmer until the potatoes are cooked through.
4. Working in batches, purée the soup in a blender until smooth, adjust seasoning. Reheat to serve.

Yield: 6-8 servings

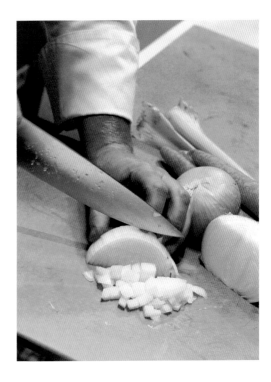

The Nelsons also own the casual eateries, Giampietro's Pizzeria and Empire Burger.

Executive Chef Todd, who studied at the Culinary Institute of America in Hyde Park, New York, brings a creative touch to a traditional chophouse menu while Ken and Chris tend to operations. Premium beef, wild game and artisanal pork, sourced regionally, are complemented by fine wines, mouth watering sides and desserts.

Briar Rose Chophouse Buffalo Short Ribs

MARINADE:
10 pounds buffalo short ribs
4 cups dry red wine
4 sprigs thyme
4 garlic cloves, crushed
2 bay leaves

1. Place short ribs in a large roasting pan. Add wine, thyme, garlic, and bay leaves; allow to marinate 12-24 hours.
2. Remove short ribs from marinade and pat dry; discard marinade.

BRAISE:
3 yellow onions, small dice
3 carrots, small dice
4 ribs celery, small dice
2 cups diced canned tomatoes
4 cups dry red wine, divided
4 sprigs thyme
2 bay leaves
2-3 quarts brown veal stock (may be purchased at specialty shops)
Marinated short ribs
Salt and pepper
Flour for dredging

1. Season short ribs with salt and pepper on both sides, dredge in flour and sear in roasting pan; do this in batches so as not to crowd the pan. Reserve the seared short ribs. Add the mirepoix to the pan.
2. Cook the mirepoix until the onions are lightly caramelized; add the tomatoes, then 2 cups of the red wine.
3. Return the short ribs back to the pan with the thyme and bay leaves. Add the stock to just cover the short ribs, cover the pan and cook in the oven at 225 degrees for 8 hours minimum.
4. Remove the short ribs from the braising liquid; add remaining 2 cups of red wine to the braising liquid and reduce the liquid by half.
5. Return the short ribs to the reduced sauce.

SERVING SUGGESTIONS: Serve on whipped potatoes, polenta, or buttered egg noodles. A gremolata makes an excellent garnish and flavor pop for this dish.

NOTE: Mirepoix is a mixture of diced carrots, onions, celery and herbs that is used to season sauces. Gremolata is a mixture of chopped parsley, finely chopped toasted walnuts or pine nuts, garlic and orange zest.

Yield: 8 – 10 servings

Mountain Berry Tiramisu

Fresh seasonal berries: 1 pint of strawberries, ½ pint of raspberries,
   blueberries, and blackberries, divided
¼ cup blackberry brandy
¼ cup Grand Marnier
½ cup water
6 egg yolks
1 cup sugar
⅓ cup Grand Marnier
5 sleeves ladyfinger cookies
2 cups heavy cream
2 pounds mascarpone cheese, at room temperature
Powdered sugar

1. Combine 1 cup of fresh berries, preferably any bruised berries, with blackberry brandy, Grand Marnier and water in a saucepan. Heat until simmering; allow to cool and purée in blender.
2. Combine egg yolks, sugar and 1/3 cup Grand Marnier in top of double boiler and heat over boiling water. Whisk mixture vigorously to incorporate air. Cook mixture until thickened to almost a soft peak stage. This should take about 8-12 minutes.
3. Whip heavy cream until thick. Fold egg yolk mixture into cream.
4. Place mascarpone in a large bowl and fold cream and egg yolk mixture into bowl. Whisk slightly to thicken mixture.
5. Layer the bottom of a 13-inch by 9-inch pan with ladyfingers. Pour half the cooked berry purée over the ladyfingers and then half the mascarpone mixture over the berry-soaked ladyfingers. Smooth with rubber spatula.
6. Arrange a second layer of ladyfingers over the mascarpone mixture. Soak ladyfingers with the remaining berry purée. Top with remaining mascarpone mixture and smooth with rubber spatula.
7. Place the remaining fresh berries on top of the mascarpone mixture and chill. Sprinkle with powdered sugar when serving.

Yield: 12 servings

Expect to be served in gracious, high country ambiance, whether you are seated in the elegant dining room or in the historic bar next to the "scandalous" portrait of the mistress of an early pioneer.

Blue River Tailgate

Tailgating is a great way to kick off a "boot scootin" fun evening at the Riverwalk Center.

Spinach and Roasted Pepper Dip
Southwest Corn Dip
Triple "R" Guacamole
T-Bar Deviled Eggs
Cheesy Chicken Wings

Old Settlers' Baked Beans
Red Potato and Green Bean Salad

Rocky Mountain Buffalo Burgers
Blue River Brisket

Strawberry Ruhbarb Pie
Chocolate Butterscotch Fudge
Cowgirl Cupcakes

Texas Sweet Tea

PAT GREEN CONCERT

Tailgating at the Riverwalk before the Pat Green concert kicked off the 2009 Breckenridge Music Festival's Blue River Summer Season. Guests indulged in chilled drinks and sweet tea and devoured buckets of nuts, tasty finger food and delicious desserts. Red bandanas tied with twine served as napkins and party favors. And flowers? Giant sunflowers in watering cans, of course!

Spinach and Roasted Pepper Dip

Serve with pita chips, wheat crackers or crudités.

2 (10-ounce) packages chopped frozen spinach, thawed, drained and squeezed dry
2 cups sour cream
1 cup real mayonnaise (a must!)
1 package vegetable soup mix

1 (4-ounce) jar of roasted red peppers, well drained and chopped
1 green onion, white section only, chopped
3 tablespoons freshly grated Parmesan cheese

1. Combine all ingredients. Cover and place in refrigerator to chill for at least 4 hours.
2. Can be made the day before, but add the spinach and Parmesan cheese only 4 hours before serving.

Yield: 25 servings

Southwest Corn Dip

A colorful prelude to a concert and simple to make.

1 pound block sharp cheddar cheese, grated
2 (11-ounce) cans Mexi corn, drained
1 cup mayonnaise (may use reduced fat mayonnaise)
4-6 green onions, chopped, including some of the green
1 jalapeno or serrano chile, seeded if desired, finely minced

1. Combine all ingredients.
2. Cover and refrigerate, if making ahead of time.
3. Serve with corn chips.

Yield: 4 cups of dip

Triple "R" Guacamole

A twist on the traditional Mexican favorite.

3 ripe avocados, halved, pitted and scooped out
½ lemon, juiced
½ medium onion, minced
2 tomatoes, diced

⅓ bunch fresh cilantro, finely chopped, some whole leaves reserved for garnish
½ cup shredded cheddar cheese
Salt and freshly ground black pepper to taste

1. Mash avocados with a fork; add lemon juice and stir well.
2. Stir in onions, tomatoes, cilantro and cheddar cheese.
3. Add salt and pepper to taste. Garnish with cilantro leaves.

Yield: 3 cups

T-Bar Deviled Eggs

A deviled egg with a kick that sets it apart.

12 hard-cooked eggs, peeled
2 tablespoons diced green onions
2 tablespoons chopped fresh cilantro
2 small serrano or jalapeno peppers, seeded and finely minced
    (more if you like the heat)
½ cup mayonnaise
2 teaspoons Dijon-style mustard
1 teaspoon salt
½ cup shredded cheddar cheese
Chili powder to taste

1. Cut eggs in half lengthwise; carefully remove yolks. Combine yolks
    thoroughly with remaining ingredients.
2. Spoon about 1 tablespoon egg yolk mixture into egg white; sprinkle
    with extra cheese and chili powder. Cover and chill.

Yield: 2 dozen servings

PREPARING THE PERFECT HARD-COOKED EGG

Cover eggs with cold water. Bring the water to a full boil. Cover and reduce heat. Simmer for 20 minutes. Plunge into ice cold water.

Cheesy Chicken Wings

A crunchy delight that stands on its own or can be dipped in a favorite sauce.

1 cup finely grated Parmesan cheese
1 cup fine bread crumbs
2 tablespoons dried parsley flakes
2 teaspoons paprika
1 tablespoon dried oregano
2 teaspoons salt
½ teaspoon freshly ground black pepper
1 cup (2 sticks) butter, melted
4 pounds chicken wings, cut at joints, discard tips

1. Preheat oven to 350 degrees. Line a baking sheet with foil.
2. Mix together cheese, bread crumbs, parsley, paprika, oregano, salt and pepper.
    Spread on plate.
3. Dip wing pieces in melted butter and then roll in cheese/bread crumb mixture.
    Coat well.
4. Place wings on baking sheet close together.
5. Bake wings for 1 hour and 15 minutes. Serve hot or at room temperature.

Yield: 15 servings

THE BLUE RIVER SERIES

The Blue River Series of the Festival is a favorite for diversified entertainment year round. Nationally known performing artists are mixed with regional talent. The program includes a broad spectrum of music beyond classical and appeals to audiences of all ages and all tastes.

Old Settlers' Baked Beans

Coat measuring cup with cooking spray for easy pouring of molasses.

4 (15-ounce) cans baked beans, drained	1 teaspoon Liquid Smoke
1 teaspoon cayenne pepper	1 tablespoon Worcestershire sauce
1½ cups chopped onion	½ teaspoon salt
¾ cup dark molasses	¼ teaspoon black pepper
¾ cup barbeque sauce	2 tablespoons spicy brown mustard
Hot pepper sauce to taste	6-7 slices crisp cooked bacon, crumbled
½ teaspoon bitters	

1. Preheat oven to 350 degrees.
2. Place drained beans in a large bowl.
3. Add remaining ingredients except for bacon. Mix well.
4. Pour bean mixture into 13-inch by 9-inch baking pan. Top with bacon.
5. Bake, uncovered, for 1 hour.

Yield: 12-16 servings

Red Potato and Green Bean Salad

No mayo, no worries …perfect for a picnic.

½ pound green beans, trimmed and cut into 1½-inch pieces	1 large shallot, chopped
3 pounds small red-skinned potatoes, unpeeled, halved	1 tablespoon coarse-grained Dijon-style mustard
2 tablespoons dry vermouth	½ cup extra virgin olive oil
2 tablespoons white wine vinegar	2 tablespoons chopped fresh parsley
	Salt and freshly ground black pepper to taste

1. Blanch beans in a large saucepan of boiling, salted water until tender crisp, about 3-4 minutes. Drain and transfer to a bowl of ice water to stop the cooking process. Pat dry with paper towels.
2. Cook potatoes in boiling, salted water until just tender, about 12-15 minutes. Drain and transfer to salad bowl.
3. Sprinkle vermouth over hot potatoes, toss gently and let stand 5 minutes.
4. In a small bowl, whisk vinegar, shallots and mustard. Gradually drizzle in the oil. Pour over potatoes and toss to coat. Cool completely.
5. Toss in green beans and parsley with the potatoes. Season to taste. Serve at room temperature or cold.

Yield: 8-10 servings

Rocky Mountain Buffalo Burgers

The smoked paprika lends a Spanish flavor to these low-fat burgers.

2 pounds ground buffalo	3 teaspoons smoked paprika, divided
½ cup grated onion	½ teaspoon ground cumin
1⅓ cups grated zucchini (about 1 small zucchini); squeeze dry	1½ teaspoons salt
⅔ cup grated carrot	¼ teaspoon cayenne pepper
8 tablespoons chili sauce, divided	⅔ cup mayonnaise

1. Mix ground buffalo, onion, zucchini, carrot, 2 tablespoons chili sauce, 2 teaspoons paprika, cumin, salt and cayenne pepper together with hands until well blended. Shape into 8 tightly packed patties.
2. Preheat grill on high; generously oil grill rack.
3. Reduce temperature to medium and cook patties about 6 minutes per side for medium, or until no longer pink inside.
4. To prepare sauce, combine mayonnaise, 6 tablespoons chili sauce and remaining teaspoon of paprika.
5. Serve burgers topped with sauce on toasted whole grain buns.

Yield: 8 servings

Blue River Brisket

Briskets are easy make-ahead entrées that work well at tailgate parties.

1 (3-pound) top cut brisket, trimmed	⅓ cup Worcestershire sauce
Celery salt	1½ cups of a favorite barbeque sauce, additional sauce for serving
Onion powder	
Garlic powder	Crusty buns
2 ounces Liquid Smoke seasoning	1 red onion, thinly sliced

1. Generously sprinkle celery salt, onion powder and garlic powder on both sides of brisket. Wrap brisket in foil and pour Liquid Smoke over meat before closing. Refrigerate overnight.
2. Preheat oven to 250 degrees. Open up brisket packet and pour Worcestershire sauce over meat. Reclose foil and place wrapped brisket in baking dish with rim.
3. Bake for 8 hours or until meat tests tender with fork.
4. Remove from oven, peel back foil and pour off extra liquid.
5. Cover meat completely with barbeque sauce and return to oven to bake for 1 hour, uncovered.
6. Remove from oven and let rest 1 hour. Slice thinly across the grain and serve on buns with additional sauce and onions, if desired.

Yield: 6 servings

SPONSORING MUSICIANS

Music patrons can bond with the Festival by sponsoring a musician. Both sponsors and musicians benefit from the match and the Festival gets a funding boost. The sponsor learns about the orchestra and what it takes for a musician to follow his or her passion. Musicians get closer to the pulse of the audience and enjoy a local's knowledge of the area.

HOW TO PREPARE RHUBARB

Choose fresh crisp stalks and remove any stringy covering before use. Refresh the stalks by standing them in cold water for an hour. Remove any leaves – they are toxic! Trim the ends. The vegetable does not need to be completely peeled. It goes nicely with a sweet partner, like strawberries and sugar.

Strawberry Rhubarb Pie

The orange zest sets this pie apart.

1¼ pounds rhubarb stalks
1½ cups strawberries, stemmed and sliced
1 cup plus 2 tablespoons sugar
3 tablespoons tapioca flour or all-purpose flour
¼ teaspoon salt
1 teaspoon grated orange zest
2 (9-inch) pie crusts

1. Preheat oven to 400 degrees.
2. Peel stringy layer off large rhubarb stalks. Trim ends and discard all leaves as they are toxic.
3. Cut stalks into ½ inch pieces for 4 cups.
4. Combine rhubarb, strawberries, sugar, flour, salt and orange zest. Let sit for 10 minutes.
5. Place 1 crust in pie pan and pour in filling. Dampen edges and cover with top crust. Crimp edges and cut slits for steam.
6. Cover edges with foil strips or a crust protector.
7. Bake for 20 minutes. Reduce heat to 350 degrees and bake 35-40 minutes longer. Remove crust protector last 20 minutes. Cool.
8. Serve at room temperature or chilled.

NOTE: Tapioca flour blends smoothly and gives a nice shine to filling.

Yield: 8 servings

Chocolate Butterscotch Fudge

A delicious morsel guaranteed to satisfy any sweet tooth!

2 cups (12 ounces) semi-sweet chocolate morsels
1 cup butterscotch chips or morsels
1 teaspoon vanilla

1 (14-ounce) can sweetened condensed milk
1 cup coarsely chopped walnuts, (optional)
½ cup raisins (optional)

1. Place morsels, vanilla and sweetened condensed milk in heavy saucepan over medium heat.
2. Stir until melted, approximately 5 minutes. Remove from heat.
3. Stir in nuts and raisins if desired.
4. Butter an 8-inch by 8-inch pan and fill with mixture.
5. Refrigerate for at least 30 minutes. Cut into 1-inch squares.

Yield: 64 one inch squares.

Cowgirl Cupcakes

These moist, carrot cupcakes can be frozen for up to one month.

CAKE:

3 cups peeled, grated carrots
   (about 5-7 carrots)

1 cup chopped walnuts

1 (8-ounce) can crushed pineapple, drained

1¼ cups canola oil

1½ cups granulated sugar

7 large eggs, plus 1 yolk, room temperature

2 tablespoons vanilla

2¼ cups all-purpose flour

1¼ teaspoons baking soda (use 2
   teaspoons at sea level)

1 teaspoon salt

2 teaspoons cinnamon

1 teaspoon nutmeg

¾ teaspoon ground ginger

½ teaspoon ground allspice (optional)

FROSTING:

1 (8-ounce) package cream cheese,
   at room temperature

1 cup (2 sticks) unsalted butter,
   at room temperature

Pinch salt

1½ teaspoons vanilla

4 cups confectioners' sugar, sifted

1. Preheat oven to 375 degrees.
2. Grate carrots using a box grater or food processor. Gently mix carrots, walnuts and pineapple.
3. In a large bowl, whisk oil, sugar, eggs and vanilla. Sift together flour, baking soda, salt and spices. Gently add dry ingredients to oil-sugar-egg mixture. Stir in the carrots, nuts and pineapple.
4. Fill cupcake liners two-thirds full with batter. Place cupcakes in oven, reduce temperature to 350 degrees and bake for 20 minutes or until toothpick inserted comes out clean.
5. Cool cupcakes completely.
6. In a food processor or a mixer, blend cream cheese and butter until creamy. Gradually add salt, vanilla and sugar, beating until smooth. Frost cupcakes.

NOTE: This recipe is adjusted for high altitude baking. Use 2 teaspoons of baking soda at sea level.

Yield: 33-36 cupcakes.

Texas Sweet Tea

Nothing like a good old glass of Southern sweet tea on a hot summer day or any other day as far as that goes.

3 quarts water

2 cups sugar

4 tea bags, 1 quart-size

1. Bring water to a rolling boil; add sugar. Stir to dissolve.
2. Add tea bags and stir. Let sit for 20 minutes.
3. Pour into a gallon size container and fill the rest with cool water.

Yield: 12 servings

FUN, FOOD, AND FROLIC

Summer brings great entertainment to Summit County. Keystone blends food and music with the Wine and Jazz Festival and later offers Bluegrass and Beer. The Breckenridge Beer Festival features microbrews and lively music. "Music on Main" in Frisco is an all day free concert. Summer is capped off at Copper Mountain on Labor Day weekend with the spirited "Copper Country".

Autumn Quest

After viewing the aspens or the bugling elk, choose from these hearty comfort foods
to enjoy back at your cozy mountain lodge.

A Hardy Bloody Mary

Avocado and Shrimp Dip
Oktoberfest Meatballs
Asparagus and Prosciutto Puffs

Minestrone á la Toscana

Apple, Nut, Stilton Cheese and Beet Salad
Green Salad with Cashews and Cranberries

Caramelized Onions
Harvest Vegetables in Ginger Butter
Jasmine Rice

Pull Apart Bread

Fresh Pasta with Red Sauce
Lamb Shish Kebabs
Osso Bucco

Alpine Bread Pudding
Chocolate and Grand Marnier Crème Brûleé

ASPEN HIKE

There's still gold in the mountains, aspen gold. Mother Nature's alchemy creates a fall display that begs for exploration. The Chihuahua Gulch hike winds through aspen forests and leads to a frozen lake. The Ptarmigan Peaks trail offers vibrant views to the west. Monte Cristo/Blue Lakes sparkle with a golden panorama and silvery lake. Every day can be a new discovery.

A Hardy Bloody Mary

Make this without alcohol and enjoy a "Contrary Mary".

1 jalapeno pepper, stem and seeds removed
1 habanero pepper, stem and seeds removed
6 tablespoons Worcestershire sauce
¼ cup steak sauce
2 tablespoons chopped fresh cilantro
1 tablespoon prepared horseradish
1 tablespoon garlic salt
1 teaspoon freshly ground black pepper
¼ teaspoon fresh oregano
Juice of ½ lemon
1 cup orange juice
1 quart tomato juice
1 cup vodka or tequila, to taste
2 teaspoons salt and 1 teaspoon mild chili powder, combined,
    for glass rims, optional
Garnish with lemon and lime slices, celery stalks or olives

1. Combine first 12 ingredients in blender; add vodka or tequila to taste.
2. Moisten rims of glasses and dip in chili/salt mixture, if desired. Fill with cocktail and garnish, as desired. Can be served over ice.

Yield: 6-8 servings

Avocado and Shrimp Dip

A combination of textures makes for an unusual dip.

3 avocados, halved, pitted, scooped out and coarsely diced
1 tablespoon lemon juice
1 pound shrimp, cooked, deveined, cut into chunks
¾ bottle (9 ounces) cocktail sauce
¾ bottle (9 ounces) chili sauce

1. In a bowl, lightly toss diced avocado with lemon juice.
2. Stir in remaining ingredients. Chill. To prevent browning, add avocado pit and cover tightly with plastic wrap.
3. Serve with corn chips or pita chips.

Yield: 3 cups

Oktoberfest Meatballs

Put on a football game, get out the toothpicks and watch these meatballs disappear.

1 pound hot bulk pork sausage
1 pound regular bulk pork sausage
1⅓ cups seasoned bread crumbs, divided in half
32 ounces sauerkraut, well-drained
2 eggs, beaten
1 jar prepared brown mustard for dipping

1. Preheat oven to 350 degrees.
2. In a large bowl, combine sausages, 2/3 cup bread crumbs, eggs and sauerkraut and mix thoroughly.
3. Form into 1-inch diameter meatballs and roll in remaining bread crumbs.
4. Place meatballs on a non-stick, rimmed baking sheet and bake for 30 minutes. Turn meatballs over and cook for an additional 30 minutes.
5. Serve with brown mustard.

Yield: 48-50 meatballs

OKTOBERFEST

Oktoberfest on Main Street Breckenridge is a lively festival of beer, food and music. It comes together with a roar to celebrate the season. Some folksy Oompah bands and lederhosen set the mood. The crowds do the rest!

Asparagus and Proscuitto Puffs

If prosciutto is too salty, substitute Black Forest ham to give a smokier taste.

½ pound thin-sliced prosciutto, cut into ½-inch wide strips
60 fresh asparagus tips, 3 inches long (save stalks to flavor soups)
1 (17.3-ounce) package frozen puff pastry, 2 sheets, thawed
Dijon-style mustard
Parsley, lettuce for garnish, optional

1. Preheat oven to 400 degrees.
2. Wrap middle of each asparagus spear with a strip of prosciutto. Set aside.
3. Lay one sheet of thawed puff pastry flat on a work surface and spread a thin layer of mustard over entire pastry.
4. Cut pastry into 2-inch squares and place an asparagus spear diagonally on each square. Roll the pastry around the asparagus, leaving the ends of the asparagus uncovered. Moisten the corners with water to seal. Continue with second sheet of pastry.
5. Cover a baking sheet with parchment paper and arrange pastry rolls 1 inch apart on sheet. Can be prepared up to 24 hours in advance to this point, covered tightly with plastic wrap and refrigerated.
6. Bake in oven 15-20 minutes until nicely puffed and browned, rotating baking sheet for even browning.
7. Transfer to garnished platter and serve warm.

Yield: 60 servings

IMAGINE: BOREAS PASS

In early mining days, Boreas Pass was a trail for burros and foot travelers carrying supplies. Twenty-three years after the gold discovery the railroad took over. Now with the gold and rails long gone, aspen thrive. Sparks from locomotives had caused fires and over time clusters of aspen emerged. The shimmer of leaves gives a new purpose to travel the Pass.

Minestrone á la Toscana

Hearty enough as a main dish yet light enough as a starter.

6-8 slices of bacon, chopped
3 celery stalks, chopped
3 carrots, sliced
1 large onion, chopped
2 garlic cloves, minced
¼ cup minced fresh parsley
2 cans beef broth or chicken broth
5-7 cups water
1 (14½-ounce) can diced tomatoes, with juices
1 (16-ounce) can pinto or kidney beans
1 teaspoon dried basil
1 teaspoon dried oregano
1 teaspoon salt
2 bay leaves
¼ teaspoon freshly ground black pepper
½ head cabbage, thinly sliced
½ cup elbow macaroni
3 medium zucchini, thinly sliced
Freshly grated Parmesan cheese
Sour cream, optional

1. Cook bacon in a large Dutch oven or 10 quart soup pot, until crisp.
2. Remove bacon from pan and reserve. Sauté celery, carrots and onion in bacon fat until soft. Add garlic and parsley and sauté 1 more minute.
3. Add broth, water, tomatoes with juices, beans, basil, oregano, salt, bay leaves and pepper. Bring to a boil and simmer for 45-60 minutes, until vegetables are tender. Discard bay leaves.
4. Remove about a third of the vegetables from the soup and purée in a blender until smooth; return puréed vegetables to soup.
5. Add cabbage and macaroni and simmer for 20 minutes more; add zucchini and cook another 10 minutes until macaroni is tender.
6. Serve in individual bowls; garnish each with reserved bacon, freshly grated Parmesan cheese and sour cream.

Yield: serves 8 as a first course, or 5 as a main course.

Apple, Nut, Stilton Cheese and Beet Salad

This classic salad can also be made with pears in place of apple.

1 cup peeled, cored and coarsely chopped apple
½ cup coarsely chopped walnut pieces
½ cup crumbled Stilton cheese
¾ cup coarsely chopped fresh white mushroom caps
3 tablespoons mayonnaise
Salt and freshly ground black pepper, to taste
1 (16-ounce) can sliced beets
1 teaspoon chopped fresh chives for garnish

1. Combine apple, nuts, cheese and mushrooms in a medium bowl.
2. Add mayonnaise, salt and pepper and mix well. Chill until ready to serve.
3. When ready to serve, drain the juice from the can of beets and divide beet slices on four plates.
4. Spoon apple/nut mixture on top of the sliced beets and sprinkle with the fresh chives. Serve chilled.
5. If preparing ahead of time, add beets just before serving.

Yield: 4 servings

IMAGINE: TRESPASSERS

"Warning: We shoot every 10th trespasser, the 9th one just left," cautioned a sign on Howard and Lura Belle Giberson's ranch before a trespasser they couldn't stop, Interstate 70, cut through their land in the 1970s. Part of the family land was previously lost to the Dillon Reservoir in the early 1960s. (quote from *Summit Pioneers*)

Green Salad with Cashews and Cranberries

Use the extra dressing as a marinade for chicken or fish.

DRESSING:
¼ cup balsamic vinegar
¾ cup extra virgin olive oil
1 tablespoon sugar
Pinch salt
Freshly ground black pepper
2 garlic cloves
5 fresh basil leaves

SALAD:
8 ounces of mixed greens
¼ cup canned mandarin oranges, drained
¼ cup toasted cashews
¼ cup dried cranberries
¼ cup crumbled feta cheese

1. Combine dressing ingredients in a blender and blend on high until basil and garlic are minced and dressing has thickened.
2. Toss all salad ingredients in large salad bowl.
3. When ready to serve, toss salad lightly with 4 ounces (½ cup) of the dressing.

NOTE: Reserve the remaining dressing for up to 10 days in the refrigerator.

Yield: 6 servings

IMAGINE: HALLOWEEN

"That first Halloween, I made a costume from gunny sacks and dressed my daughter up as a little monkey. It sure didn't take her long to go trick or treating because there weren't that many houses in town" recalled Helen Foote on Frisco circa 1950 when the population was between 60 and 70. Today, 2700 people call Frisco home. (*Summit Pioneers*)

Caramelized Onions

These mild flavored onions make an excellent side dish.

4 tablespoons unsalted butter
1 pound pearl onions, frozen
1 tablespoon minced fresh
  thyme

½ teaspoon each of salt and freshly
  ground black pepper
1½ tablespoons sugar
¼ cup red wine

1. Preheat oven to 350 degrees.
2. In an ovenproof skillet, melt butter over medium heat. Add frozen pearl onions, reduce heat to low and cook, turning often until slightly golden, 5-10 minutes. Cover the onions and cook another 3-4 minutes.
3. Add thyme, salt and pepper and cook 3-4 minutes, until onions are lightly browned and barely soft.
4. Sprinkle with sugar and cook, stirring often, until onions are caramelized and a thick syrup has formed, 3-4 minutes.
5. Add red wine and deglaze the pan. Simmer 1-2 minutes.
6. Place skillet in oven and bake until golden brown and very tender, about 15 minutes. Cool briefly before serving.

Yield: 8 Servings

Harvest Vegetables in Ginger Butter

The ginger and dressing make this dish special. Mmmm!

½ cup each of carrots, parsnips, turnips
  and butternut squash; cut into
  ¼-inch x 2-inch matchsticks
1 tablespoon butter
½ tablespoon vegetable oil

1 tablespoon grated fresh ginger
2 tablespoons honey
2 tablespoons fresh lemon juice
Salt and freshly ground black
  pepper, to taste

1. Blanch vegetables separately in boiling salted water for 3-5 minutes. Remove with slotted spoon and rinse under cold water. Pat dry and set aside.
2. In a large skillet or wok, heat butter and oil over medium heat.
3. Add ginger and stir fry until fragrant, about 1 minute.
4. Add blanched vegetables and stir fry for about 5 minutes, until crisp-tender.
5. Transfer to a serving dish.
6. Combine honey, lemon juice, salt and pepper and mix well.
7. Add to vegetables and stir to coat.

Yield: 4 Servings

Jasmine Rice

This recipe can easily be doubled and be made ahead and kept warm.

1 cup jasmine rice
2 cups chicken broth
1 tablespoon salted butter
1 tablespoon extra virgin olive oil
¼ cup diced sweet onion
¼ cup peeled and diced Granny Smith apple

2 tablespoons diced red bell pepper
Salt and freshly ground black pepper,
   to taste
Fresh basil leaves, chopped, optional

1. Rinse the rice in cold water until water runs clear and drain.
2. In medium size saucepan, bring chicken broth, butter, and rice to a boil; cover partially.
3. Reduce heat and simmer about 18 minutes or until the rice is tender but firm to the bite.
4. While the rice is cooking, heat olive oil in a small pan and add the onion, apple, pepper and sauté 3 minutes on medium heat.
5. When the rice is cooked, stir in the vegetable mixture and season with salt and pepper to taste. This can be made ahead and kept warm.
6. Garnish with fresh basil leaves, if using.

Yield: 4 Servings

Pull Apart Bread

This bread is fun for everyone to make.

5½ - 6½ cups all-purpose flour, divided
3 tablespoons sugar
2 teaspoons salt
½ (1⅛ teaspoons) package yeast; (at sea level,
   use 1 package yeast)

1½ cups warm water
½ cup milk
3 tablespoons butter, divided

SPECIAL THANKS

Bob Winsett is renowned in Summit County for his professional photography. Since 1984, he has captured mountain scenery, golfers, skiers, hikers, rafters and fly fisherman in addition to architectural photography. Bob accepted the challenge of capturing our local chefs at work in their restaurants, and through his photos, we get a feeling for each of these fine establishments.

1. In a large bowl, mix together 2 cups flour, sugar, salt and yeast.
2. Combine the water, milk and 2 tablespoons butter in a saucepan.
3. Heat over low heat until 120-130 degrees; butter does not need to melt.
4. Gradually add heated liquids to dry ingredients and beat 2 minutes at medium speed. Add ¾ cup more flour and beat for 2 more minutes. Stir in enough of the remaining flour to make stiff dough.
5. Turn out onto a lightly floured surface and knead until smooth and elastic.
6. Place in a greased bowl and turn to evenly grease the top of the dough. Cover and let rise until doubled, about 1 hour.
7. Punch dough down, divide in half. Cover and let rest on floured surface for 15 minutes. Meanwhile melt 1 tablespoon butter.
8. Roll each half into a 12-inch by 8-inch rectangle and brush with melted butter. Cut crosswise into 4 equal strips, 8 inches long. Stack strips, cut crosswise again into 4 equal pieces.
9. Place stacks on edge in a greased 8½-inch by 4½-inch by 2½-inch loaf pan. Repeat with remaining dough.
10. Cover and let rise in a warm place, until doubled, about 1 hour.
11. Preheat oven to 400 degrees. Bake about 30 minutes. Remove from pans and cool on a wire rack.

NOTE: This recipe has been adjusted for high altitude baking. Use 1 package of yeast at sea level.

Yield: 2 Loaves

COOKING PASTA AT ALTITUDE

The best technique for cooking pasta is the taste test. Boil the pasta based on the maximum time in the package directions. Then stand over the pot testing periodically to catch it at the perfect texture. A real benefit for pasta lovers!

Fresh Pasta with Red Sauce

Semolina flour can be purchased at natural foods stores.

RED SAUCE:	FRESH PASTA:
3 garlic cloves, peeled and left whole	2 cups semolina flour
3 tablespoons extra virgin olive oil	2 eggs
1 (14½-ounce) can diced tomatoes	3-6 teaspoons extra virgin olive oil
1 (12-ounce) can tomato paste	All-purpose flour for dusting
1 cup red wine	2 quarts boiling water
⅓ cup sugar	
2 bay leaves	

RED SAUCE:

1. Heat olive oil in a large saucepan over medium-high heat.
2. Reduce heat to medium-low, add garlic and cook until soft and fragrant, 8-10 minutes.
3. Remove garlic (use in another dish). Add tomatoes, tomato paste, wine, sugar and bay leaves. Simmer at least 3 hours. Remove bay leaves before serving.

FRESH PASTA:

1. Put semolina flour in a medium mixing bowl. Make a well in the middle of the flour and drop in eggs. Stir together until mixed.
2. Add oil one teaspoon at a time until mixture forms a ball. Cover, let rest fifteen minutes.
3. Roll out pasta by machine or by hand; roll out on a lightly floured surface and cut into desired pasta shape.
4. Boil water in a large pot. Drop in pasta; boil until the pasta rises to the surface of the boiling water (3-5 minutes). Drain.
5. Serve pasta topped with sauce and freshly grated Parmesan cheese.

NOTE: This side dish can become an entrée by adding 1 pound of cooked meat of your choice. Meatballs that have been browned can be added the last hour of cooking.

Yield: 6 servings

Lamb Shish Kebabs

Your guests will want to take just 'one more bite'.

MARINADE:	LAMB KEBABS:
¾ cup extra virgin olive oil	1 pound lamb from leg, cut
⅓ cup sherry or wine vinegar	into 1 inch cubes
1 teaspoon salt	8 cherry tomatoes
2 teaspoons dry mustard	8 mushroom caps
4 teaspoons Worcestershire sauce	1 large onion, cut into 8 wedges
2 large garlic cloves, peeled and lightly crushed	2 green bell peppers, cubed
½ teaspoon dried oregano	4 (12-inch) metal skewers

1. Whisk together all marinade ingredients in a bowl.
2. Place marinade and cubed lamb in a re-sealable plastic bag and refrigerate for 6 hours or overnight, turning occasionally.
3. Remove lamb from marinade and discard marinade. Prepare kebabs by alternately threading lamb and vegetables on skewers.
4. Preheat grill on high and grill about 10 minutes, turning after 5 minutes to cook evenly.

Yield: 4 to 6 servings

Osso Bucco

This is the perfect dish to fill your home with delicious aromas.

6-8 large veal shanks, each tied securely with string to keep the
    meat on the bone
Salt and freshly ground black pepper to taste
Flour to coat shanks
5 tablespoons butter
2 tablespoons extra virgin olive oil
1½ cups finely chopped onion
¾ cup peeled, chopped carrots
¾ cup chopped fennel
1 garlic clove, minced
1½ cups white wine
3-4 cups chicken broth
1½ cups canned plum tomatoes, drained
Bouquet garni: place 6 parsley sprigs, 4 fresh thyme sprigs and
    1 bay leaf in cheesecloth and tie securely

GREMOLATA GARNISH:
½ cup minced parsley
2 tablespoons lemon zest
1 tablespoon minced garlic

1. Preheat oven to 250 degrees.
2. Season shanks on both sides with salt and pepper; dredge in flour.
3. Heat butter and oil in a Dutch oven and brown the shanks on both sides, adding
    more fat as needed. Remove shanks to a warm platter.
4. Sauté onions, carrots, fennel and garlic in the same pan, stirring often.
5. Deglaze the pan by stirring in the wine and scraping browned bits from the
    pan bottom.
6. Add the shanks, 3 cups of broth, tomatoes and herb bouquet into the pan. Cover.
7. Braise in oven 5-6 hours.
8. Remove and discard the herb bouquet.
9. Transfer shanks to a serving platter and carefully remove the string. Cover with foil, set
    aside and keep warm.
10. Put vegetables and liquid into a blender and purée until smooth. Return to saucepan,
    simmer until thick.
11. Serve the shanks with sauce and generous spoonful of gremolata.

Yield: 6-8 servings

"Everyone must take time to sit and watch

the leaves turn."

Elizabeth Lawrence, (garden designer and writer,

1904-1985)

IMAGINE: CROSSING THE DIVIDE

There's a special thrill to crossing the Continental Divide in places like the Loveland, Argentine, Boreas and Hoosier Passes. Brace for high winds and imagine early travelers making the trek over the daunting Rockies, often blown down on hands and knees, fighting the chill. They were fueled by a sense of adventure, dreams of riches and the search for a better life.

Alpine Bread Pudding

An apple bread pudding that warms the body.

PUDDING:
4-5 cups white bread cubes
2 tart apples, peeled and sliced thin
¼ cup dried cherries
2 large eggs, beaten
1½ cups (12-ounce can) evaporated milk
    (may use fat free)
2 tablespoons butter
½ cup apple cider
½ cup sugar
1 teaspoon cinnamon
¼ teaspoon salt

CUSTARD SAUCE:
⅜ cup sugar
⅛ cup flour
⅛ salt
⅛ teaspoon ground nutmeg
1⅜ cups milk (use 2%)
2 egg yolks, beaten
½ teaspoon vanilla
1 tablespoon bourbon (may use
    dark rum)

PUDDING:
1. Preheat oven to 325 degrees.
2. Combine bread cubes, apple slices and cherries in a large mixing bowl.
3. Beat eggs in smaller bowl using whisk. Set aside.
4. Melt butter in medium saucepan. Add evaporated milk, cider, sugar, cinnamon and salt. Heat mixture until sugar is dissolved, but do not boil.
5. Pour over bread cubes, stirring gently. Add beaten eggs. Let stand for 5 minutes.
6. Spray 1½ quart casserole or an 11-inch by 7-inch baking dish with cooking spray; pour in bread mixture.
7. Bake for about 55-60 minutes or until set and apples are tender and when knife inserted in center comes out clean.
8. Serve warm with or without custard sauce.

CUSTARD SAUCE:
1. Stir together sugar, flour, salt and nutmeg in a suacepan.
2. Gradually stir in milk, egg yolks and vanilla.
3. Cook and stir over medium heat until thickened and bubbly. Continue to cook for 2 more minutes, stirring constantly.
4. Remove from heat. Add bourbon (or rum, if desired) and stir.
5. Cover surface with plastic wrap. Chill 4-6 hours.

Yield: 8 servings

Chocolate and Grand Marnier Crème Brûlée

This melt-in-your-mouth dessert will bring sighs of pleasure from all.

2 cups heavy cream
1 vanilla bean, split lengthwise
4 (1-ounce) squares semi-sweet chocolate, chopped
4 large egg yolks
12 tablespoons superfine or baker's sugar, divided
1 tablespoon Grand Marnier
Raspberries for garnish
6 (1-cup) ramekins

1. Preheat oven to 325 degrees. Place ramekins in a 2-inch rimmed baking pan. Set aside.
2. Combine cream and vanilla bean in a saucepan and slowly bring to a simmer. Remove from heat and take out the vanilla bean. Using the tip of a small knife, scrape the seeds from the inside of the vanilla bean and stir into the cream.
3. Add the chopped chocolate to the pan and stir until melted and combined well. Set aside.
4. In a small bowl, whisk the egg yolks and 6 tablespoons of superfine sugar until thick and creamy.
5. Add the warm cream mixture slowly to the egg yolk/sugar mixture, whisking constantly.
6. Pour the custard through a fine-mesh sieve into a bowl and add Grand Marnier and mix well.
7. Pour custard into ramekins, filling them almost to the top.
8. Place baking pan in oven and pour boiling water into pan reaching half-way up the sides of the ramekins. Bake for 25 minutes, until custard starts to set around the edges, but is still soft in the center.
9. Remove baking dish from oven and place ramekins on a wire rack. Cool for 1 hour, then cover and refrigerate for at least 3 hours.
10. When ready to serve, remove from refrigerator and evenly sprinkle 1 tablespoon of superfine sugar on top of each ramekin.
11. Using a kitchen torch, melt and caramelize the sugar. The broiler may also be used, placing the ramekins 4 inches away from the broiling unit for 1-2 minutes, until the top is a dark caramel color and brittle.
12. Garnish with raspberries and serve at once.

Yield: 6 servings

SUMMIT AUTUMN BREW

Mix:

Golden aspen

Deep green spruce

Willow covered fields

And snow dusted peaks

Toss in wind blown leaves

Brush with sage

Serve with spirits

Keystone Ranch

Executive Chef Jason Kassib

Roasted Butternut Squash and Pear Soup

Arugula and Pomegranate Salad

Caramelized Onion, Apple and Duck Confit Pierogi

Roasted Pork Tenderloin

Cherry Compote

Calvados Pan Sauce

Black Walnut Risotto

Wander two miles down the long and winding road to reach Keystone Ranch Restaurant, where you will find a critically acclaimed fine dining experience in the rustic elegance of an original 1930s ranch homestead adjacent to the Keystone Ranch Golf Course in Keystone.

Roasted Butternut Squash and Pear Soup

1 large butternut squash
1 pear, cored, cut into pieces
½ yellow onion, cut into matchstick strips
1 tablespoon butter
4 cups chicken stock or water
1 pint heavy cream
2 tablespoons fresh minced sage
1 tablespoon butter
¼ cup sweet white wine
Kosher salt and pepper

1. Cut the butternut squash in half; scoop out seeds. Roast in a 350 degree oven until fork tender and golden brown, about half an hour.
2. Sweat the onions with butter in a saucepan until translucent.
3. Once the squash is done, scoop out the meat of the squash; discard the skin. Add meat to saucepan with onions, stir and then add pear.
4. Add the white wine to the saucepan and reduce by half (reduce more if you prefer less wine flavor).
5. Add stock, half the cream, and 1 tablespoon of sage and simmer for half an hour.
6. Pureé soup in blender; add remaining cream to reach a consistency you prefer.
7. Strain through fine mesh strainer and reheat. Salt and pepper to taste.
8. Serve and sprinkle with additional sage.

NOTE: "To sweat" is a cooking technique by which ingredients are cooked over low heat and the end result is a translucent product without browning.

Yield: 4-6 servings

Arugula and Pomegranate Salad

3 cups arugula
1 pomegranate, seeds removed
   and reserved
½ ounce extra virgin olive oil
Salt and pepper

1. Toss the arugula and pomegranate seeds together with the olive oil and season to taste.
2. Put a handful of the salad on a plate and put a pierogi on the side.
3. Enjoy as a salad or an appetizer.

Yield: 6 servings

Caramelized Onion, Apple and Duck Confit Pierogi

DOUGH:

1 cup sour cream

1 tablespoon salt

4 cups all-purpose flour

1 tablespoon extra virgin olive oil, for crisping

FILLING:

2 tablespoons extra virgin olive oil

½ large yellow onion, cut into matchstick strips

½ Granny Smith apple, peeled, cored and diced

¼ cup duck confit, diced

2 ounces Boursin cheese

DOUGH:

1. Add sour cream and salt to a mixing bowl.
2. Add the flour slowly, initially mixing with a fork. Once half the flour is added, mix by hand (all of the flour may not be needed). Continue adding flour until the dough is firm and not sticky.
3. Wrap the dough in plastic wrap and refrigerate for an hour or longer.
4. Roll the dough out on a floured surface to 1/6 of an inch. Cut twelve 3-inch circles out of the sheets of dough. Chill circles for later use.

FILLING:

1. Caramelize the onion in oil and butter over very low heat (this will take about an hour).
2. Add the apple to the onions and cook this mixture until the apples are soft.
3. Add the duck confit and the cheese to the mixture and mix until everything is well distributed.

ASSEMBLY:

1. Drop a walnut sized piece of the filling onto six of the chilled dough circles.
2. Use the other six circles to cover the filling (like ravioli). You may need to do a little stretching to get the top and bottom to meet evenly. Use a fork to crimp the edges.
3. Just before eating, drop the pierogi into boiling water. When they float count to 30 and remove them to an oiled cookie sheet.
4. Heat a large sauté pan and add a tablespoon of oil; place the pierogi in the pan to crisp the top side.
5. Serve with a handful of salad.

Yield: 6 servings

Executive Chef Jason Kassib will wow you with a four or six course inventive dinner. Educated locally at the Colorado Mountain College Culinary Institute, Kassib became executive chef in 2007, after impressive tutelage and sous chef experience.

The Ranch is truly a dining destination with dinner served to you on delicate Limoges china. Top features are Colorado rack of lamb, King Canyon buffalo, North American elk, wild game birds and perfectly balanced wines.

Roasted Pork Tenderloin

Enjoy this entrée of pork tenderloin on black walnut risotto with Calvados pan sauce and cherry compote.

PORK TENDERLOINS:
2 (1 pound) pork tenderloins
2 tablespoons salt
1 teaspoon black pepper
1 tablespoon fresh thyme
Extra virgin olive oil for searing

1. Mix the salt, pepper and thyme and rub on both tenderloins.
2. In a hot sauté pan (medium heat) with a little oil, sear the first tenderloin, remove and sear the next. (Be careful not to burn the bits in the pan as they will be used later.)
3. Put the pan aside (do not wash).
4. Roast both tenderloins in a 350 degree oven until they reach an internal temperature of 140 degrees.

Cherry Compote

1 cup frozen cherries
1 ounce Grand Marnier
1 teaspoon salt
1 teaspoon black pepper
1 tablespoon sugar

1. Add all of the ingredients for the compote to a small saucepan and cook over low heat, mashing with a fork every once and a while, until it takes on a jam-like consistency. Set aside.

Calvados Pan Sauce

1 shallot, minced
1 cup Calvados (apple brandy)
2 cups beef stock
1 tablespoon cornstarch
2 ounces butter, cold
1 teaspoon fresh thyme

1. Heat the pan used for searing the pork over medium heat and sauté shallots until transparent.
2. Add the Calvados to the pan and reduce to 2 ounces. Combine beef stock and cornstarch together and add to the sauce. Reduce to 1 cup; check seasonings and add thyme.
3. Remove sauce from heat, add butter and mix with a whisk.

Black Walnut Risotto

2 ounces butter
2 cups Arborio rice
6 cups chicken stock
½ cup black walnuts
Salt and pepper

1. In a medium sized saucepan, melt butter on medium heat. Add the Arborio rice and stir while heating for 1 minute.
2. In a separate pan, bring chicken stock to a simmer.
3. Add a third of the stock to the rice. Stir until most of the liquid is absorbed by the rice.
4. Add half of the remaining chicken stock and continue stirring once again until most of the liquid is absorbed.
5. Add the last of the chicken stock to the rice, continue cooking and stirring until it takes on the consistency of porridge.
6. Season the risotto to taste and stir in the black walnuts. Serve immediately.

TO SERVE:
1. Pour the risotto onto a serving platter.
2. Slice the pork and lay it on top of the risotto.
3. Pour the sauce over the pork and finally the cherry compote on top.

Yield: 6-8 servings

Keystone Ranch is highly rated by the renowned Zagat Survey, recognized by Wine Spectator Magazine and rated as AAA Four-Diamond restaurant.

Raid The Cellar

Raid your cellar for wine pairings and select from among these elegant entrées to create a memorable menu.

Brie and Chutney Pastry Flowers
Succulent Mushroom Caps
Smoked Trout Pâté in Endive

Frisée Salad with Blue Cheese and Dried Cherries

Broccoli-Spinach Timbale
Garnet Sweet Potatoes
Oven Baked Risotto

Lavender, Honey and Caper Scallops

Crusty French Bread

Spicy Pork Tenderloin
Individual Beef Wellington

Coconut Flan
Decadent Chocolate Cake with Raspberry Sauce

PASTY PUFF AT ALTITUDE

When working with puff pastry, keeping it cold is crucial to avoid the butter melting prematurely. Work quickly with one piece at a time and keep the rest covered with plastic wrap in the refrigerator. The tools and working area should also be kept cold.

Brie and Chutney Pastry Flowers

A lovely twist on a brie recipe. This can be easily doubled.

All-purpose flour, for rolling

1 (17.3-ounce) package frozen all-butter puff pastry, thawed but cold

8 ounces brie cheese, trimmed of rind and cut into 16 pieces

1 egg, lightly beaten

8 ounces mango chutney or chutney of your choice

2 tablespoons chopped pistachios, toasted

1. Preheat oven to 400 degrees.
2. On a lightly floured work surface, roll out the puff pastry 1/8-inch thick into a 12-inch by 12-inch square. Cut into sixteen 3-inch squares. Place squares into the tins of a mini-muffin pan, crimping and turning out corners to form a flower-like shape. Freeze for 5 minutes.
3. Fill each pastry with a piece of brie. Brush the exposed pastry with egg.
4. Bake in center of oven for about 15-20 minutes, or until puffed and golden.
5. Cool slightly. Top with a spoonful of chutney and chopped pistachios.

Yield: 16 pieces

Succulent Mushroom Caps

This is a classic appetizer to begin the evening.

½ cup (1 stick) unsalted butter; additional butter for brushing

36 medium mushrooms, stems removed, minced and reserved

2 teaspoons minced shallots

2 tablespoons minced fresh parsley

2 tablespoons fresh lemon juice

¾ cup bread crumbs

1 teaspoon salt

5 ounces crumbled herbed goat cheese

1. In a skillet, melt butter and sauté minced mushrooms stems and shallots until soft.
2. Remove from heat and stir in parsley, lemon juice, bread crumbs and salt. Cool to room temperature.
3. Stir cheese into crumb mixture. May be refrigerated at this point; remove 30 minutes before final assembly.
4. Preheat oven to 450 degrees.
5. Fill mushroom caps with crumb mixture and place in a 13-inch by 9-inch baking dish. Brush with melted butter.
6. Bake 10-12 minutes until lightly browned.

Yield: 36 mushrooms

Smoked Trout Pâté in Endive

Smoked trout is available in gourmet food stores or can be ordered from your local grocer.

1 pound of smoked trout, skinned
and boned

3 ounces cream cheese, room temperature

½ cup half-and-half

1 tablespoon prepared white horseradish

1 tablespoon fresh lemon juice

¼ teaspoon freshly ground black pepper

2 teaspoons chopped fresh parsley

2 heads of Belgian endive

1 lemon, sliced

Fresh edible flowers – pansies or violas

1. Using a food processor, grind the smoked trout.
2. Combine cream cheese, half-and-half, horseradish, lemon juice, pepper and parsley in a large bowl and blend until smooth.
3. Add trout and stir to combine the ingredients. Cover bowl and chill.
4. Cut the base from each endive and separate into individual spears.
5. Spread a heaping teaspoon of trout on the wide end of each spear.
6. Arrange on platter and garnish with lemon slices and pansies – a Summit County favorite for a beautiful presentation.

Yield: about 20 pieces

"Close friends contribute to our personal growth. They also contribute to our personal pleasure, making the music sound sweeter, the wine taste richer, the laughter ring louder because they are there."

Judith Viorst, (author, b. 1931)

Frisée Salad with Blue Cheese and Dried Cherries

A variety of packaged gourmet salad mixes can be substituted.

⅓ cup dried tart cherries

2 tablespoons minced shallot (1 medium)

2 tablespoons sherry wine vinegar

1 teaspoon Dijon-style mustard

Kosher salt and freshly ground
black pepper

6 tablespoons walnut oil

2 tablespoons extra virgin olive oil

8 ounces frisée or gourmet salad mix

4 ounces crumbled blue cheese

1. In a small bowl, soak dried cherries in ½ cup hot water about 10 minutes Drain.
2. In another small bowl, whisk together the shallots, vinegar and mustard.
3. Season with salt and pepper and drizzle in the walnut and olive oils while continuing to whisk.
4. In a salad bowl, toss bite-size greens with dressing until lightly coated.
5. Plate salad and top each serving with cherries and blue cheese.

Yield: 6 servings

Colorado has more than 70 vineyards and wineries covering all corners of the state. The soil and weather enable the region to produce award winning wines. The grapes are the highest-grown in the world. Seventy-five percent of Colorado's premium wine grapes come from vineyards in the Palisades region which is often called the "Heart of Colorado's Fruit and Wine Country".

Broccoli-Spinach Timbale

This side dish is a perfect complement to any entrée.

½ cup chicken stock

1 cup heavy cream

¾ cup cooked, well-drained and chopped fresh spinach (or frozen and thawed)

1 cup cooked, well-drained and chopped fresh broccoli (or frozen and thawed)

5 ounces Boursin cheese

5 eggs, lightly beaten

½ teaspoon dry mustard

½ teaspoon Worcestershire sauce

¼ teaspoon hot pepper sauce

¼ cup grated Parmesan cheese

3 tablespoons snipped fresh chives

1. Preheat oven to 350 degrees. Butter eight 6-ounce ramekins or a large soufflé dish.
2. In a small bowl, mix stock and cream. Set aside.
3. In food processor, combine spinach, broccoli, Boursin cheese and ¼ cup of stock mixture. Process until smooth. Set aside.
4. In a bowl, whisk eggs, mustard, Worcestershire, hot pepper sauce and remaining 1¼ cups of stock. Fold in spinach-broccoli mixture. Add Parmesan cheese, chives and mix thoroughly.
5. Fill buttered ramekins three-fourths full or use soufflé dish.
6. Place ramekins or dish in a deep roasting pan. Fill with hot water up to three-fourths of the height of the ramekins or soufflé dish.
7. Bake for 45 minutes. Remove from oven and let rest for 5 minutes.
8. Invert onto individual plates, or spoon from soufflé dish.

Yield: 8 servings

Garnet Sweet Potatoes

Garnet is the darker skinned variety of a sweet potato.

8 Garnet sweet potatoes, about 3 pounds

Extra virgin olive oil

Salt to taste

TOPPING:

1 cup sour cream

2 tablespoons maple syrup

1-2 jalapenos, seeded and minced, depending on taste

2 tablespoons lime juice

Salt and freshly ground pepper, to taste

1. Preheat oven to 400 degrees.
2. Scrub and dry potatoes and brush them with olive oil; lightly salt. On a cookie sheet, bake potatoes for about 40-50 minutes until they are soft.
3. In a small bowl, combine topping ingredients. Chill.
4. To serve, cut top off each potato and top with sour cream mixture.

Yield: 8 servings

Oven Baked Risotto

Enjoy the company of your friends while the risotto is baking.

8 ounces fresh mushrooms, chopped
    into ½-inch chunks

8 ounces fresh asparagus, cut on bias,
    2 inches long (may substitute other
    favorite vegetables)

1 medium yellow or red onion, finely
    chopped

2 tablespoons extra virgin olive oil

2 tablespoons butter

1 cup Arborio rice

2½ cups chicken broth

1 cup dry white or Madeira wine

1 tablespoon salt and freshly ground
    pepper to taste

2 tablespoons freshly grated
    Parmesan cheese

Grated Parmesan cheese for garnish

1. Preheat oven to 325 degrees. Coat a 9-inch square shallow baking dish with nonstick cooking spray.

2. In a medium saucepan, add olive oil and butter and heat over low heat; add onion and cook for 5 minutes. Add mushrooms and asparagus, stir well and cook for 10 minutes.

3. Meanwhile, put dish in oven to warm. Add rice to saucepan and stir, coating rice well. Add chicken broth, wine, salt and pepper and bring to a simmer.

4. Remove warmed dish from oven and transfer rice and liquid mixture to dish. Place in center of oven and bake for 20 minutes. Remove from oven and gently stir in Parmesan cheese. Return to oven and bake another 15 minutes or until liquid is absorbed.

5. Remove from oven and serve immediately. Sprinkle servings with grated Parmesan cheese.

Yield: 4-6 servings

Lavender, Honey and Caper Scallops

Large peeled tail-on shrimp may be substituted for the scallops.

1 pound large sea scallops

3 tablespoons capers

2 tablespoons pickling liquid from capers

½ cup honey

¼ cup sherry

1 tablespoon lavender blossoms, dried

1 lime, zested

1 teaspoon sea salt

¾ cup extra virgin olive oil

1 tablespoon capers for garnish

1 whole lime for garnish

1 bunch lavender, for garnish

1. Rinse scallops and remove muscle.

2. Put scallops in a bowl or re-sealable plastic bag. Set aside.

3. In a food processor, purée capers, pickling liquid, honey, sherry, lavender blossoms, lime zest and sea salt.

4. While the motor is running, add the olive oil in a slow, steady stream. Reserve ¼ cup of the marinade for presentation.

5. Toss the scallops in the remaining marinade and marinate in the refrigerator for at least 1 hour and up to 24 hours.

6. Grill or pan-sear scallops over medium heat for about 1 minute per side or until opaque and golden.

7. To serve: plate scallops, drizzle on some of the reserved marinade, and add a few whole capers and a lime wedge. Garnish with lavender sprigs.

Yield: 6 servings

FOODIES AND

FRISCO WINE MERCHANT, FRISCO

Susanne Johnston cares about wine. As owner of this specialty shop, she tastes every wine to ensure quality. She tests the integrity of the fruit source. Did the farmer do everything possible to grow the very best fruit and did the winery honor that? Does the wine have personality? Does the price reflect what's in the bottle? While food holds a place in Susanne Johnston's business, her establishment is about wine and the symbiotic relationship it shares with food, people, the earth and the overall enjoyment.

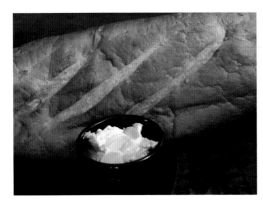

"The sky is the daily bread of the eyes."

Ralph Waldo Emerson

Crusty French Bread

Baking at high altitude can yield mixed results. This recipe is a winner.

1 packages active dry yeast (use 2
   packages for sea level baking)
½ cup warm water, 110 degrees
2 cups hot water
3 tablespoons sugar

1 tablespoon salt
6½ to 7 cups all-purpose flour
1 egg white, lightly beaten
1½ tablespoons cornmeal

1. Soften yeast in the warm water.
2. Combine hot water, sugar, salt and 3 cups of flour in a large bowl. Mix well.
3. Add yeast mixture and 3½ cups flour, stirring until well mixed. Add up to ½ cup more
    flour if dough is too sticky.
4. Let dough rest 10 minutes. Punch down.
5. Repeat resting and punching a total of five times.
6. Turn dough onto a lightly floured surface; knead only enough to coat dough with flour
    to prevent sticking.
7. Divide dough in half and roll each piece into a rectangle. Roll tightly beginning at long
    side and seal well. Taper the ends.
8. Place each loaf, seam side down, on a greased baking sheet and let rise in warm place
    for 30 minutes.
9. Preheat oven to 400 degrees.
10. Remove loaves to cutting board. With sharp knife, carefully cut 3 diagonal slashes
    across the top of each loaf. Brush with beaten egg whites. Sprinkle baking sheets with
    cornmeal before placing loaves back on sheets.
11. Bake for 30 minutes.

NOTE: This recipe has been adjusted for high altitude baking. Use 2 packages for sea level baking.

Yield: 2 loaves

Spicy Pork Tenderloin

An Asian alternative to a classic entrée makes for a very tasty dish.

1-inch piece fresh ginger, peeled and
   minced
1 jalapeno pepper, seeded and minced
⅓ cup honey

3 tablespoons soy sauce
3 tablespoons sesame oil
2 pork tenderloins (about ¾ pound each)

1. In a small bowl, mix together ginger, jalapeno pepper, honey, soy sauce and sesame oil.
2. Pour all but 2 tablespoons marinade into a re-sealable plastic bag; add meat and
    refrigerate at least 1 hour or overnight. Use reserved marinade for basting.
3. Preheat grill to medium-hot heat. Remove tenderloins from marinade.
    Discard marinade.
4. Grill about 10 minutes on each side, turning once. Baste with reserved marinade.
    Total grilling time is 15-20 minutes. Cut into ¼ to ½ inch slices.

Yield: 6-8 servings

Individual Beef Wellington

This is a "labor of love" and your guests will love you for it. You can easily adjust this for whatever size crowd you have.

WELLINGTON:

4 filet mignons, 1½-inch thick, center-cut (5-6 ounce)

Salt and freshly ground black pepper to taste

1-2 tablespoons canola oil

1 tablespoon unsalted butter

4 large mushrooms, thinly sliced

1 tablespoon finely chopped shallots

1 tablespoon minced garlic

1 large egg

1 sheet frozen puff pastry sheet (from 17.3 ounce package), thawed

4 tablespoons crumbled Gorgonzola cheese, about 2½ ounces

SAUCE:

1 cup beef or veal demi-glace (or reduce 3 cups low-sodium beef stock to 1 cup)

1 cup dry red wine (pair with your dinner choice)

"Music is the wine which inspires one to new generative processes, and I am Bacchus who presses out this glorious wine for mankind and makes them spiritually drunken."

~Ludwig van Beethoven

1. Pat filets dry and season with salt and pepper.

2. In a large heavy skillet, heat oil until very hot. Sear filets until nicely browned on each side, about 3-4 minutes per side. Remove from pan and cool. Chill filets, covered, for about 1 hour. May be done up to a day ahead.

3. Melt butter in a large heavy skillet over moderate heat and add mushrooms, shallots, garlic, salt and pepper to taste, stirring until mushrooms are lightly browned. Transfer mushroom mixture to a bowl and cool completely. May be done up to a day ahead.

4. In a small bowl, lightly beat egg to make an egg wash.

5. On a lightly floured surface, roll out pastry sheet into a 14-inch square. With a very sharp knife, trim edges to form a 13-inch square and cut square into four 6½-inch squares. Save trim to decorate tops of Wellington (optional).

6. To assemble, put 1 tablespoon Gorgonzola in center of each square of pastry and top with ¼ of the mushroom mixture and then the filet mignon. Press down gently and wrap 2 opposite corners of pastry over filet, overlapping them. Seal seam with egg wash. Bring remaining 2 corners of pastry over filet and seal with egg wash. Seal any gaps with egg wash and press pastry around filet to enclose completely. Arrange Wellington, seam side down, in a non-stick baking pan.

7. Chill remaining egg wash for brushing on pastry just before baking.

8. Chill Wellington, loosely covered for at least 1 hour or up to 1 day. Make a decorative topping from the pastry trimmings and use the egg wash to secure.

9. Preheat oven to 425 degrees. (Do not place Wellington in a cold oven.) Brush tops and sides of each Wellington with egg wash and bake 20 minutes or until golden.

10. In a saucepan, heat demi-glace or reduced beef stock and wine until it reaches a thick sauce consistency. Keep warm. Serve on the side.

Yield: 4 servings

"I'm like old wine. They don't bring me out very often, but I'm well preserved."

Rose Kennedy

Coconut Flan

Take care when caramelizing sugar and always use potholders to handle hot glassware.

1 cup sugar, divided
6 tablespoons water, divided
10 drops lemon juice, divided
3 large eggs, thoroughly whisked
1 (14-ounce) can condensed milk
   (fat free or regular)
1 (13.5-ounce) can unsweetened
   coconut milk
¼ cup shredded coconut
1½ teaspoons vanilla

Six (6-ounce) ramekins

1. Preheat oven to 325 degrees.
2. To caramelize sugar: place ½ cup sugar, 3 tablespoons water and 5 drops lemon juice in microwave-safe 2 cup measuring cup; mix well with a wooden spoon. Place in microwave and cook on full power for around 4 minutes. Stir after first 2 minutes, continue to cook for 1 minute and stir. For last minute, stir every 30 seconds. When the caramel is light golden brown (honey colored), remove it and pour evenly into the ramekins, coating bottom and sides. Caution: Caramelized sugar is very hot, so use potholders.
3. Whisk eggs, condensed milk, coconut milk, coconut and vanilla together in a large bowl.
4. Ladle custard into ramekins. Set ramekins in a large roasting pan or 15-inch by 10-inch baking dish and place on center rack in oven. Carefully add hot water to the baking pan, filling two-thirds of the way up the sides of the ramekins.
5. Bake 55 minutes. Custard is set when knife inserted into center comes out clean.
6. Carefully remove the pan from the oven and set on counter; do not empty out water for 10 minutes. Remove ramekins from pan and cool completely.
7. Refrigerate until chilled and fully set, about 4 hours.
8. To serve: Run knife around edges, place dessert dish over top of ramekin and invert.

NOTE: This recipe has been adjusted for high altitude baking.

Yield: 6 servings

Decadent Chocolate Cake
with Raspberry Sauce

This is a moist "must have" for chocolate lovers.

CAKE:

1 cup plus 3 tablespoons boiling water

3 (1-ounce) unsweetened chocolate

½ cup (1 stick) unsalted butter

1 teaspoon vanilla

1⅔ cups granulated sugar

3 large eggs, separated

½ teaspoon baking soda (use 1 teaspoon at sea level)

½ cup sour cream

2 cups sifted unbleached, all-purpose flour

½ teaspoon baking powder (use 1 teaspoon at sea level)

FROSTING:

1¼ cups sifted, confectioners' sugar, or as needed

1 teaspoon vanilla

2 tablespoons unsalted butter

6 tablespoons heavy cream

¾ cup semisweet chocolate morsels

RASPBERRY SAUCE:

1 (10-ounce) package frozen raspberries, thawed

1 tablespoon sugar

2 tablespoons Grand Marnier

1 pint fresh raspberries for garnish

CAKE: May be baked a day ahead. Cover completely and frost before serving.

1. Preheat oven to 375 degrees. Set baking rack in middle of oven.
2. Butter and flour a 10-inch tube pan (not a Bundt pan).
3. Place chocolate and butter in a large mixing bowl and pour in boiling water; let stand until melted.
4. Stir in vanilla and sugar; whisk in egg yolks, one at a time, blending after each addition.
5. Mix baking soda and sour cream and whisk into chocolate mixture.
6. In a medium bowl, sift flour and baking powder together and add to batter, mixing thoroughly.
7. Beat egg whites to form soft peaks. Fold a quarter of the whites thoroughly into the batter and then the remaining whites.
8. Pour batter into the prepared pan.
9. Bake for 40-45 minutes, or until the edges pull away from the sides of the pan or a cake tester comes out clean.
10. Cool in pan for 10 minutes; turn out of pan and cool completely.

FROSTING:

1. Place confectioners'' sugar, vanilla, butter, cream and chocolate morsels in a heavy saucepan over low heat and whisk until smooth.
2. Cool slightly; add more sugar if necessary for a spreadable consistency. While still warm, frost.

Raspberry Sauce: May be prepared one day ahead. No need to refrigerate.

1. Working in small amounts, strain raspberries through a fine sieve.
2. Add sugar and Grand Marnier to the raspberry juice. Mix well.

ASSEMBLY:

1. Place frosted cake on serving platter, fill the center with fresh raspberries and serve sauce on the side.

NOTE: Can be frozen, unfrosted, for one week. This recipe has been adjusted for high altitude baking. At sea level use 1 teaspoon of baking soda and 1 teaspoon baking powder.
Yield: 12-16 servings.

WINE IN THE PINES

Wine in the Pines started over twenty-five years ago to raise funds for Colorado's Cerebral Palsy programs, and has raised millions of dollars. The two day event is held in Keystone's finest restaurants in October. Described as enchanting, it features more than 500 exquisite wines, elegant cuisine and a Moonlight Masquerade.

High Country Baking

Vera Dawson
Chef Instructor, Culinary Institute, CMC
Baking Columnist, Summit Daily News and Vail Daily News

Apple-Walnut Tart

Summit Shortbread

Dark Rye Bread with Walnuts

Vera Dawson shares her culinary skills as a Chef Instructor at the Colorado Mountain College Culinary Institute and as the baking columnist for the Summit Daily News and Vail Daily News.

Apple-Walnut Tart

Make in a 9 inch tart pan with a removable bottom.

CRUST:

2 cups bleached all-purpose flour
  (spoon and level)
½ cup of confectioners' sugar

Pinch salt
1 generous teaspoon vanilla
1 cup (2 sticks) unsalted butter, cold, cut
  into small pieces

1. Place the flour, sugar, and salt in the bowl of a food processor and pulse to combine. Add butter and vanilla to the processor. Pulse to mix and, then, process ONLY until dough starts to form a ball on top of processor's blade. Remove dough and use it immediately or, if it is too soft to work with, pat it into a disc and refrigerate until it is easy to handle.

2. Lightly grease the bottom of tart pan. Break off tablespoon-size pieces of dough and pat them into pan, leveling and smoothing as you go. Or, roll dough into a circle about 11 inches in diameter and gently fit it into tart pan. In both cases, trim top of dough even with pan rim. Freeze or refrigerate pan until dough is quite firm. Preheat oven to 375 degrees with a rack in center position.

3. Blind bake the crust: Line dough with non-stick foil or lightly greased regular foil, (non-stick or greased side against the dough). Fill liner with pie weights or dried beans. Place pan on a cookie sheet and bake until dough is firm. Start checking at about 20 minutes. Remove tart shell from oven (leave oven on) and let it rest for about 3-4 minutes (this allows it to firm up a bit). Carefully remove pie weights and foil liner, return pan to oven, and continue baking until shell is lightly golden and set. Remove it to a cooling rack to cool completely.

FILLING:

3 Golden Delicious apples, peeled,
  cored and diced (¼ -⅓ inch dice)
¼ cup unsalted butter
½ cup granulated sugar
¾ cup chopped walnuts, separated
2 tablespoons granulated sugar

1 large egg
½ cup heavy cream
1 tablespoon Calvados or 1¼ teaspoons
  vanilla extract
¼ teaspoon salt
⅓ cup apricot preserves
2 teaspoons Calvados

4. Preheat oven to 350 degrees with a rack in center position.

5. In a large skillet, combine unsalted butter and ½ cup sugar and stir over low-moderate heat until butter melts and combination is bubbly. Keep cooking and stirring about 2 more minutes so sugar dissolves. Add diced apple and stir until juices evaporate and apples turn color slightly and soften, about 7-9 minutes. Spread mixture of apples over bottom of cooled tart shell.

6. Set aside ½ cup of chopped walnuts. In a food processor, pulverize remaining ¼ cup of walnuts with sugar. Pour them into a bowl; add egg, cream, Calvados or vanilla, and salt. Whisk to combine well and pour over the apple mixture in tart shell. Sprinkle ½ cup walnuts on top and bake until custard is set (it should jiggle slightly in the center when pan is moved), about 23-27 minutes. Start checking earlier. Remove tart to a cooling rack.

7. Make the glaze: Whirl apricot preserves in a food processor until smooth. Bring preserves to a boil in a microwave oven or in a small saucepan on the stove. Remove from heat and stir in Calvados. Let cool slightly and brush on tart while tart filling is still slightly warm. Cool completely. Refrigerate, lightly.

NOTE: This elegant tart can be prepared over a two-day period: Make and bake the tart shell on the first day and fill it on the second. The finished tart can be refrigerated up to a day before serving.

Yield: 12-16 servings.

Summit Shortbread

This tender, buttery cookie will remind you of Walkers Shortbread, the famous, commercial pastry that's sold in a red plaid package. Perfect plain, Summit Shortbread is also delicious dipped in white or dark chocolate.

Make in an 8 or 8 ½-inch springform pan

1¼ cups plus 2 tablespoons of bleached, all-purpose flour

½ cup of confectioners' sugar

1 tablespoon of granulated sugar, preferably superfine or Baker's

¼ teaspoon of salt

⅓ cup of cornstarch

12 tablespoons (1½ half sticks) cold unsalted butter

1 teaspoon of vanilla

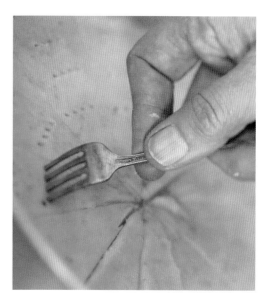

1. Butter the bottom and sides of the springform pan.
   To make with a food processor: Place the flour, both sugars, salt, and cornstarch in the bowl of the food processor and pulse several times to aerate and combine thoroughly. Cut the cold butter into about 24 pieces and add it, with the vanilla, to the bowl. Process until the dough smooths out and starts to come together. Stop just before it forms a ball on the food processor blade.
   To make with a mixer: Let the butter come to room temperature. Beat it with the two sugars, cornstarch, vanilla and salt until it is light in color and thoroughly combined. Add the flour and stir or beat until it is completely absorbed into the dough.
2. Gently spread the dough into the prepared pan, smoothing and leveling the top. (Pressing the dough through a sheet of plastic wrap is an effective way to do this.) Cover the dough and refrigerate it for about 30 minutes. Preheat the oven to 300 degrees, with a rack in the center position.
3. Remove the chilled dough from the refrigerator. Using a thin, sharp knife, score it into 10-12 wedges, cutting into the dough at least one-fourth of an inch. Prick the dough uniformly with a fork to prevent air bubbles from lifting it. Place the pan on a cookie sheet and bake until the shortbread is lightly golden all over, the edges are slightly browned, and the dough is completely set. This takes from about 55-65 minutes, depending on the size of your pan. Shortbread can appear fully baked when it isn't, so err on the side of more time in the oven. Remove the pan from the oven, cool the shortbread for ten minutes or so, then cut it into wedges along the scored lines and let the cookies cool completely. Remove the wedges from the pan. The cookies can be stored for at least a week in an airtight container at cool room temperature or frozen for up to two months.

Yield: 10-12 wedges

Vera's passion for cooking began as a child in a family of gourmet cooks. While she pursued public education as a vocation, she expanded her culinary skills through years of cooking and baking classes and the careful digestion of countless cookbooks.

Dark Rye Bread with Walnuts

This nontraditional, dark rye bread eliminates the usual caraway seeds and replaces them with walnuts, resulting in a milder flavor and a moist crumb. Good sliced, it's wonderful toasted and slathered with jam at breakfast time.

Today, Vera combines her teaching experience with her culinary knowledge to the benefit of eager culinary students in Summit County. At home, she shares her love of cooking with her husband, Michael Babnik. Their busy lives epitomize the active Summit County lifestyle, cherishing the outdoors, friends and food.

2 teaspoons of instant yeast (no sea level adjustment)
¼ cup of dark brown sugar
¾ cup of stone ground, whole grain rye flour (available at Natural Grocers and health food stores)
2 teaspoons of salt
2 tablespoons of unsweetened cocoa powder
½ teaspoon baking powder

½ cup broken walnuts
Approximately 1¾ cups of bread flour, divided (The amount of flour used will depend upon the humidity in your kitchen on the day the bread is made)
1¾ cups water

GLAZE
1 egg
2 tablespoons milk

1. Add the yeast, brown sugar, rye flour, salt, cocoa powder, baking powder, walnuts, and half a cup of the bread flour to a large mixing bowl (large enough to knead the bread in the bowl). Warm the water to 110 degrees and add it to the bowl, stirring until fully combined.

2. Slowly add about one-fourth cup of the remainder of the bread flour, stirring and adding more flour until the dough clings, in a large ball, around your spoon. Use some of the rest of the flour to coat your hands and knead the dough for 12 minutes, adding more flour each time the dough becomes sticky (this will happen several times during the kneading process).

3. Cover the bowl with plastic wrap. Let the dough rise in the mixing bowl for 1 hour. It will double in bulk.

4. Preheat the oven to 400 degrees, with a rack in the center position. With oiled hands, divide the dough into two equal pieces, shape each piece into an oval and place them as far apart as possible on a flat baking sheet. Cover them with a dry, clean towel and let the dough rise for exactly 20 minutes.

5. While the dough is rising, make the glaze: Beat the egg and milk together in a small bowl until combined. Slash the tops of the loaves down the center (make a tree of life pattern, if you choose) with a sharp knife and brush the glaze all over them (you will not use it all). Bake for 35 minutes. Remove to a cooling rack to cool completely. Serve at room temperature. Store loaves in a plastic bag for about 5 days or freeze.

NOTE: No Adjustment for sea level.

Yield: Two medium lovees

Colorado Mountain College

Director of Culinary Education Kevin Clarke
Center for Lifelong Learning Doug Schwartz

*"Food is becoming the focus of many events including
farmers' markets, food festivals and elegant black tie affairs."*

In Summit County, we enjoy food. We are fortunate to have two campuses of the Colorado Mountain College, in Dillon and the newest facility, in Breckenridge. Among the many programs offered are the Culinary Arts Institute and the Culinary Workshop Series.

The Colorado Mountain College Culinary Institute at Keystone is America's finest apprenticeship-based culinary degree program. Kevin Clarke, a 1996 graduate of the first Culinary Arts Class, has been the director since 2000. In this rigorous hands-on program, students train under world class chefs while working in a variety of Keystone's award winning restaurants. Many of our local chefs completed their training at the school and now have successful careers in the culinary world.

Taught from Colorado Mountain College's new state of the art teaching kitchen, the recently launched recreational cooking program has been a great success. With classes open to the public,

students can take classes on simple skill development such as Knife Skills to more advanced classes such as Classical Stocks and Sauce.

Doug Schwartz moved to Summit County in 1977, and directs and teaches in the recreational cooking program. He has 30 years of experience in the food service industry; Doug was the original director of the Colorado Mountain Culinary Institute at Keystone. His goal is to offer classes that are educational, affordable, fun and meant to "satisfy" the strong interest in the community for recreational cooking.

Local food personality, Chef Carolyn Deal, Le Grand Diplôme, Le Cordon Bleu, is known for her demonstration-style cooking classes with tastings. Asian specialties, Thai cuisine and Barbequing with Beer are just a few of her popular classes. Besides her work at CMC, Chef Deal donates her time and talents to the community, including the Breckenridge Music Festival.

Moveable Feast

An early fund raiser for Applause! was a progressive gourmet dinner with each course served in a different Summit County home. These delicious recipes are suited for such an evening.

Asparagus with Meyer Lemon Sauce
Crab Bisque
Vietnamese Summer Rolls

Leek and Endive Salad
Spinach Salad with Spicy Pecans

Glazed Carrots
Green Beans with Dill
Provençal Roasted Potatoes
Baked Almond Rice

Stir Fried Shrimp with Spicy Orange Sauce
Blue Cheese Beef Tenderloin with Port Wine Sauce

Orange Napoleons with Strawberries
Limoncello-Mint Sorbet with Blackberries
Cappuccino-Chocolate Mousse

APPLAUSE!

Applause! is the volunteer fundraising committee of the Breckenridge Music Festival. Since 1990, the group has sponsored year round social fundraising events that are vital to the fiscal health of the Festival. Membership is open to all.

Asparagus with Meyer Lemon Sauce

Serve as an enticing appetizer or side dish.

Zest and juice of two Meyer lemons
    or regular lemons
1 teaspoon Dijon-style mustard
1 green onion, minced
Salt and freshly ground black pepper
1 cup extra virgin olive oil

ASPARAGUS:
1 pound jumbo asparagus, ends
    removed and peeled
Coarse sea salt
Freshly ground black pepper to taste

1. Whisk together zest, juice, mustard, onion, salt and pepper.
2. Drizzle in olive oil in a slow stream, whisking constantly. Season to taste and set aside.
3. In a large pot, bring salted water to a boil, add asparagus and cook for about 6 minutes. Drain and immerse asparagus in ice water until cool. Drain.
4. If serving chilled, toss the asparagus with sauce and season to taste.
5. If serving warm, toss the asparagus with the sauce. Heat a large skillet over medium high heat. Add dressed asparagus and sauté until warmed through. May also be served at room temperature.

Yield: 4 to 6 servings

Crab Bisque

Serve this rich soup in little cups.

4 tablespoons butter
2 cups lump crab meat
1 large onion, grated
Salt and white pepper to taste
½ teaspoon mace
5 ribs of celery, grated
4 cups milk

1 cup heavy cream
1 teaspoon Worcestershire sauce
4 teaspoons all-purpose flour
2 tablespoons water
6 tablespoons sherry
6 teaspoons chopped fresh chives,
    for garnish

1. In a saucepan or double boiler, melt butter and add crab, onion, salt, pepper, mace and celery. Simmer for 5 minutes.
2. Heat milk 2 minutes on medium in microwave and add to crab mixture. While stirring, add cream and Worcestershire sauce.
3. Mix flour and water into a paste and add to crab mixture, stirring until thickened and smooth. Add sherry.
4. Cook over low heat for 30 minutes.
5. Correct seasonings and garnish with chopped chives.

Yield: 8-10 servings

Vietnamese Summer Rolls

The bright cilantro, the sweet shrimp, the crispy carrots, lettuce and the spicy dipping sauce create a light appetizer that is well-balanced in taste and texture.

DIPPING SAUCE:

2 tablespoons low-sodium soy sauce

2 tablespoons fish sauce

2 tablespoons water

2 tablespoons rice wine vinegar

2 tablespoons fresh lime juice

2 tablespoons sugar

2 teaspoons chili sauce

ROLLS:

4 ounces uncooked rice noodles, broken
　　into 3-4 inch pieces (may use vermicelli)

12 large raw shrimp (26/30 count),
　　peeled completely and deveined

3 carrots, peeled, shredded or julienned

3 cups shredded iceberg lettuce

¼ cup diagonally chopped green onions

¼ cup chopped fresh cilantro, plus extra
　　sprigs for garnish

12 (8-inch) round sheets of rice paper

1. Whisk together the dipping sauce ingredients and set aside.
2. Cook noodles in 6 cups of salted boiling water. Remove the noodles, shock in cold water and drain.
3. Cook the shrimp in same boiling water until done, about 3 minutes. Shock the shrimp in cold water and slice in half lengthwise.
4. Toss the noodles, carrots, lettuce and green onions with 1-2 teaspoons of the dipping sauce just to coat; drain away excess liquid.
5. To assemble rolls, immerse 1 rice paper in warm water to moisten and place on a flat surface. Place 2 tablespoons of noodle mixture in center of paper, top with 2 shrimp halves and sprinkle with chopped cilantro. Fold up end of paper over filling, fold in both sides and roll to completely encase the filling (burrito-style fold).
6. Cut rolls in half on a diagonal. Place each piece, seam side down on a serving platter; cover to keep from drying.
7. Repeat rolling procedure with remaining ingredients to assemble 12 rolls. Refrigerate rolls and dipping sauce until needed.
8. Serve rolls with dipping sauce; garnishing platter with extra cilantro sprigs.

Yield: 12 servings

SOCIAL FEST

Life in Summit County is a social fest that the Applause! Committee of the Breckenridge Music Festival enhances. Through the creativity and energy of the volunteers. The offerings have become social highlights for the community and a great place for locals to meet new people and mingle with friends.

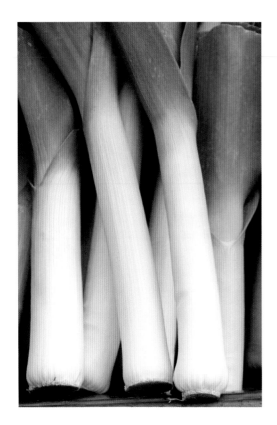

PARTY ON THE MOVE

Applause! cooked up a summertime moveable feast, a party on the move, in the mid 1990s. One year, 200 people shuttled from home to home on trolleys in Spruce Valley Ranch, Blue River. As the crowd grew to over 300, the venue changed from neighborhoods to resort venues of Keystone, Copper and Beaver Run. Now, it is a lovely Gala held annually each summer.

Leek and Endive Salad

Leeks with a tarragon vinegar dressing create a delicious salad

DRESSING:
1 cup extra virgin olive oil
6 tablespoons tarragon vinegar
2 tablespoons snipped chives
3 teaspoons salt
2 teaspoons sugar
½ teaspoon freshly ground black pepper
1 teaspoon dry mustard

SALAD:
8 leeks, outer layer removed, trimmed, cleaned and cut in ½-inch slices
1 teaspoon salt
3 Belgian endives, rinsed, drained and stored in refrigerator until crisp
¼ red bell pepper, finely diced
Fresh chive spears, for garnish

DRESSING:
1. Combine dressing ingredients in a small bowl or tightly covered jar.
2. Whisk or shake until well blended. Refrigerate.

SALAD:
1. In a 4-quart saucepan, bring 2 quarts of water to a boil. Add leeks and salt and simmer covered for 13 to 15 minutes, or until tender. Drain.
2. Place warm leeks in a bowl and toss with just enough dressing to coat. Refrigerate, covered, until well chilled (about 2 hours). Reserve remaining dressing.
3. To serve, arrange endive leaves on salad plates. Spoon dressed leeks into leaves and drizzle with reserved dressing.
4. Garnish salad with red pepper. Add chive spears for extra garnish.

Yield: 8 servings

Spinach Salad with Spicy Pecans

A tasty spinach salad is dressed with balsamic, sherry and honey.

PECANS:
2 tablespoons unsalted butter
2 tablespoons brown sugar
1 teaspoon cayenne pepper
¾ cup pecan pieces

DRESSING:
2 tablespoons balsamic vinegar
2 tablespoons sherry vinegar
½ cup extra virgin olive oil
1 tablespoon honey
½ tablespoon kosher salt and freshly ground black pepper, to taste

SALAD:
1 (16-ounce) package baby spinach leaves
2 avocados, halved, pitted, scooped out and coarsely chopped
20 strawberries, thinly sliced

1. In a skillet, melt butter over medium heat. Add brown sugar, cayenne and pecans and sauté for 3 minutes, stirring to coat the pecans well. Remove pecans and cool.
2. Whisk together the vinegars, olive oil, honey, salt and pepper. Set aside.
3. Place 1 cup of spinach leaves on each of 8 plates. In a small bowl, gently mix avocado and strawberries. Divide equally among 8 plates.
4. Drizzle each salad with 1½ tablespoons of dressing and top with 2 tablespoons of spicy pecans.

Yield: 8 servings

Glazed Carrots

The glaze is sugar and spice and everything nice.

2 pounds fresh carrots, peeled, cut into
    quarters lengthwise, then in half

1½ cups water

1 teaspoon salt

¼ cup (½ stick) butter

1 teaspoon grated orange zest

¼ cup brown sugar

½ teaspoon ground cardamom

1. In a large saucepan, heat water and salt to a boil.
2. Add carrots, turn heat to medium and cook until tender, then drain.
3. Melt butter over low heat in a skillet. Add orange zest, brown sugar, cardamom and carrots. Stir gently until carrots are coated with glaze.

Yield: 8 servings

Green Beans with Dill

Fresh green beans are served with creative flavors.

4 tablespoons extra virgin olive oil

1 small onion, sliced thinly

2 garlic cloves, minced

2 pounds fresh green beans, ends snapped

⅔ cup water

⅔ teaspoon chopped fresh dill

4 tablespoons chopped fresh parsley

Salt and freshly ground black pepper to taste

Dash cayenne pepper

1. In a medium saucepan, heat olive oil. Add sliced onion and garlic and sauté for 5 minutes.
2. Add green beans and water. Cook without stirring on medium high heat for about 8 to 10 minutes or until liquid is absorbed and beans are tender.
3. Stir in dill, parsley, salt, pepper and cayenne pepper. Serve immediately.

Yield: 8 servings

Provençal Roasted Potatoes

This recipe can easily be increased for a crowd or decreased for an intimate group.

10-12 medium Yukon Gold potatoes,
    scrubbed and diced (1-inch dice), skin on

½ cup extra virgin olive oil

½ cup Dijon-style mustard

2 tablespoons herbes de Provence

2 tablespoons kosher salt

1 tablespoon freshly ground black pepper

1. Preheat oven to 400 degrees.
2. Combine all ingredients in a large bowl and mix to coat potatoes evenly.
3. Place coated potatoes on a large rimmed baking sheet; spreading evenly in one layer (may need to use more than one baking sheet).
4. Roast in oven for 45-50 minutes or until potatoes have a nice crust and are tender; turning potatoes after about 25 minutes.
5. Serve immediately or can be made in advance and held in warming oven (covered) until ready to serve.

Yield: 10-12 servings

SANDY KUSCHNERUS

Sandy Kuschnerus was instrumental in editing and cooking for the cookbook. She prepared over 50 beef Wellingtons for the Wine Pairing Dinner – no small feat! In addition to a Master's in Business Administration, she graduated from The Art Institute of Colorado as a Gold Medal Certified Culinarian and a Certified Cellar Manager. Her catering business, Bon Vivant! by Chef Sandy K, is devoted to refined taste and providing enjoyment of superb food and wine.

MOVEABLE FEAST

"If you are lucky enough to have lived in Paris…, then wherever you go for the rest of your life, it stays with you, for Paris is a moveable feast." A. E. Hotchner inspired the title of Hemingway's Paris memoirs as he described their 1920s life there. Substitute "Summit County" for "Paris" to describe how locals feel about life here.

Baked Almond Rice

This rice is baked in the oven for easy preparation.

½ cup (1 stick) butter
1 medium onion, chopped
½ cup slivered almonds
1 cup rice
1 (14-ounce) can beef consommé
1 cup water

1. Preheat oven to 325 degrees.
2. In a heavy oven proof dish, melt butter and sauté onions and almonds for three minutes.
3. Add rice, consommé and water and mix well; bring to a boil.
4. Remove from heat and place in oven, uncovered and bake for 45-60 minutes, until liquid is absorbed and rice is cooked.
5. Remove from oven, fluff and return to oven for additional 5-10 minutes.

Yield: 8 servings

Stir Fried Shrimp with Spicy Orange Sauce

Easy to prepare, this shrimp dish has a definite "kick".

½ cup orange juice
4 tablespoons low-sodium soy sauce
4 tablespoons honey
2 tablespoons rice wine vinegar
½ tablespoon chili paste with garlic
  (such as sambal oelek)
3 pounds large shrimp, peeled and

deveined
2 tablespoons cornstarch
4 tablespoons peanut oil, divided
2 tablespoons peeled, minced fresh ginger
5 garlic cloves, minced
⅔ cup diagonally sliced green onions

1. Whisk together orange juice, soy sauce, honey, vinegar and chili paste. Set aside.
2. In medium bowl, toss shrimp with cornstarch, coating well.
3. In skillet, heat peanut oil over medium-high heat. Add ginger and garlic and stir-fry for 15 seconds until fragrant.
4. In two batches, add shrimp and stir-fry each batch for 3 minutes. Remove first batch and add additional peanut oil as needed. Remove second batch of shrimp.
5. To skillet, add juice mixture and onions and cook until sauce thickens; return cooked shrimp to pan and mix to coat well.
6. Serve over rice, if desired. Garnish with green onions.

Yield: 8 servings

Blue Cheese Beef Tenderloin with Port Wine Sauce

A wonderful dish for blue cheese lovers.

TENDERLOIN:

4 pound beef tenderloin, trimmed

¼ teaspoon salt

¾ teaspoon freshly ground black pepper, divided

¾ teaspoon dried thyme, divided

2 cups crumbled blue cheese

⅓ cup bread crumbs

Butcher's twine or string

1 tablespoon extra virgin olive oil

PORT WINE SAUCE:

1 cup port wine

1 cup chicken broth

1 teaspoon cornstarch, dissolved in 1 teaspoon water

1. Preheat oven to 425 degrees. Place rack in lower third of oven.
2. Slit tenderloin lengthwise, (not all the way through) to create a pocket for stuffing. Sprinkle inside with salt and ½ teaspoon each of pepper and thyme.
3. Mix cheese, bread crumbs and remaining ¼ teaspoon of pepper and thyme.
4. Stuff pocket with cheese mixture. Tie tenderloin crosswise at 1½-inch intervals. Coat outside with oil, pepper and salt.
5. In large roasting pan over medium-high heat, sear tenderloin until well-browned (2 minutes per side). Place in oven.
6. Roast tenderloin until meat thermometer inserted in thickest portion registers 120 (medium-rare) or 125 (medium), 30-35 minutes. Remove roast from oven and let rest on a cutting board for 25 minutes.
7. Pour port wine into roasting pan, scraping to loosen brown bits. Add 1 cup broth and simmer until reduced to 1 cup. Whisk in cornstarch-water mixture and cook until sauce has thickened.
8. To serve, cut beef into 1 inch slices and serve with sauce.

Yield: 8 to 10 servings

BEAR ALERT

Every summer Applause! sponsors a Pig Roast at a member's home in woodsy Blue River. There could be more than pork for dinner. A highlight is how the host holds a shotgun as he patiently presides over the roasting pit, just in case a neighborhood bear crashes the party!

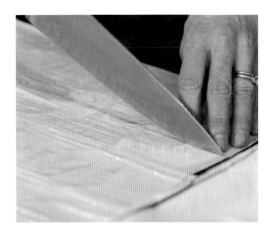

"Life itself is the proper binge."

Julia Child (chef, author, 1912-2004)

Orange Napoleons with Strawberries

Each component can be prepared in advance and the results are a lovely ending to a special dinner.

PASTRY RECTANGLES:
½ cup (1 stick) unsalted butter, melted
    and kept warm
10 phyllo sheets, thawed, stacked between 2 sheets
    waxed paper, covered with damp towel

STRAWBERRY SAUCE:
1 (12-ounce) package of frozen strawberries
Sugar to taste
2 tablespoons Grand Marnier
Fresh strawberries for garnish

PASTRY CREAM:
2 cups milk
¾ cup sugar
½ vanilla bean, split lengthwise
4 egg yolks
2 eggs
2 teaspoons orange zest
¼ cup cornstarch
¼ cup unsalted butter, softened
2 tablespoons Grand Marnier
½ cup heavy cream, chilled

PASTRY RECTANGLES: Can be prepared up to 4 days ahead; keep in airtight container.
1. Preheat oven to 400 degrees. Prepare two baking sheets by brushing with melted butter.
2. Working with one baking sheet, lay 1 sheet of phyllo lengthwise and brush with butter. Keep other pastry sheets covered with damp towel while working.
3. Lay a second sheet on top of buttered first sheet. Butter this sheet, repeat 3 more times.
4. With a sharp knife, cut the 5 layers of dough into 12 equal rectangles.
5. Fold in the 2 short sides of each rectangle ¼-inch to hold the sheets together. Brush folded edges with butter. Repeat process with remaining 5 sheets to form 12 more rectangles.
6. Bake immediately for 7-10 minutes, until golden. Cool on racks.

PASTRY CREAM: Can be prepared up to 2 days ahead; keep chilled
1. In a heavy saucepan, combine milk, sugar and vanilla bean and bring to a boil, stirring occasionally. Let stand for 10 minutes. Scrape the seeds from vanilla bean into mixture. Discard vanilla bean pod.
2. In a separate bowl, whisk egg yolks, whole eggs, orange zest and cornstarch. Whisking constantly, slowly add hot milk mixture in a steady stream to egg mixture.
3. Put mixture back in saucepan and bring to boil, over medium high heat, whisking constantly. Boil 2 minutes then strain mixture into a bowl; stir in butter and Grand Marnier until well combined.
4. Cover pastry cream with buttered waxed paper and chill at least 2 hours.
5. Several hours before serving, in a chilled bowl, beat heavy cream until it holds soft peaks. Fold gently into chilled pastry cream, cover and chill until ready to use.

STRAWBERRY SAUCE: Can be prepared up to 1 day ahead, refrigerate.
1. Defrost strawberries in package.
2. Place strawberries in a fine-mesh sieve. Over a bowl, press strawberries to strain juice. Continue until all juice is removed. Discard remaining strawberry pulp.
3. To the juice, mix in sugar (as needed) and Grand Marnier.

BUILDING NAPOLEONS: Prepare immediately before serving.
1. Pour strawberry sauce on each plate and place a phyllo rectangle on top of sauce.
2. Gently spread a generous layer of pastry cream on phyllo; top each with another phyllo rectangle (smooth side up). Add a small dollop of pastry cream on top.
3. Garnish with fresh strawberries and drizzle sauce over top.

Yield: 12 servings

Limoncello-Mint Sorbet with Blackberries

A sweet dessert finishes off a lovely evening.

2 cups water

1¹/₃ cups sugar

½ cup Limoncello

1 cup fresh lemon juice (about 6 lemons)

½ cup chopped fresh mint

2 cups fresh blackberries

Sprigs of mint for garnish

1. In a medium saucepan, combine water, sugar and Limoncello. Bring to a boil and stir until sugar dissolves.
2. Remove from heat, add lemon juice and mint. Cover and chill overnight or up to 24 hours.
3. Strain juice mixture through a sieve. Discard solids and pour strained mixture into a freezer-safe container and cover. Freeze for at least one hour. If using an ice cream maker, process according to manufacturer's instructions.
4. Place 3 small scoops in nice glasses. Garnish with blackberries and a sprig of mint.

Yield: 8 to 10 servings

TRACKING YOUR SUCCESS

Keep a personal record of your entertaining. On cards, list problems you encountered, your solutions and include your calculations for beverages and food amounts. Keep a file — you will thank yourself later.

Cappuccino-Chocolate Mousse

Another make ahead dessert that can be served in wine glasses for an elegant gourmet touch.

4 egg yolks

½ cup sugar

½ cup Marsala wine or dry sherry

2 cups whipping cream

¹/₃ cup boiling water

1 tablespoon instant espresso coffee

6 (1-ounce) squares semi-sweet chocolate

Shaved white chocolate (optional)

1. Whisk together egg yolks and sugar in a saucepan; add wine, whisking until smooth.
2. Cook over low heat until mixture thickens (about 2 minutes), whisking constantly.
3. Cool and refrigerate mixture for several hours.
4. In a large chilled bowl, whip cream to stiff peak stage.
5. Gently fold whipped cream into cooled egg mixture.
6. In a saucepan, dissolve instant espresso into boiling water.
7. Add chocolate to saucepan and reduce heat to low; stir until chocolate melts (about 3 minutes). Remove from heat.
8. Gently fold into whipped cream/egg mixture.
9. Spoon mousse into a serving bowl or individual wine glasses. Refrigerate overnight. Top with shaved white chocolate, if desired.

Yield: 6-8 servings

Let's Give Thanks

*Choose between these impressive entrées, then mix and match
from the delicious sides to complete the meal.*

Pumpkin Bread
Apple Pie Bread
Prosecco Sparkler

Mushroom Crostini
Faux Ceviche
Butternut Apple Soup

Five Green Salad with Walnut Vinaigrette

Artichoke and Hearts of Palm Salad
Brussels Sprouts with Pancetta
Mashed Potatoes with Horseradish
Wild Rice with Hazelnuts and Cranberries

Thanksgiving Capon
Turkey Chowder
Gingered Pork with Cranberry Chutney

Bourbon Pumpkin Cheesecake
Grandmother Donahue's Gingerbread
Chocolate Pecan Pie

IMAGINE: HOLIDAY DELICACIES

Holiday delicacies, gleaned from newspaper advertisements by grocers in 1897, might include the following: "fancy turkeys – 12 cents/pound; oysters – 45 cents/quart; fancy cranberries – three quarters for 25 cents; English walnuts – 10 cents/pound; dates – three pounds for 25 cents." (*SUMMIT* by Mary Ellen Gilliland)

Pumpkin Bread

Early morning treats for the Thanksgiving cooks to nibble on while preparing the meal.

2 cups sugar	1 teaspoon cinnamon
1 cup vegetable oil	1 teaspoon nutmeg
3 large eggs	½ teaspoon baking soda
1 (16-ounce) can pure pumpkin	½ teaspoon salt
3 cups all-purpose flour	½ teaspoon baking powder
1 teaspoon ground cloves	1 cup chopped walnuts (optional)

1. Preheat oven to 350 degrees.
2. Line two 9-inch by 5-inch by 3-inch loaf pans with foil and grease well.
3. Beat sugar and oil in a large mixing bowl. Mix in eggs and pumpkin.
4. In a separate bowl, combine dry ingredients.
5. Stir flour mixture into pumpkin mixture in two additions, blending well each time. Add walnuts, if desired.
6. Pour batter into pans, bake about 1 hour and 10 minutes or when tester comes out clean. Cool for about 10 minutes and remove from pans.

NOTE: This recipe is adapted for high altitude. Use 3 cups sugar, 2 eggs and 1 teaspoon baking soda for sea level baking.

Yield: 2 loaves

Apple Pie Bread

Autumn's favorite fruit makes this bread hard to resist.

1 teaspoon baking powder	1 large egg
6 teaspoons cinnamon	2 cups milk
3 cups all-purpose flour	2 tablespoons vegetable oil
2 cups sugar	2 cups diced apples
1 teaspoon salt	2 tablespoons raw sugar

1. Preheat oven to 350 degrees.
2. Line two 9-inch by 5-inch by 3-inch loaf pans with foil and grease well.
3. Combine dry ingredients in a large bowl.
4. Combine egg, milk and oil in a small bowl.
5. Blend liquids into flour mixture. Fold in apples.
6. Pour batter into pans and bake 1 hour and 40 minutes or when tester comes out clean. Cool for 10 minutes and remove from pans.

NOTE: This recipe is adapted for high altitude. Use 3 teaspoons of baking powder for sea level baking.

Yield: 2 loaves

A crisp and refreshing cocktail to toast the start of the holiday season.

⅔ cup pomegranate liqueur
1 (750 ml.) bottle of Prosecco, chilled
Raspberries for garnish

1. Pour 3 tablespoons liqueur into each champagne flute.
2. Fill with Prosecco about two-thirds full. Garnish with berries.

Yield: 9 servings

The addition of blue cheese and prosciutto make this a festive appetizer.

"Thanksgiving dinners take eighteen hours to prepare. They are consumed in twelve minutes. Half-times take twelve minutes. This is not coincidence."

Erma Bombeck (humorist and writer 1927-1996)

3 tablespoons unsalted butter
½ pound shitake mushroom caps, chopped
4 ounces cremini mushroom caps, chopped
2 garlic cloves, minced
½ cup whipping cream

½ cup crumbled blue cheese
½ cup chopped thinly-sliced prosciutto
Salt and freshly ground black pepper to taste
Sourdough baguette, sliced diagonally into ¼-inch slices
Chopped parsley for garnish

1. Melt butter in a large skillet over medium high heat. Sauté mushrooms and garlic until brown, about 10 minutes.
2. Add cream and boil until liquid is completely absorbed, about 2 minutes. Remove from heat.
3. Add blue cheese and stir until melted. Mix in prosciutto; season with salt and pepper. Transfer to bowl. May be prepared 1 day ahead, covered and refrigerated.
4. Preheat oven to 375 degrees. Bake bread slices about 5 minutes until golden. Mound a tablespoon of mushroom topping on each toasted slice.
5. Return to oven and bake until just heated through, about 6 minutes. Sprinkle with parsley.

Yield: 20-25 appetizers

HOSPITALITY

Sue Chamberlain, an early resident of Summit County, described the character of the area. "My mother kept track of how many extra people were at our house for meals. Everybody was always welcome." Summit County has a history of hospitality. Today, houses are filled with visitors year round. A destination with the draw of Summit Country keeps friendships fresh and family close.

(quote from *Summit Pioneers*)

Faux Ceviche

A sumptuous appetizer that can double as a salad course.

2 tablespoons salt	½ red onion, peeled and diced
1 pound large raw shrimp, peeled and deveined	½ medium cucumber, peeled, seeded and diced
½ cup lime juice	1 ripe mango, peeled, pitted and diced
½ cup ketchup	1 avocado, halved, pitted, scooped out and diced
½ tablespoon hot pepper sauce, or more to taste	⅓ cup chopped fresh cilantro
2 tablespoons extra virgin olive oil	6 small sprigs cilantro for garnish
½ teaspoon salt	

1. Bring 2 quarts of water to a boil. Add salt and shrimp and cook until they just begin to turn pink (about 30 seconds). Drain and cool.
2. Combine the lime juice, ketchup, hot pepper sauce, olive oil and salt in a large bowl.
3. Add onion, cucumber, mango, avocado and cilantro. Toss well.
4. Add shrimp and gently toss. Taste and adjust seasonings; chill for at least 1 hour.
5. Serve in stemmed glasses or salad plates; garnish with sprigs of cilantro.

Yield: 6 servings

Butternut Apple Soup

Visually appealing when topped with sour cream and crumbled bacon.

1 large yellow onion, chopped	3 cups low-sodium chicken broth
3 tablespoons butter	1½ cups whole milk
3 cups diced butternut squash	Juice of 1 fresh orange
1 Granny Smith apple, peeled and chopped	Salt, pepper, and sugar to taste
3 tablespoons all-purpose flour	2 slices bacon, cooked until crispy and crumbled
1-2 teaspoons curry powder	Sour cream (optional)
Pinch nutmeg	

1. In a large saucepan, sauté the onions in the butter for about 5 minutes or until soft.
2. Add squash and apple and sauté until the butter is absorbed, about 3 minutes, stirring occasionally.
3. Stir in flour, curry powder, and nutmeg. Cook for 2 minutes.
4. Add chicken broth, milk and orange juice. Simmer slowly, uncovered, for 15-20 minutes until vegetables are tender.
5. Remove from heat and purée in a blender. Return to saucepan and reheat.
6. Add salt, pepper and sugar to taste. Serve hot, topped with crispy crumbled bacon and a spoonful of sour cream, if desired.

Yield: 6-8 Servings

Five Green Salad with Walnut Vinaigrette

For convenience, use a bag of mixed green salad and fresh watercress.

VINAIGRETTE:

¼ cup red wine vinegar

1 tablespoon Dijon-style mustard

1 tablespoon heavy cream

1 teaspoon salt

1 teaspoon pepper

¾ cup walnut oil or extra virgin olive oil

¾ cup safflower oil or canola oil

SALAD:

1 head Boston lettuce

1 head red-leaf lettuce

1 head radicchio

1 head curly endive

1 head watercress, stems removed

½ cup toasted, coarsely chopped walnuts

½ cup crumbled Gorgonzola or Feta cheese

VINAIGRETTE:

1. Combine red wine vinegar, mustard, cream, salt and pepper in blender or food processor.
2. With food processor running, slowly pour oils in a steady stream until well blended and smooth.
3. Vinaigrette may be stored in refrigerator up to one week. To use, bring to room temperature and whisk well.

SALAD:

1. Tear lettuce leaves into bite-size pieces. Toss together in a large salad bowl with walnuts.
2. Dress with vinaigrette and toss well. Sprinkle with Gorgonzola or Feta cheese.

Yield: 10 servings

GOBBLER FEST

The Copper Mountain Gobbler Fest is a great kickoff to the holiday season with family activities like crafts and games. The main event is the Gobbler Chase snowshoe fun walk. The race helps burn off those Thanksgiving meal calories, as long as participants don't eat too many of the Thanksgiving leftovers offered along the way.

Artichoke and Hearts of Palm Salad

This salad is a lovely compliment to many different entreés.

1 garlic clove, chopped

½ teaspoon salt

6 tablespoons extra virgin olive oil

2 tablespoons lemon juice

¼ teaspoon freshly ground black pepper

1 (14-ounce) can artichoke hearts, drained, coarsely chopped

1 (14-ounce) can hearts of palm, drained, coarsely chopped; cut into bite-size pieces, reserve several for garnish

3 ounces crumbled blue cheese

¼ cup finely chopped parsely

1 head romaine lettuce, torn into bite-size pieces, chilled

½ head iceberg lettuce, torn into bite-size pieces, chilled

1. Combine garlic and salt in large bowl and rub together into a paste. Blend in olive oil, lemon juice and pepper.
2. Add artichoke hearts and hearts of palm to dressing. Cover and chill.
3. To serve, toss vegetable mixture with lettuces. Serve on chilled plates and top with blue cheese crumbles. Garnish with reserved palm hearts.

Yield: 10 servings

"Today gives us a chance to love, to work,

to play, and to look up at the stars."

Henry Van Dyke (author, educator 1852-1933)

Brussels Sprouts with Pancetta

Italian bacon transforms ordinary sprouts.

1 tablespoon extra virgin olive oil
1 shallot, chopped
2 garlic cloves, chopped
3 ounces sliced pancetta, coarsely
  chopped

1 pound fresh Brussels sprouts, trimmed
  and cut into halves
1 cup low-sodium beef broth

1. In a large skillet, sauté chopped shallot and garlic in oil.
2. Add pancetta and stir until cooked through; about 5 minutes.
3. Add the Brussels sprouts, cook for about 3 minutes, until they turn darker green and the edges begin to brown.
4. Add the beef broth. Lower heat to medium, cover and simmer for about 12 minutes, or until tender when pierced with a fork.

Yield: 4 Servings

Mashed Potatoes with Horseradish

A unique potato dish that can be prepared ahead and easily doubled for a larger crowd.

2½ pounds Yukon Gold potatoes,
  peeled, cut into 2-inch pieces
1 tablespoon plus 1 teaspoon kosher
  salt, divided
4 ounces bacon, diced
2 cups lightly packed coarsely chopped
  fresh parsley, stems removed

½ cup hot water
1 cup chopped green onions
¾ cup buttermilk
¼ cup (½ stick) unsalted butter
¼ teaspoon freshly ground black pepper
1-2 tablespoons prepared white
  horseradish

1. Preheat oven to 375 degrees and butter a shallow 2-3 quart glass or ceramic baking dish.
2. Place potatoes in large pot with enough cold water to cover; add 1 tablespoon salt. Bring to boil over medium-high heat and boil about 20 minutes until potatoes are tender. Drain and set potatoes aside. Reserve pot for later use.
3. Cook bacon until nearly crisp in a large skillet over medium high heat; drain on paper towels. Pour off half of the drippings. Add parsley and hot water to the skillet; cook 5 minutes or until liquid evaporates and parsley is tender. Add green onions; cook 30 seconds.
4. Place buttermilk, butter, remaining one teaspoon salt and pepper in reserved pot and bring to simmer over medium heat. Buttermilk will look curdled. Add potatoes; coarsely mash, then stir in parsley mixture, horseradish and bacon.
5. Spread potatoes in dish, leaving top uneven so potato peaks brown.
6. Bake 30 minutes or until browned on edges and peaks. Serve warm.
7. Can be prepared through step 5 one day ahead; cover and refrigerate and increase baking time 10-15 minutes.

Yield: 8-10 servings

Wild Rice with Hazelnuts and Cranberries

If unable to find hazelnuts, substitute chopped pecans.

¼ cup (½ stick) butter

1 large onion, diced

1 garlic clove, minced

4 cups chicken broth

1 teaspoon salt

1 cup (6½ ounces) wild rice

1 cup (6 ounces) long grain brown rice

1 cup (4 ounces) dried cranberries

¼ cup chopped fresh parsley

1 tablespoon chopped fresh thyme or 1 teaspoon dried

1½ cups (6 ounces) hazelnuts, toasted and coarsely chopped

8 green onions, trimmed and sliced

¼ teaspoon freshly ground black pepper

1. Melt butter in a large, heavy pot; add onions and garlic and sauté until tender.
2. Add the chicken broth and salt. Bring to a boil.
3. Add wild rice. Reduce heat to low, cover and simmer for 45 minutes.
4. Add brown rice to pot; cover and simmer gently for 45 minutes or until both rices are just tender adding more broth if necessary.
5. Stir in cranberries, parsley and thyme.
6. Cover and cook for 5 more minutes or until all the liquid has been absorbed.
7. Mix in the hazelnuts, green onion and pepper.
8. Taste and adjust seasoning.
9. If the rice is made in advance, it can be reheated in the oven.

Yield: 8 servings

Built in 1875, the Edwin Carter home is now a museum located at 111 N. Ridge Street in Breckenridge. A gold miner turned naturalist, Carter spent his life collecting and preserving Rocky Mountain wildlife. He was concerned about the negative impact mining had on the environment and preserved almost 3,300 specimens in order to document the changes. Alas, Carter died in 1900 due to arsenic poisoning from the chemicals he used for his taxidermy.

Thanksgiving Capon

An alternative entrée for an intimate holiday celebration.

1 (9-pound) capon, frozen

2 tablespoons kosher salt

freshly course-ground black pepper

1 celery stalk, cut into 3 pieces

1 small onion, quartered

½ lemon, quartered

½ orange, quartered

2 cloves garlic, peeled and smashed

2 sprigs fresh thyme

1. Rub frozen capon on all sides with kosher salt and place in a large plastic bag. Seal tightly. Allow five days for the capon to defrost in the refrigerator. Once each day massage the thawing juices into the skin and muscles of the capon (through the sealed bag).
2. Three hours before roasting, remove the capon from the bag, dry carefully with paper towels and place on a platter. Put back into the refrigerator, uncovered for two hours. Remove from refrigerator one hour before roasting to allow capon to come to room temperature. Season generously with coarse pepper.
3. Preheat oven to 450 degrees.
4. Fill the cavity with celery, onion, lemon, orange, garlic and thyme and tie legs together.
5. Roast at 450 degrees for thirty minutes; then lower oven temperature to 325 degrees and roast for two more hours or until juices run clear. Remove and allow to rest up to one hour before carving.
6. Cut each breast section away from the breast bone and slice across the grain. Serve with favorite stuffing.

Yield: 6 servings

COMMUNITY GIVING

The Breckenridge Community Thanksgiving Dinner serves locals, visitors and those in need. Between donations from residents and food from local restaurants, 350 people were fed in 2009. Fifty turkeys were served, 170 pounds each of mashed potatoes and green beans, 75 pounds each of squash, stuffing and cranberry sauce, and 90 gallons of gravy — all in elegant chafing dishes and on lovely linen.

Turkey Chowder

A tasty and filling soup that is the perfect solution for leftover turkey.

2½ cups water
¾ cup wild rice (about 5 ounces), rinsed and drained
¼ teaspoon salt
1 tablespoon extra virgin olive oil
2 (3-ounce) packages sliced pancetta, diced
5½ cups sliced cremini mushrooms (may use baby bellas)
¼ cup (½ stick) butter
2 carrots, sliced
2 celery stalks, chopped
1 cup chopped shallots
⅓ cup all-purpose flour
10 cups turkey or chicken stock
2 teaspoons crushed fresh rosemary
2-4 cups chopped cooked turkey (may use chicken)
1½ cups frozen corn kernels
1 cup heavy whipping cream
Salt and freshly ground black pepper to taste
¼ cup dry sherry
Finely chopped fresh parsley, for garnish

1. Bring water, rice and salt to boil in a medium saucepan. Reduce heat to low, simmer until rice is tender but still firm to bite, about 45 minutes. Drain, set aside.
2. Heat olive oil in large heavy pot over medium heat. Add pancetta and cook until browned, stirring often, about 8 minutes. Drain on paper towels.
3. Add mushrooms to pot and cook until beginning to brown, about 8 minutes. Transfer to medium bowl.
4. Melt butter in same pot. Add carrots and celery and cover pot; cook until vegetables begin to soften, about 5 minutes, stirring often. Add shallots, stir and cook until soft, about 9 minutes.
5. Sprinkle flour over vegetables and cook for 1 more minute.
6. Return mushrooms to pot. Stir in stock and rosemary; bring to a full boil, stirring occasionally. Reduce heat to medium-low, partially cover, and simmer 15 minutes.
7. Add cooked rice, pancetta, turkey and corn to soup. Simmer to blend flavors, about 10 minutes. Stir in cream. Salt and pepper to taste.
8. Stir in sherry; sprinkle with parsley, if desired.

NOTE: May make ahead through step 7. Cool slightly and chill uncovered until cool, then cover and keep refrigerated. Bring to room temperature, reheat and add sherry.

Yield: 8 servings

Gingered Pork with Cranberry Chutney

Lambrusco is a lovely wine to pair with this pork entrée.

MARINADE:

1 (14-ounce) can low sodium chicken broth
½ cup lite soy sauce
½ cup dark brown sugar, firmly packed
6 tablespoons ketchup
½ cup peeled, chopped fresh ginger
4 garlic cloves, chopped
2 tablespoons balsamic vinegar
2 (1-pound) pork tenderloins, trimmed

CRANBERRY CHUTNEY:

1 (20-ounce) can crushed pineapple, drained, reserve juice
1½ cups sugar
1 (12-ounce) bag fresh cranberries, washed
1 cup dried currants
½ teaspoon cinnamon
¼ teaspoon ground ginger
¼ teaspoon ground allspice
¾ cup chopped walnuts or pecans, toasted

A three-year old gave this reaction to her dinner: "I don't like the turkey, but I like the bread he ate." ~Anonymous

1. Whisk together marinade ingredients; pour into a large re-sealable plastic bag.
2. Add tenderloins and seal. Marinate in refrigerator, turning bag occasionally, for 24 hours. When ready to cook, remove tenderloins from bag and discard marinade.
3. Preheat the grill to medium heat.
4. Grill tenderloins to an internal temperature of 155 degrees, about 20 minutes. Turn meat to cook evenly on all sides.
5. Transfer to a cutting board and let stand; loosely cover with foil for 5 minutes.

CRANBERRY CHUTNEY:

1. In a large saucepan, mix the reserved pineapple juice with the sugar, cranberries, currants, cinnamon, ginger and allspice. Bring to a boil, reduce heat and simmer for 30 minutes, uncovered.
2. Remove pan from heat; add crushed pineapple and nuts and chill until serving.
3. To serve, slice pork and serve chutney on side.

Yield: 6-8 servings

FIRST TRACKS

Give thanks for abundant snow in Summit County. Some local residents take pride in being part of Opening Day and set goals each year for how many slope days they can clock in. Resorts in Summit County open in November, offering visitors a great Thanksgiving holiday. And, true snow lovers can extend the season into June at Arapahoe Basin.

Bourbon Pumpkin Cheesecake

A committee favorite and fabulous finale to a family gathering.

CRUST:
5 graham crackers, crushed
½ cup chopped pecans
¼ cup light brown sugar, firmly packed
¼ cup sugar
¼ cup (½ stick) unsalted butter, melted

FILLING:
1½ cups canned solid-pack pumpkin
3 large eggs, room temperature
½ cup light brown sugar, firmly packed
1 teaspoon vanilla
1 tablespoon bourbon
½ cup sugar
1 tablespoon cornstarch
1½ teaspoons cinnamon
½ teaspoon freshly grated nutmeg
½ teaspoon ground ginger
¼ teaspoon salt
3 (8-ounce) packages cream cheese,
    room temperature

TOPPING:
2 cups sour cream
2 tablespoons sugar
1 tablespoon bourbon

CRUST:
1. Combine the 5 ingredients in a medium bowl. Mix well.
2. Pat down evenly in buttered 9-inch springform pan.
3. Preheat oven to 350 degrees.

FILLING:
1. Combine pumpkin, eggs, brown sugar and cream together. Add vanilla and bourbon.
2. In another large bowl, combine sugar, cornstarch, cinnamon, nutmeg, ginger and salt. Mix well.
3. Using an electric mixer on high speed, combine cream cheese and cornstarch mixture and mix until creamy. Reduce speed to medium and add pumpkin mixture and beat until smooth.
4. Pour filling into crust. Place springform pan on a rimmed cookie sheet and bake until set, about 50-60 minutes.
5. Transfer to rack and cool for 5-10 minutes. Leave oven on.
6. Combine sour cream, sugar and bourbon in a medium bowl. Mix well.

TOPPING:
1. Mix ingredients and spread on top of cheesecake and bake for 5 minutes. Remove from oven.
2. Cool cheesecake in pan completely for about 3 hours.
3. Cover and place in refrigerator for at least 4 hours.
4. Remove sides of pan and bring to room temperature before serving.

Yield: 12 servings

Grandmother Donahue's Gingerbread

An Irish turn of the century recipe, equally delicious with cream cheese frosting or whipped cream.

½ cup (1 stick) butter, at room temperature

½ cup sugar

1 large egg

1 cup dark molasses

1 teaspoon ground ginger

2 cups all-purpose flour

½ teaspoon baking soda (adjusted for altitude; at sea level, use 1 teaspoon)

1 cup boiling water

1. Preheat oven to 350 degrees.
2. Grease and flour an 8-inch or 9-inch square pan
3. Using a mixer, cream butter and sugar. Beat in egg. Add molasses and ginger.
4. Dissolve baking soda in boiling water and add alternately with flour to mixture.
5. Pour into prepared pan and bake for about 45 minutes or until done.

NOTE: This recipe has been adjusted for high altitude baking. Use 1 teaspoon baking soda for sea level baking.

Yield: 9 servings

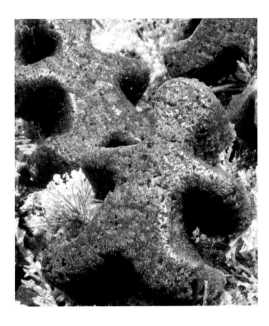

"An optimist is a person who starts a new diet on Thanksgiving Day."

Irv Kupcinet (Columnist 1912-2003)

Chocolate Pecan Pie

A deliciously rich version of a favorite Southern dessert.

1 cup sugar, less 1 tablespoon

½ cup flour

2 large eggs, slightly beaten

½ cup (1 stick) butter, melted

1 teaspoon vanilla

1 cup chopped pecans

⅓ cup semi-sweet chocolate morsels

Unbaked 9-inch pie shell

Whipped cream

1. Preheat oven to 325 degrees.
2. In a mixing bowl, combine sugar and flour.
3. Whisk in eggs.
4. Stir in melted butter and mix well.
5. Add vanilla, pecans and chocolate morsels.
6. Pour into unbaked pie shell and bake for 35 minutes.
7. Allow to set for 30 minutes; serve warm.
   Top each serving generously with whipped cream.

Yield: 8 servings

Hearthstone Restaurant

Executive Chef Michael Halpin
General Manager/Managing Partner Peter Bakken

Beef Wellington

Striped Bass

Elk Chops with Blackberry Sauce

Garlic Mashers

Ginger Scallops

Coconut Basmati Rice

HEARTHSTONE
restaurant

For over 125 years, the building that now houses the Hearthstone Restaurant has been perched up on Ridge Street overlooking the Town of Breckenridge and Ten Mile Range. Originally a residence, the charming Victorian has held restaurants since the late sixties, around the time the ski resort opened. Alexandra Storm and Dick Carleton took ownership in 1989.

Beef Wellington

1½ ounces extra virgin olive oil
3 ounces beef tenderloin cubes (1½-inch size)
½ teaspoon chopped garlic
½ teaspoon chopped shallots
½ ounce Point Reyes blue cheese
2 sheets puff pastry (5-inches by 5-inches)
1 egg

SAUCE:
1 teaspoon chopped shallots
1½ ounces Madeira wine
2 ounces veal demi-glace

GARNISH:
1 small onion, sliced thin
Flour to coat slices
Extra virgin olive oil for frying

1. In a hot pan, heat olive oil and sear beef cubes with the shallots and garlic, for about 2-3 minutes but do not cook past rare. Set aside and cool in refrigerator.
2. Lay out one sheet of puff pastry and brush with egg wash around sides.
3. Put beef in middle of sheet with the cheese on top. Place the other puff pastry sheet on top and use a circle mold to cut around sides making a nice circle. Egg wash the top of pastry.
4. Preheat oven to 400 degrees.
5. Cook in oven for about 8 minutes or until golden brown.
6. For the sauce, sweat shallots in a hot sauté pan.
7. Add Madeira and reduce wine by three-fourths.
8. Add demi-glace and bring to a simmer for 5 minutes.
9. Coat onion slices with flour and fry until crispy in oil. Use to garnish Wellington.

Yield: 1 serving

Striped Bass

PURÉED TOMATOES:
2 tomatoes, cut in half
1 teaspoon extra virgin olive oil
1 teaspoon chopped shallots
1 teaspoon chopped garlic

BREADING:
½ cup panko bread crumbs
4 large basil leaves
1 filet of fresh striped bass

SAUCE:
1 teaspoon chopped shallots
1 teaspoon extra virgin olive oil
1 cup white wine
½ cup heavy cream
3 ounces butter

POTATO FENNEL HASH:
1 Yukon gold potato, peeled, cut into
    ¼-inch cubes
¼ bulb fennel, cut into ¼ -inch cubes
¼ ounce butter
pinch salt and pepper

GARNISH:
3 grape tomatoes, cut in half
¼ red onion, cut as thinly as possible
1 basil leaf, sliced thin
¼ teaspoon balsamic vinegar
½ teaspoon extra virgin olive oil
pinch salt and pepper
¼ red onion, thinly sliced

In a warm, richly decorated Victorian ambience, diners are offered innovative American cuisine of well-presented wild game, fresh seafood and hand-cut steaks.

1. Preheat oven to 275 degrees.
2. Roast tomatoes, shallots and garlic in olive oil for 2 hours.
3. Purée tomatoes, shallots and garlic in a food processor. Set aside.
4. Preheat oven to 400 degrees.
5. Purée bread crumbs and basil in a food processor.
6. Coat the fish with crumb mixture and sear in a hot sauté pan, until slightly brown. Flip over and finish in oven for about 6-8 minutes.
7. For the sauce: sweat off the shallots in olive oil in a hot sauté pan.
8. Add white wine and previously puréed tomatoes, then reduce mixture by two-thirds.
9. Add cream and reduce by two-thirds again. Slowly whisk in butter and season to taste.
10. For the hash: Blanch potatoes in boiling water for 6 minutes, then remove and cool.
11. Blanch fennel for ten minutes, then remove and cool.
12. In a hot pan, add butter, potatoes, and fennel and sauté for 5 minutes.
13. Finish in 400 degree oven for about 6-8 minutes.
14. Sauce the plate, then plate fish on sauce. Mix garnish ingredients together and serve over fish fillet. Plate the potato hash as a side dish.

Yield: 1 serving

Executive Chef Michael Halpin's culinary creations highlight the Rocky Mountain region's locally farmed seasonal products, including meats, fish, artisan cheeses and fresh produce.

Elk Chops with Blackberry Sauce

2 elk chops
1 tablespoon soybean oil for searing

BREADING:
1 tablespoon minced garlic
1 tablespoon extra virgin olive oil
2 ounces granola
1 ounce panko bread crumbs

SAUCE:
5 blackberries
2 ounces demi-glace

1. Preheat oven to 400 degrees.
2. To make the breading: first slowly sauté garlic and oil on very low heat for about 20 minutes.
3. Then strain the oil and coat the granola with the oil. Let cool.
4. In a food processor, combine granola and bread crumbs and mix well.
5. Coat elk chop with this mixture and sear in olive oil in a sauté pan until golden brown.
6. Finish in oven for about 5 minutes for a medium rare chop.
7. To make sauce: Combine blackberries and demi-glace and bring to a simmer.
8. Serve over chop.

Yield: 1 serving

Garlic Mashers

1 Yukon gold potato
1 teaspoon minced garlic
1 tablespoon heavy cream
1 tablespoon butter
Pinch salt and pepper

1. Boil potato in boiling water until a knife easily slides out.
2. Add the rest of ingredients and mash to desired consistency.

Yield: 1 serving

Ginger Scallops

6 large scallops

Breading for scallops:
1 teaspoon chopped ginger
1 teaspoon dried ginger
1 teaspoon pickled ginger
1½ cups panko bread crumbs
1 egg mixed with 1 tablespoon water for wash
1 tablespoon soybean oil for searing

SAUCE:
1 teaspoon chopped shallots
1 cup white wine
¼ cup orange juice concentrate
½ cup heavy cream
¼ cup (½ stick) butter

Take in the view from the upstairs at happy hour or request a table in one of the grand bay windows.

1. Wash and clean scallops.
2. In a food processor, add the three different gingers and purée with the panko bread crumbs. Place on a cookie pan and let dry overnight.
3. To bread the scallops: coat scallops with flour, then dip in egg wash.
4. Coat scallops with the ginger bread crumbs.
5. Sear the scallops in soybean oil in a hot pan until golden brown.
6. To make sauce: sweat the shallots in oil.
7. Add white wine and orange juice concentrate and reduce by three-fourths.
8. Add cream and reduce again by three-fourths.
9. Whisk in butter and season with salt and pepper.

Yield: 1 serving

Coconut Basmati Rice

4 ounces cooked basmati rice
2 ounces coconut milk
1 green onion, sliced

1. Heat coconut milk and add rice and sliced green onion.
2. Stir until liquid is absorbed.
3. Serve with scallops.

Yield: 1 serving

Hut Trip

*Hut trips require creativity and menu planning; most of these recipes
can be made ahead of time and easily reheated at the hut.*

Summit County Caviar
Fabulous Hummus

Francie's Sandwich
Janet's Turkey and Avocado Wrap

Quinoa, Corn and Tomato Salad

Garlic Dipping Sauce
Cheese Pepper Bread

Chili Blanco
Hearty Sausage and Vegetable Soup

Maggie Pond Cookies

Oat Bran Applesauce Muffins
Deconstructed Omelets

SUMMIT HUTS

Recreational enthusiasts utilize a long network of backcountry huts as the Summit Huts Association connects with the 10th Mountain Division Huts in the Vail Pass area. Summit Huts operates four huts stretching from the Copper Mountain area to south of Breckenridge.

Summit County Caviar

A versatile dip that can be served inside Pita bread or used as a vegetable when warmed.

SALAD:
1 (4-ounce) can diced mild green chiles, well drained
1 (4-ounce) jar diced pimientos, drained
1 (16-ounce) can red pinto beans, rinsed and drained
1 (16-ounce) can black beans, rinsed and drained
1 (16-ounce) can black eyed peas, rinsed and drained
1 (10½ to 12-ounce) can shoepeg corn, washed and drained
1 (14½ to 16-ounce) can diced tomatoes, no flavor, with juices
1 cup chopped green pepper
1 cup chopped celery
1 cup sliced green onions

DRESSING:
½ cup sugar
½ cup cider vinegar
¾ cup extra virgin olive oil

1. Combine salad ingredients in a large bowl and mix well.
2. Combine dressing ingredients in a saucepan and bring to a boil. Cook until sugar dissolves and allow to cool.
3. Pour cooled dressing over salad and mix well. Refrigerate overnight.
4. Drain excess dressing before serving.
5. Serve with corn scoops.

Yield: 8 servings

Fabulous Hummus

A spread that could not be easier!

2-3 tablespoons extra virgin olive oil
3-4 tablespoons lemon juice
1-3 garlic cloves
¼ cup tahini

1 (15-ounce) can garbanzo beans, rinsed, drained (reserve some liquid)
1 (7-ounce) jar roasted red bell peppers (optional)

1. In a food processor, blend all ingredients until creamy. Add additional reserved liquid or more olive oil if necessary to reach desired consistency.

Yield: 2 cups

Francie's Sandwich

For a lighter approach, use sandwich wraps and make individual servings.

1 loaf sourdough bread
2 ounces extra virgin olive oil
1 garlic clove, minced
2 teaspoons dried Italian seasoning
1 medium eggplant, peeled and sliced
1 tablespoon olive oil
1 cup ricotta cheese
¼ cup grated Parmesan cheese

1 cup chopped, pitted black olives
   (may use kalamata olives)
1 cup chopped pimento stuffed
   green olives
2 tablespoons chopped fresh basil
8 ounces salami, sliced
8 ounces provolone cheese,
   thinly sliced

1. Slice top off of bread and remove inside of loaf leaving a ¾-inch shell.
2. Combine olive oil, garlic and Italian seasoning and brush inside of bread shell.
3. Sauté sliced eggplant in a small amount of olive oil on both sides until golden brown. Drain on paper towel and allow to cool.
4. Combine ricotta and Parmesan cheese in a bowl.
5. Spread inside of bread shell with the cheese mixture.
6. Place half of eggplant slices in shell, then half the olives, fresh basil, half the salami and all the cheese slices. Repeat with remaining eggplant, olives and salami.
7. Replace top of bread and wrap loaf tightly with plastic wrap.
8. Place loaf between 2 baking sheets and top with a weight to flatten the sandwich slightly. Refrigerate at least 2 hours.
9. Remove from refrigerator and unwrap. Cut into 8 portions, re-wrap with plastic wrap to transport.

Yield: 8 servings

FOUR SUMMIT HUTS

Janet's Cabin is nestled into a roadless area near Copper Mountain. Francie's Cabin sits near Crystal Lakes. Both are named in memory of long time residents. The Section House at Boreas Pass is the restored 1882 house of railroad workers and their families. Nearby the restored 1860s wagon cabin, Ken's Cabin, is named to honor a young doctor who was a victim of an avalanche. Reservations required at www.summithuts.org.

Janet's Turkey Avocado Wrap

Wraps are made for skiers or snowshoers; they are easy to carry and tasty as well.

8 (8 or 10-inch) tortilla wraps, whole wheat or
   choice of flavor
Black cherry preserves or cranberry relish
1 pound deli turkey breast

½ pound pepper jack cheese, thinly sliced
1-2 ripe avocados, halved, pitted, scooped
   out and sliced
1 cup shredded romaine lettuce

1. Spread each tortilla wrap with preserves or relish. Add turkey, cheese and avocado slices; top with lettuce.
2. Roll into a wrap sandwich, hold together with toothpicks and slice in half. Wrap in plastic wrap to transport.

Yield: 8 wraps

10TH MOUNTAIN DIVISION

Scattered over 350 miles of the Rocky Mountains, the 10th Mountain Division hut system honors the US Army's 10th Mountain Division which trained for alpine warfare during World War II at Camp Hale, near Leadville. The soldiers exploited the harsh terrain and weather conditions to hone skills in rock climbing, downhill and nordic skiing and winter and mountain survival techniques.

Quinoa, Corn and Tomato Salad

A fresh salad so simple yet so colorful is the essence of a sunny day.

CHIVE-INFUSED OIL:
¼ cup extra virgin olive oil
½ cup fresh chives, sliced into
    1-inch pieces
½ teaspoon salt

SALAD:
1½ cups water
1 cup quinoa, uncooked
1 cup fresh corn kernels (about 2 ears)
1 cup cherry tomatoes, halved
¼ cup finely chopped fresh parsley
Chive spears, for garnish

DRESSING:
2 tablespoons chive-infused oil
2 tablespoons lime juice
2 tablespoons white wine vinegar
1 garlic clove, minced
Salt and freshly ground black pepper
    to taste

1. Place the olive oil, chives and salt in a blender and pulse until chives are very finely minced. Strain mixture through a fine sieve into an airtight container and discard the solids. The infused oil can be refrigerated for 2 weeks.
2. Combine water and quinoa in a medium saucepan; bring to a boil. Cover, reduce heat and simmer 10-15 minutes or until liquid is absorbed. Remove from heat; let stand 10 minutes. Fluff with a fork.
3. Combine quinoa, corn, tomatoes and parsley in a medium bowl.
4. Whisk together dressing ingredients. Season to taste.
5. Drizzle dressing over salad; toss well to coat.
6. Let stand 10 minutes before serving or may make ahead, cover and refrigerate until ready to serve. Garnish with chives.

Yield: 8 servings

Garlic Dipping Sauce

A savory dip for crusty breads.

7 garlic cloves, finely chopped
1 cup extra virgin olive oil, divided
⅛ teaspoon crushed red pepper
Freshly ground black pepper to taste

⅛ teaspoon dried oregano
⅛ teaspoon dried basil
⅛ teaspoon dried thyme

1. Sauté garlic in 2 -3 tablespoons olive oil over moderate heat until golden brown.
2. Cool and combine with remaining ingredients in a jar. Shake when ready to use.

Yield: 1 cup

Cheese Pepper Bread

This is foolproof bread for high altitude bakers.

1 teaspoon plus ¼ cup sugar, divided

1¾ cups warm water, divided

½ envelope yeast (1⅛ teaspoons)

1 teaspoon salt

1 teaspoon freshly ground pepper

½ teaspoon dried basil

½ cup non-fat powdered milk

5½ cups all-purpose flour, divided

2 tablespoons butter, at room temperature

1 egg, lightly beaten

1 cup grated sharp cheddar cheese

"The clearest way into the Universe is through a forest wilderness."

John Muir (naturalist, 1838-1914)

1. Dissolve 1 teaspoon sugar in ¼ cup of warm water. Add yeast and let stand 10 minutes.
2. Mix ¼ cup sugar, salt, pepper, basil, powdered milk and 1½ cups of flour. Add to yeast mixture. Stir.
3. Add 1½ cups of warm water, butter and egg and stir.
4. Stir in up to 4 more cups of flour to make dough fairly stiff.
5. Place on lightly floured surface and knead until smooth, about 8 – 10 minutes.
6. Place in warm place, covered, until double in size, about 1½ hours.
7. Turn out on lightly floured surface and press flat with palms of hands.
8. Cover dough with ½ cup sharp cheddar cheese. Knead in the cheese and then add another ½ cup of cheddar cheese and knead again.
9. Shape into two loaves and put in greased loaf pans. Cover and let rise until double in size, about 1½ hours.
10. Bake at 350 degrees for about 55 minutes.

NOTE: This recipe is adjusted for high altitude baking. Use 1 envelope of yeast at sea level.

Yield: 2 loaves

Chili Blanco

A chicken chili that is best when made ahead; perfect for a hut trip!

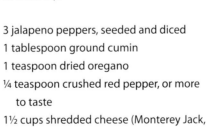

1 tablespoon extra virgin olive oil

1 pound chicken breast, chopped into bite-size pieces

1 medium onion, chopped

2 garlic cloves, finely chopped

3 (15-ounce) cans Great Northern white beans, drained

3 (14-ounce) cans chicken broth

1 (7-ounce) can diced green chiles

3 jalapeno peppers, seeded and diced

1 tablespoon ground cumin

1 teaspoon dried oregano

¼ teaspoon crushed red pepper, or more to taste

1½ cups shredded cheese (Monterey Jack, cheddar)

8 ounces sour cream

1 cup chopped fresh cilantro, if desired

1. Heat oil in large skillet. Add chicken and sauté until no longer pink. Add onion and garlic; cook 2-3 minutes.
2. Stir in 2 cans of beans, chicken broth, chiles, jalapenos, cumin, oregano and red pepper.
3. Purée the third can of beans and add to the mixture. Bring to a boil, reduce heat to low and simmer 45 minutes.
4. If making ahead, cool chili in pot; cover and refrigerate. Reheat to serve.
5. Just before serving, stir in cheese and sour cream. Garnish with cilantro, if desired.

Yield: 6-8 servings

FOOD FOR A HUT TRIP

It takes creativity to plan food for hut trips. Everything gets hauled up the mountain, cooking is rustic and water is limited. Zip lock bags hold frozen homemade soups, stews or chilis. Pre-cooked rice or pasta carry well. Cold cuts make a fuss free lunch. Pre-made baked goods offer a sweet treat. Granola packs well, and pre-shelled eggs scramble up for a hearty breakfast.

Hearty Sausage and Vegetable Soup

A soup that is better made ahead; add the pasta when ready to serve.

1 pound sweet Italian sausage
1 tablespoon extra virgin olive oil
1 cup chopped onion
2 large carrots, chopped
1 large zucchini, chopped
1 garlic clove, minced
1½ teaspoons dried basil
¾ teaspoon dried oregano

1 (32-ounce) carton beef broth
1 cup water
1 (28-ounce) can crushed tomatoes
½ cup dry red wine (optional)
1 (15-ounce) can garbanzo beans, drained and rinsed
Grated Parmesan cheese, for garnish
1/2 pound macaroni, cooked al dente

1. In a large soup pot, brown the sausage, breaking into small pieces. Remove sausage, drain and reserve. Discard fat.
2. Heat olive oil in the same pot and sauté onion and carrots until crisp tender. Add zucchini, garlic, basil and oregano and sauté another 2-3 minutes.
3. Add broth, water, tomatoes and wine to the vegetables and bring to a boil. Reduce heat, cover and simmer for 30 minutes.
4. Add reserved sausage to the pot. Heat through. If making ahead, cool soup in pot, cover and refrigerate until ready to use.
5. Reheat soup when ready and add pasta at that time. Cook until pasta is done. Garnish with cheese.

Yield: 6 servings

Maggie Pond Cookies

A variety of your favorite goodies make these cookies scrumptious.

2½ cups old-fashioned oats
1 (4-ounce) milk-chocolate bar
1½ cups (3 sticks) butter, room temperature
½ cup brown sugar
½ cup sugar
2 eggs
1 teaspoon vanilla

½ teaspoon salt
½ teaspoon baking powder
½ teaspoon baking soda
2 cups all-purpose flour
3 cups total of a mix of chopped nuts, dried cranberries, raisins, coconut, chocolate morsels and white chocolate morsels

1. Preheat oven to 350 degrees. Do not grease cookie sheets.
2. In a food processor, pulse oats with chocolate bar. Reserve ½ the mixture in an airtight container for your next batch of cookies.
3. In a mixer, cream butter and sugars until well blended.
4. Continue to mix while separately adding eggs and vanilla.
5. Combine salt, baking powder, baking soda and flour. Stir into creamed mixture.
6. Add the oat and chocolate mix, and then add the goodies (about 3 cups or so of your favorite things).
7. Place tablespoons of cookie dough on baking sheet about 2 inches apart.
8. Bake for about 10-13 minutes.

NOTE: This recipe is adjusted for high altitude baking. Use 1 teaspoon of baking powder and 1 teaspoon of baking soda at sea level.

Yield: 6 Dozen cookies

Oat Bran Applesauce Muffins

This cereal can be found at specialty food stores.

½ cup brown sugar
1½ cups Hodgson Mill Oat Bran Cereal
1½ cups whole wheat flour
½ tablespoon baking powder
½ tablespoon baking soda
½ teaspoon salt
4 egg whites

1 cup chilled applesauce (unsweetened)
1 cup shredded carrots
½ cup chopped walnuts
3 small bananas, mashed
2 (8-ounce) cans crushed pineapple, drained

1. Preheat oven to 400 degrees.
2. Spray a muffin pan with non-stick spray.
3. Mix all ingredients together. Pour into muffin pan.
4. Bake 18 minutes.

NOTE: There is no need to adjust this muffin recipe for high altitude baking.

Yield: 12 muffins

ROCKY MOUNTAIN HIGH

John Denver describes a Rocky Mountain High as "the elation, celebration of life, or the joy in living that one feels when he observes....a moonless, cloudless night, when there are so many stars you have a shadow from the starlight, and you are out camping with your friends, your best friends, and introducing them to one of nature's most spectacular light shows for the first time."

Deconstucted Omelets

A unique way to cook omelets for outdoor cookouts as well as for a large crowd; double or triple the recipe with extra pots of boiling water.

8 (one-quart size) re-sealable freezer bags; mark each guest's name with a Sharpie pen
8-16 eggs or egg whites (1-2 per serving)

OPTIONAL GARNISHES:
1½ cups shredded cheddar or Monterey Jack cheese
1½ cups finely chopped green bell pepper
1½ cups finely chopped tomatoes
1½ cups finely chopped green onions
½ - 1 cup finely chopped jalapeno peppers
1½ cups finely chopped mushrooms
1½ - 2 cups diced cooked ham

1. Fill a large soup pot with water and bring to a boil.
2. Place each freezer bag in a cup and add 1-2 eggs or egg whites into the bag.
3. Add choice of garnishes to the egg. Seal the bag removing all the air. Massage the bag to combine all ingredients and break up the eggs. Prepare bags ahead and refrigerate until ready to use.
4. Place the 8 freezer bags into the boiling water and continue to boil for 15-18 minutes or until done. (Boiling time will be less at sea level.)
5. Remove the bags, open and serve omelet on a plate.

Yield: 8 servings

Ski Tip Lodge

Executive Chef Kevin McCombs

Rosemary Pine Honey Corn Muffins

Pot Roast and Portobello Cassoulet

Apple Cobbler
with Streusel Topping

The historic Ski Tip Lodge, located within Keystone Resort on Montezuma Road, is now the oldest operating ski lodge in North America. The legendary ski pioneers Max and Edna Dercum transformed the former 1860s stage coach stop from a rustic home to a charming ski lodge in the 1940s.

Today, diners enjoy a romantic four course meal, created by Executive Chef Kevin McCombs, locally trained at the Colorado Mountain College Culinary Institute. Chef McCombs uses fresh and sustainable ingredients to present tantalizing flavor combinations in new and exciting ways.

Rosemary Pine Honey Corn Muffins

1 cup fine cornmeal
1¼ cups all-purpose flour
1 tablespoon chopped fresh rosemary
3 tablespoons toasted pine nuts
1½ teaspoons baking powder
¼ teaspoon baking soda

½ teaspoon salt
2 large eggs
4 tablespoons pine honey
6 ounces milk
4 tablespoons melted butter

1. Preheat oven to 400 degrees.
2. Place first seven ingredients in mixing bowl and mix until incorporated.
3. In a second mixing bowl, beat eggs and then add honey and milk. Add wet ingredients to dry and mix until incorporated being careful not to over mix.
4. Add melted butter and mix one more time. Scoop mixture into well oiled muffin pans.
5. Bake for 15 minutes.

Yield: 16 muffins

Pot Roast and Portobello Cassoulet

2 pounds beef chuck pot roast
2 ounces vegetable oil
1 (15-ounce) can low sodium beef broth
1 medium onion, large dice
1 carrot, large dice
1 celery stalk, large dice
Water to cover
2 tablespoons butter
2 carrots, small dice
1 bulb celery root, small dice

1 pound portobello mushrooms, cleaned and small dice
2 medium onions, small dice
2 garlic cloves, minced
12 ounces heavy cream
3 (15-ounce) cans Great Northern Beans
Reserved braising liquid
6 ounces grated Parmigiano Reggiano cheese
2 tablespoons chopped chives

1. Preheat oven to 300 degrees.
2. In a large sauté pan over medium high heat, sear pot roast in oil on all sides until well browned, approximately 10 minutes. Remove from heat and place in deep roasting pan along with the next five ingredients, making sure to cover roast completely with water. Cover roasting pan.
3. Cook in oven for six hours until the meat will pull apart with a fork. Cooking time will vary depending on size of the roast. Cool roast and strain vegetables from braising liquid, being sure to save braising liquid. Roast can be braised from one to five days in advance, and can also be done in a slow cooker if available.
4. In large sauté pan over medium heat, melt butter and sweat carrots, celery root, mushrooms, onions and garlic. Turn heat to low and add cream, beans, braising liquid and begin to reduce.
5. Pull pot roast apart with a fork into bite-size pieces and add to pan. Continue to cook over very low heat until cream becomes thick and a tight stew consistency is reached, about twenty minutes.
6. Serve hot and garnish with grated cheese and chives.

Yield: 6-8 servings

Apple Cobbler with Streusel Topping

APPLE FILLING:

10 apples, Granny Smith, peeled, cored and sliced into 10 pieces

4 ounces (1 stick) butter

1 cup brown sugar

1 tablespoon cinnamon

1 teaspoon ground cloves

1 teaspoon nutmeg

1 teaspoon allspice

1 teaspoon ground coriander

STREUSEL TOPPING:

½ cup ground pecans

5 tablespoons butter

¼ cup brown sugar

2½ tablespoons granulated sugar

½ tablespoon cinnamon

½ cup flour

½ box white cake mix

1. Preheat oven to 350 degrees.
2. In a large sauté pan, melt butter and add sugar. Cook on medium heat for five minutes then add all 5 spices and apples. Cook over low heat for approximately 30 minutes until apples are tender.
3. Place first 6 ingredients for streusel topping in food processor and pulse until pecans are ground and well incorporated. If food processor is not available, cut the butter into flour, sugars and cinnamon. Chop nuts very fine and then add to butter and flour mixture.
4. Follow cake mix directions to make batter being sure to cut ingredients in half. Pour into a well-greased 13-inch by 9-inch pan, being sure to spread evenly. Layer apples and jus (French for "juice") evenly over cake batter. Sprinkle streusel topping evenly over the apples.
5. Bake at 350 degrees for thirty minutes until cake batter is cooked through. Serve hot with your favorite ice cream.

Yield: 8-10 servings

Returning guests enjoy an ever changing menu based on the highest quality products available. Ski Tip is known for thoughtful service and fine wine selections.

To top off the memorable evening, a friendly and attentive staff invites you to take your dessert in the log-lined great room, warmed by the cozy fire.

White Christmas

Here in Summit County, we always enjoy a White Christmas, with family and friends from near and far.

CHRISTMAS EVE DINNER
Apples with Brie and Rosemary
Olivita
Poinsettia Cocktail

Clementine Salad

Seafood Chowder with Sherry

Peppermint Pavlova

CHRISTMAS MORNING
Christmas Day Strata

Danish Almond Coffee Cake

Irish Soda Bread

CHRISTMAS DINNER
Champagne Powder

Spicy Pecans
Smoked Salmon and Lemon Pepper Cream on Crostini

Pear and Goat Cheese Salad with Champagne Vinaigrette

Stir-Fried Snow Peas and Carrots
Roasted Red Potatoes with Garlic
Cauliflower Gratin

Easy Croissants

Slow Roasted Prime Rib of Beef
Yorkshire Pudding
Horseradish Cream Sauce
Crown Roast of Pork with Stuffing

Frozen Holiday Bombe
Chocolate Whiskey Balls

HOLIDAY IN THE MOUNTAINS

The mountains of Summit County are the ideal place to enjoy the holidays. The brisk air, sparkle of snow, a cozy fire and the festive spirit of a town provides the perfect backdrop for sharing the joy of the season with family and friends.

Apples with Brie and Rosemary

Make these brie treats ahead of time, cover and allow to rest at room temperature until broiling.

2 large Honeycrisp or Fuji apples, cored, cut into ½-inch slices

2 large Granny Smith apples, cored, cut into ½-inch slices

Diet lemon lime soda

1 (10-ounce) Brie, rind removed and cut into thin slices

1 small package fresh rosemary, ½ chopped; reserve sprigs for garnish

Freshly ground black pepper

1. After slicing apples, sprinkle with diet soda to prevent browning.
2. Preheat broiler.
3. Arrange slices on baking sheet. Top each apple slice with a slice of brie; sprinkle with chopped rosemary and pepper.
4. Broil until cheese melts, rotating sheet to ensure even cooking, about 1 minute. Garnish with sprigs of rosemary and serve immediately.

Yield: 20 servings

Olivita

These appetizers can be frozen then heated before serving.

1 baguette or cocktail pumpernickel rye bread

TOPPING:

1 (4.25 ounce) can chopped black olives

½ cup chopped pimento-stuffed green olives

¾ cup shredded Monterey Jack cheese

4 tablespoons butter, softened

1 tablespoon extra virgin olive oil

½ cup grated Parmesan cheese

2 garlic cloves, chopped

¼ cup chopped Italian flat leaf parsley

1. Preheat oven to 350 degrees.
2. Mix all topping ingredients.
3. If using a baguette, slice into thin slices. Spread mixture to edges of bread. May be frozen at this point.
4. Bake in oven for 5-8 minutes, until melted and golden around edges. Serve warm.

Yield: 12 servings

Poinsettia Cocktail

A glamorous cocktail, bubbly and beautiful; perfect for the holiday season.

¼ cup lemon-flavored vodka

½ cup cranberry juice

¼ cup champagne

2 strips orange zest, each about ¼-inch by 2-inches

1. In a cocktail shaker filled with ice, combine vodka and cranberry juice. Cover and shake vigorously.
2. Strain into a martini glass and top with champagne. Twist the orange strips over the glass, drop them in, and serve.

Yield: 1 serving (1 cocktail)

Clementine Salad

A simple yet distinctive salad; watercress could also be used.

5½ teaspoons white wine vinegar

1 garlic clove, minced

¼ teaspoon kosher salt

¼ teaspoon freshly ground black pepper

⅓ cup extra virgin olive oil

1 (9-ounce) package of baby arugula

1 pound Belgian endive, cut crosswise into ½-inch pieces

8 clementines, peeled and separated

½ cup pine nuts, toasted (optional)

1. Whisk together vinegar, garlic, kosher salt and pepper.
2. Add olive oil in a slow steady stream, whisking until emulsified.
3. Just before serving, toss arugula and endive with just enough dressing to coat. Add clementines and pine nuts.

Yield: 8 servings

Seafood Chowder with Sherry

Sherry adds a sophisticated touch for the holidays.

4 cups milk

2 cups heavy cream

8 slices bacon

5-6 (6½-ounce) cans chopped clams, strain and reserve juice and clams separately

3 large potatoes, peeled and diced

2 cups chopped onions

2 teaspoons dried dill

½ teaspoon celery salt

½ teaspoon pepper

2 teaspoons instant chicken bouillon granules (or 4 cubes)

½ cup shredded carrots

1 pound bay scallops

¼ cup dry sherry

1. Combine milk and cream in pot and heat slowly, uncovered, to almost boiling.
2. Cook bacon, drain on paper towels and crumble for garnish. Reserve 2 tablespoons of warm grease.
3. Combine clam juice, potatoes, onions, dill, celery salt, pepper and chicken bouillon in a large separate pot. Cover and bring to a boil.
4. Add bacon grease when clam juice is boiling. Reduce heat and simmer until potatoes are slightly tender.
5. For remainder of recipe, do not cover pot.
6. Add milk/cream mixture and carrots to soup and heat until bubbly.
7. Stir in clams and scallops. Return to a slow boil. Cook 1-2 minutes until clams and scallops are opaque.
8. Remove pot from heat; stir in sherry and serve. Garnish with crumbled bacon. If reheating, do so in an uncovered pot.

Yield: 8-10 servings

IMAGINE: TREE CUTTING

Settler families would plunge into the woods at Christmastime to cut that special tree. It would be carried by wagon, or sometimes on a sheet of burlap, pulled by the family horse or mule. The tree would be lit only once – with wax candles – on Christmas Eve. The threat of fire was too great to light the tree more than once.

SNOW IN THE MOUNTAINS

Three hundred is the magic number for Summit County. An average of 300 inches of snow falls annually, achieved while the area enjoys an average of 300 days of sunshine.

Peppermint Pavlova

A famous Australian dessert that lends itself to many toppings but at Christmas, crushed peppermint bark is perfection.

MERINGUE:

3 egg whites, at room temperature
6 ounces very superfine sugar
½ teaspoon peppermint extract
½ teaspoon white vinegar
2 teaspoons cornstarch
1 cup heavy cream, whipped

OPTIONAL TOPPINGS:

Fresh fruits such as strawberries, pitted cherries, kiwi fruit
Chocolate sauce, trickled over meringue
Peppermint bark, coarsely chopped

1. Preheat oven to 300 degrees.
2. Line a baking sheet with parchment paper and draw an 8-inch circle on it. Turn parchment paper over.
3. With an electric mixer, beat the egg whites until foamy.
4. Add the sugar in 2 batches, ensuring that the foam is firm after each addition.
5. Continue beating while adding peppermint extract, vinegar and cornstarch, until stiff peaks form. Do not overbeat.
6. Spread the meringue on the paper circle, piling it up around the edges to form a nest.
7. Bake for about 1 hour until the exterior is firm. Turn off oven, open the door and allow meringue to rest for 5 minutes. Remove from the oven and cool, away from drafts.
8. Carefully remove the meringue nest from the paper and place on a serving dish.
9. Just before serving, top meringue with whipped cream and choice of toppings.

Yield: 8 servings

Christmas Day Strata

Use white bread or sourdough for this delicious egg dish.

6 slices bread, crusts removed and torn into bite-size pieces
6 tablespoons butter, melted
8 eggs, beaten
1 cup milk
1 teaspoon dry mustard
½ teaspoon salt
½ teaspoon black pepper

Dash cayenne pepper
3 green onions, chopped
4 ounces cream cheese, cubed
6 mushrooms, sliced
1 medium tomato, chopped
4 ounces grated cheddar cheese
½ pound crab meat

1. Preheat oven to 375 degrees.
2. Butter or spray with non-stick spray a 13-inch by 9-inch oven-proof dish.
3. Cover bottom of dish with torn bread; pour melted butter over bread.
4. Beat eggs in a large mixing bowl, add milk and mix well.
5. Add mustard, salt, peppers, onions, cream cheese, mushrooms, tomato and cheddar cheese to mixture. Mix well.
6. Add crab and stir gently. Pour mixture over bread.
7. Cover with foil and bake for 15-20 minutes. Remove foil and bake an additional 30-40 minutes.

Yield: 6 servings

Danish Almond Coffee Cake

A delicious holiday treat.

FILLING:

½ cup plus 2 tablespoons sliced almonds

1 (7-ounce) roll almond paste

¼ cup brown sugar

2 teaspoons cinnamon

CAKE:

1 cup sugar

½ cup (1 stick) butter, softened

2 eggs

1 teaspoon almond extract

2 cups all-purpose flour

½ teaspoon baking powder

½ teaspoon baking soda

½ teaspoon salt

1 cup sour cream

Confectioners' sugar to decorate

1. Preheat oven to 350 degrees.
2. Grease and flour 10-12 cup Bundt pan. Sprinkle 2 tablespoons almonds into Bundt pan and set aside.

TO MAKE FILLING:

1. In a food processor, blend almond paste, ½ cup almonds, brown sugar and cinnamon until it resembles coarse meal.
2. To make cake batter, combine sugar and butter in a mixer. Beat on high speed until blended.
3. Add eggs, one at a time, followed by almond extract. Beat until batter is light and fluffy, about 3 minutes.
4. Sift flour with baking powder, baking soda and salt into a bowl. Add flour mixture and sour cream to egg mixture. Beat until combined.
5. Spoon one-third batter into Bundt pan; sprinkle half filling on top. Repeat with another one-third batter and remaining half filling; spoon remaining batter over filling.
6. Bake 45-50 minutes or until toothpick inserted near middle of cake comes out clean.
7. Cool in pan on wire rack for 15 minutes. Unmold carefully onto wire rack and cool completely. Dust with confectioners' sugar.

NOTE: This recipe is adjusted for high altitude. Increase baking powder and baking soda to 1 teaspoon each for sea level baking.

Yield: 12 servings

IMAGINE: CHRISTMAS MORNING

A child in early-day Summit County might awake on Christmas morning to find.....an orange! Fresh fruit, particularly citrus fruit, was expensive and difficult to get so was often a once a year treat!

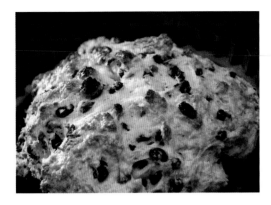

"Bread deals with living things, with giving life, with growth, with the seed, the grain that nurtures. It is not coincidence that we say bread is the staff of life."

Lionel Poilane (artisan baker, 1945-2002)

Irish Soda Bread

A traditional bread that is perfect for holiday celebrations.

4 cups all-purpose flour
½ cup sugar
1 teaspoon baking powder
½ teaspoon baking soda
¾ teaspoon salt
¼ cup (½ stick) butter
3 cups raisins, or golden raisins, dried cranberries or mixture of dried fruit

2 large eggs, beaten slightly
1¼ cups buttermilk
½ cup sour cream
1 large egg with 1 tablespoon water for egg wash

1. Combine flour, sugar, baking powder, baking soda and salt. Cut in butter until it resembles small peas.
2. Add fruit. Mix well.
3. Mix eggs, buttermilk and sour cream. Stir into the flour mixture until just moistened. Knead 2-3 minutes.
4. Preheat oven to 350 degrees.
5. Shape into a ball, place in greased cast iron skillet. Cut a cross shape on top about 1-inch deep and brush with egg wash.
6. Bake 65-75 minutes or until tester comes out clean; cool in skillet 10 minutes and then on cooling rack.

NOTE: This recipe is adjusted for high altitude baking. Use 2 teaspoons baking powder and 1 teaspoon baking soda for sea level baking.

Yield: 1 loaf

Champagne Powder

A simple punch that is beautiful to serve.

2 oranges, sliced
2 lemons, sliced
2 (750 ml.) bottles champagne
2 quarts lemon lime soda, chilled
1 pint pineapple sherbet, chilled

1. A day before serving, make an ice ring using a decorative mold, water and fruit slices. Freeze until firm.
2. In a large punch bowl, combine champagne and soda. Mix well.
3. Add sherbet and gently stir.
4. Unmold ice ring and slide into punch. Serve immediately.

Yield: 24 servings

Spicy Pecans

Sweet and peppery pecans are a perfect complement to a holiday cocktail.

2 tablespoons cold water
2 egg whites, beaten
2 pounds pecan halves
1½ cups sugar

2 teaspoons cinnamon
2 teaspoons salt
1½ teaspoons crushed red pepper

1. Preheat oven to 225 degrees; cover 2 cookie sheets with foil.
2. Mix cold water and egg whites; fold in pecans until coated.
3. In another bowl, mix remaining ingredients. Fold in coated pecans.
4. Spread pecans in a single layer, on cookie sheets. Bake for 1 hour, stirring occasionally. Cool and store in an airtight container.

Yield: 2 pounds pecans

Smoked Salmon and Lemon Pepper Cream on Crostini

A delicious holiday treat.

CROSTINI:
1 French baguette, thinly sliced diagonally
Extra virgin olive oil

LEMON PEPPER CREAM:
2 teaspoons black peppercorns
⅓ cup mascarpone cheese
¼ cup milk
Zest of 1 lemon
Juice of 2 lemons, divided
½ pound smoked salmon, thinly sliced
2 tablespoons chopped fresh dill
Sea salt

CROSTINI:
1. Preheat oven to 400 degrees.
2. Lightly brush both sides of each slice of bread with olive oil.
3. Bake on a baking sheet for 8-10 minutes until crisp and golden.
4. Cool and store in an airtight container until ready to use.

LEMON PEPPER CREAM:
1. Pound or grind the peppercorns as finely as possible.
2. In a small bowl, mix mascarpone cheese and ground pepper.
3. Add milk and lemon zest, mixing well.
4. Season with salt and lemon juice to taste. Chill until needed.

TO SERVE:
1. Spread crostini with the lemon pepper cream and place a slice of smoked salmon on top.
2. Sprinkle dill and lemon juice over the salmon and serve immediately.

Yield: 6 servings

SKI SPECTACULAR

In December, Breckenridge and Copper Mountain host the world's largest winter sports event for people with disabilities, the Hartford Ski Spectacular. The event provides adaptive ski/snowboard programs, youth mentorship, competitions and instructor training. American and British Wounded Warriors join over 700 participants. The program helps injured veterans, many of whom are amputees, to enjoy the sense of freedom and accomplishment that comes from floating down slopes and mastering a sport.

Pear and Goat Cheese Salad with Champagne Vinaigrette

A lovely presentation that makes a holiday dinner so special.

HOLIDAY GARNISH

Liven up platters with small holiday ornaments, edible plants or gorgeous small fruits and vegetables. But watch out, poinsettias are poisonous!

SUGARED WALNUTS:
1½ cups walnut halves
¾ cup sugar

SALAD:
2 (5-ounce) bags gourmet mixed salad greens
⅓ cup sweetened dried cranberries
1 ripe Bosc or Bartlett pear, peeled, cored and sliced thinly
4 ounces crumbled goat cheese

VINAIGRETTE:
¼ cup extra virgin olive oil
¼ cup champagne vinegar
2 tablespoons Dijon-style mustard
2 teaspoons honey
½ teaspoon salt
¼ teaspoon freshly ground black pepper

1. In a heavy saucepan over medium heat, stir walnuts and sugar until sugar melts and turns golden brown (8-10 minutes).
2. Spread mixture in a single layer on lightly greased waxed paper; cool. Break into small, bite-size pieces; store in an airtight container up to 3 days.
3. Whisk together olive oil, vinegar, mustard, honey, salt and pepper.
4. Combine salad greens and cranberries in a large bowl and toss with vinaigrette. Arrange greens on individual salad plates.
5. Place the pear slices on each serving; then sprinkle with the sugared walnuts and crumbled goat cheese.

Yield: 8 servings

Stir-Fried Snow Peas and Carrots

This colorful side dish may be served warm or at room temperature.

2 carrots cut into thin julienne strips, 2 inches in length
1½ tablespoons butter
1½ tablespoons finely minced shallots

1 pound snow peas, trimmed
1-2 tablespoons water
Salt and freshly ground black pepper to taste

1. Blanch carrots in boiling water for 2 minutes. Remove from heat, drain and store in refrigerator.
2. Heat a wok or medium-sized skillet and add butter. Stir-fry shallots for 1 minute.
3. Add the carrots, snow peas and stir-fry 2 minutes.
4. Add water and stir-fry until vegetables are crisp-tender.
5. Remove from wok and season with salt and pepper. Serve warm or at room temperature.

Yield: 6 servings

Roasted Red Potatoes with Garlic

A unique dressing adds a special zest to a holiday favorite.

2½ pounds small red potatoes, halved

1 teaspoon salt, divided

8 sprigs fresh rosemary

8 tablespoons extra virgin olive oil, divided

8-12 garlic cloves, unpeeled

2 tablespoons white wine vinegar

4 teaspoons Dijon-style mustard

½ teaspoon pepper

4 green onions, sliced thinly

1. Preheat oven to 450 degrees.
2. Mix potatoes, ½ teaspoon salt, rosemary, 2 tablespoons olive oil and garlic cloves. Toss to coat. Spread on baking sheet.
3. Roast 30-40 minutes until potatoes are tender and browned.
4. In a large bowl, whisk together vinegar, mustard, ½ teaspoon salt and pepper. Gradually add 6 tablespoons olive oil and whisk until emulsified.
5. Squeeze garlic out of skins; mash and add to dressing.
6. Add potatoes and green onions to dressing. Serve warm.

Yield: 12 servings

Cauliflower Gratin

The horseradish flavor is a perfect match for the beef roast.

3½ pounds cauliflower, about 8 cups

6 tablespoons unsalted butter, divided

3 tablespoons flour

2 cups half-and-half

7 tablespoons prepared white horseradish, divided

1 teaspoon white vinegar

Ground nutmeg, salt and pepper to taste

1 cup crumbled Fontina cheese, about 4 ounces

½ tablespoon Dijon-style mustard

2 cups bread crumbs

1. Preheat oven to 375 degrees.
2. Steam cauliflower until tender crisp, about 15-20 minutes. Transfer to a 13-inch by 9-inch baking dish.
3. Melt 3 tablespoons of butter in a heavy saucepan, add flour and stir 2 minutes.
4. Gradually whisk in half-and-half. Cook until sauce boils and thickens, whisking constantly, about 4 minutes.
5. Add 5 tablespoons horseradish and 1 teaspoon vinegar. Season to taste with nutmeg, salt and pepper.
6. Pour sauce over cauliflower and mix to coat. Sprinkle cheese over the top. If making a day ahead, refrigerate at this point.
7. Melt 3 tablespoons butter in saucepan and add mustard and remaining horseradish. Add bread crumbs, stir until bread crumbs are golden brown.
8. Top gratin with bread crumbs and bake until thoroughly heated, about 30 minutes.

Yield: 8-10 servings

SPECIAL THANKS

John and Linda Mirro have turned a favorite hobby into a profitable photography career. They moved to Summit County in 2002, and have been active in numerous non-profit groups, including the Breckenridge Music Festival, Summit Public Radio and Summit County Animal Control Shelter. This active couple enjoys fly fishing, photography, travel and hiking; Linda plays golf and John develops web sites and marketing plans. They have generously donated their time and talents to provide quality photography for this book.

BUTTER IS THE REAL THING

Do not substitute margarine for butter;

it will affect texture and taste.

Easy Croissants

The herbs in these croissants pair nicely with the entrées.

Croissants:
5 cups all-purpose flour, divided
2 teaspoons dry yeast
⅓ cup sugar
1½ teaspoons salt
1 cup warm water
¾ cup evaporated milk (may use
   evaporated skim)
1¼ cups (3 sticks) butter, divided
2 eggs, divided
1 tablespoon water

Herbs (optional):
2 tablespoons chopped fresh oregano
2 tablespoons chopped fresh basil
2 tablespoons minced onion

1. In large bowl, mix 1 cup flour, yeast, sugar and salt. Set aside.
2. In a saucepan, heat water, milk, and ¼ cup butter until warm and add to flour mixture. Add 1 egg and mix at low speed for about 3 minutes. Set aside.
3. In another bowl, cut remaining butter into remaining 4 cups flour until butter is size of peas. Pour yeast mixture over butter/flour mixture and fold in until all of the flour is moistened. Cover bowl tightly with plastic and wrap in aluminum foil; refrigerate 2 to 24 hours.
4. Remove from refrigerator and place dough on floured surface. Knead 5 or 6 times to release air bubbles. Divide dough into 4 parts.
5. Roll each part into a 14-inch circle. With a sharp knife, cut into 10 wedges. If using herbs, sprinkle herbs on wedges.
6. Starting at the long edge of each wedge, roll dough towards the point to create the croissant. Place point side down on ungreased cookie sheets.
7. Cover prepared croissants with a cloth and allow to rise in a warm place until doubled, 1 to 1½ hours.
8. Combine the other egg and 1 tablespoon water and mix well. Brush lightly on croissants.
9. Bake at 350 degrees for 15 to 18 minutes. Remove to rack to cool. Croissants freeze well.

NOTE: This recipe has been adjusted for high altitude. Use 4 teaspoons yeast for sea level baking.

Yield: 40 croissants

Slow Roasted Prime Rib of Beef

This is a foolproof recipe for a holiday favorite.

1 (3 bone-in) beef rib roast, about
  6 pounds
3 tablespoons kosher salt
1½ tablespoons coarsely ground
  black pepper
1 tablespoon extra virgin olive oil

8-10 sprigs fresh rosemary
8-10 sprigs thyme
10 medium garlic cloves, peeled
  and smashed
3 tablespoons unsalted butter, cut into
  ½-inch cubes

1. Bring beef to room temperature, about 2 hours before cooking. Thirty minutes later, season the meat on all sides with salt and pepper.
2. Position rack in the center of the oven and preheat to 325 degrees.
3. Heat a large skillet over high heat for 1 minute. Add the olive oil, swirl to cover the pan, and when first whiffs of smoke appear, add beef to the pan. Use tongs to turn the beef, sear exterior until well-browned, about 9 minutes total. NOTE: If using a cast iron skillet, it may go straight to the oven after searing.
4. Transfer the roast to a roasting pan, bone side down. Arrange the rosemary, thyme, garlic and butter evenly over the top of the roast.
5. Roast the beef, basting every 30 minutes until a meat thermometer inserted into the center reads 120-125 degrees for rare, about 2 hours. For medium rare, cook to 130-135 degrees, about 2¼ hours. For medium, roast about 2½ hours to 140-145 degrees.
6. Let the roast rest out of the oven for 15-30 minutes before carving. Save the pan drippings for making Yorkshire pudding.

Yield: 8 servings

"The ornament of a house is the friends who frequent it."

Ralph Waldo Emerson (author, philosopher, 1803-1882)

Yorkshire Pudding

Allow plenty of time for this batter to set up before baking.

⅞ cup all-purpose flour
½ teaspoon salt
½ cup milk
½ cup water
2 eggs, well beaten (until fluffy)
¼ cup reserved pan drippings (or ¼ cup butter)

1. In a deep bowl, stir flour and salt and make a well in the center.
2. Mix milk and water together and stir into the dry ingredients.
3. Add eggs and continue to beat until large bubbles rise to the surface. Cover and refrigerate for 1 hour. Bring to 70 degrees and beat again.
4. After removing roast, increase oven temperature to 400 degrees.
5. Using a 13-inch by 9-inch ovenproof dish (for larger roasts use 2 pans) pour pan drippings into dish and heat in oven.
6. Pour batter into hot dish to ½-inch deep. Bake for 20 minutes.
7. Reduce heat to 350 degrees and continue baking 10-15 minutes longer. Pudding will deflate when out of oven; cut into 3-inch squares and serve immediately.

Yield: 6-8 servings

STAYING WARM AT ALTITUDE

It's tough to get food to the table warm in Summit Country. The heat of the moisture of cooked food makes it hot. Since water boils at around 190° F here, the steam is 18° cooler than at sea level. Because the air pressure is lower, moisture evaporates rapidly. Heat plates and keep food covered, but it's best to seat your guests quickly. Locals say "Good Luck".

Horseradish Cream Sauce

A versatile sauce that is perfect for either prime rib or roast pork.

2 cups sour cream	Dash hot pepper sauce
1 cup prepared horseradish	1 teaspoon kosher salt
Dash Worcestershire sauce	

1. In a medium bowl, whisk all ingredients together until smooth.
2. Cover and refrigerate; stir before serving.

Yield: 3 cups

Crown Roast of Pork with Stuffing

No dinner party can equal the elegance of a succulent Crown Roast of Pork, festively garnished and presented to the table before carving.

ROAST:
1 (12-rib) crown roast of pork (5-6 pounds)
Extra virgin olive oil for rubbing
Kosher salt and ground pepper
2 sprigs fresh rosemary
1 cup dry white wine, for basting

GARNISH:
3-4 pears, halved and cored
Lingonberries
2-3 sprigs fresh rosemary

STUFFING:
½ pound ground pork
6 breakfast sausages, cooked and thinly sliced
1 medium onion, diced
1 cup celery, diced
1 cup frozen corn, thawed or ½ cup chopped dates
¾ cup chopped walnuts or pecans
2 tablespoons chopped fresh parsley
7 ounces (½ package) seasoned, cubed bread stuffing
1 cup chicken stock
Butter

1. Remove roast from refrigerator one hour before roasting. Rub roast with olive oil and season well with kosher salt and pepper. Preheat oven to 350 degrees.
2. Place crown roast (cover the protruding rib bones in foil to avoid scorching) in oiled broiler pan in the middle of oven. Insert rosemary springs in the center of the roast, cover with foil. Baste with wine every 30 minutes.
3. The roast will be thoroughly cooked when juices run clear and meat thermometer reads 155-160 degrees, approximately 2 hours.
4. Prepare stuffing by sautéing pork, sausage, onion and celery. Add corn or dates, nuts, parsley and bread cubes. Add enough chicken stock to moisten bread cubes.
5. Reserve enough stuffing to fill the cavity in the center of the roast. Fill the cavity 30 minutes before end of roasting period. Place remaining stuffing in a buttered casserole, dot with butter and bake at 350 degrees for 25 minutes before serving.
6. Allow roast to rest for 30 minutes before carving. Garnish with pears, lingonberries and rosemary.

Yield: 6-8 servings

Frozen Holiday Bombe

This classic French dessert is an attractive finale for your holiday dinner.

¾ cup macaroons, crushed
¾ cup half-and-half
¼ cup confectioners' sugar
pinch salt
1 cup heavy whipping cream
3 teaspoons Amaretto liqueur
3 cups raspberry sorbet, softened
1½ cups raspberries

1. In a large bowl, combine macaroons, half-and-half, confectioners' sugar and salt. Let stand for 1 hour.
2. Chill a 2 quart dome mold or a 2 quart stainless steel dome-shaped bowl for 30 minutes.
3. Using a chilled mixing bowl, whip cream to soft peaks.
4. Fold macaroon mixture into whipped cream and add liqueur.
5. Fill chilled bombe mold with softened sorbet. Fill the rest of the mold with the macaroon/whipped cream mixture. Cover with foil and freeze for at least 6 hours or overnight.
6. Thirty minutes before serving, remove from mold by immersing in hot water, running a knife around the edges; place decorative plate on mold and turn upside down. Gently remove mold.
7. Garnish with raspberries and refrigerate until ready to serve.

Yield: 8 servings

AN INSPIRATION

"I try to share the spirit and beauty of the mountains with my students," explains Freda Nieters, a 1962 pioneer ski instructor at Keystone and Arapahoe Basin who's still out there. She's listed in Skiing magazine's top 100 instructors, honored by the Colorado Ski and Snowboard Hall of Fame and in the Guinness World Book for skiing 78,000 vertical feet in one day, at age 74.

Chocolate Whiskey Balls

Make these treats up to a month in advance; they get better with age.

6 (1-ounce) squares semi-sweet chocolate, broken into bits
3 tablespoons dark corn syrup
½ cup whiskey (scotch, bourbon or Irish)
2½ cups crushed chocolate wafers
1 cup finely chopped pecans
¼ cup finely chopped candied cherries
½ cup confectioners' sugar
Granulated sugar, for rolling

1. Melt chocolate in top of double boiler. Remove from heat and add corn syrup and whiskey.
2. Combine cookie crumbs, nuts, cherries and confectioners' sugar in a large bowl and mix well.
3. Add melted chocolate mixture and mix well. Let stand 30 minutes.
4. Form the mixture into ¾-inch balls and roll in granulated sugar.
5. Store the balls in waxed paper-lined tins in a cool place.
6. To keep moist, add a few sugar cubes soaked in whiskey to each tin.

Yield: 6 dozen balls

Ski Weekend

Ski weekends are for fun and leisure. These make ahead recipes need little last minute attention. Hit the slopes!

BREAKFAST
Cheddar and Cream Scones
Miner's Muffins
Bubble Bread

SKI SNACK
Pepperoni Pockets

APRÈS SKI
Mulled Wine
Wild Mushroom and Feta Pâté
Chicken Pesto Bites

Tomato Bisque
Mixed Green Salad with Fruit

Southwestern Pork Chili
Beef Stew
Chicken Tagine
Corn Spoon Bread

Double Black Diamond Cake
Colorado Cookies
Amen Fudge

ARAPAHOE BASIN

It's called "white gold". And just like mining, it took a vision and a lot of determination to see it prosper. By 1982, Summit County was named Colorado's number one skiing destination. It started in 1945 when a few skiing locals and two national ski pioneers from the US Army's 10th Mountain Division collaborated to launch Arapahoe Basin. Lift tickets were $1.25.

Cheddar and Cream Scones

Freshly baked scones are a special treat with or without butter.

2 cups all-purpose flour
½ teaspoon baking powder (for sea level use 1 teaspoon)
¼ teaspoon salt
2 teaspoons sugar

½ cup (1 stick) butter, cut into cubes
1 cup (packed) grated sharp cheddar cheese
¾ cup whipping cream, chilled
1 large egg

1. Preheat oven to 375 degrees.
2. Blend dry ingredients in food processor and pulse to cut in butter until it resembles coarse meal. Pulse in grated cheese.
3. Whisk cream and egg in small bowl.
4. Pulse in cream mixture through the feed tube, using only as much as is necessary for dough to begin to form together.
5. Turn dough out onto lightly floured surface. Gather dough together, divide in half. Pat each into a 6 inch circle and cut into 6 wedges. Transfer to ungreased baking sheet about 2 inches apart.
6. Bake until golden about 20 minutes. Transfer to rack and cool.

NOTE: This recipe has been adjusted for high altitude baking. Use 1 teaspoon baking powder at sea level.

Yield: 12 scones

Miner's Muffins

This delicious breakfast sandwich can be put together before the weekend.

½ pound bulk sausage
8 large eggs
3-4 tablespoons milk

2 cans large biscuits, flaky style
2 jalapenos, diced, optional
1 cup finely grated cheddar cheese

1. Preheat oven per directions on biscuit package. Spray muffin pans with nonstick spray; prepare 16 muffin cups.
2. Brown sausage breaking it into crumbles. Remove and drain on paper towels.
3. In a bowl, beat eggs and whisk in milk. In a medium pan, scramble the egg mixture until cooked but still soft.
4. Cut each biscuit horizontally. Press bottom halves in prepared cups leaving a slight edge extending over the top of each cup.
5. Fill each cup with 1 tablespoon browned sausage; add one heaping tablespoon of eggs. Top with ½ teaspoon diced jalapenos and 1 heaping teaspoon of cheese.
6. Place other half of biscuit over the top and press edges together sealing well. Make a mark on those without jalapenos to distinguish them.
7. Bake for 12-15 minutes; until biscuits are golden brown. Muffins can be refrigerated for several days and reheated in microwave. They can be frozen. Remove from freezer the night before and reheat in microwave.

Yield: 16 biscuits

Bubble Bread

Great for breakfast, this bread is also a perfect complement to a mug of steaming hot chocolate beside a roaring fire later in the day.

BREAD:
5-5½ cups of all-purpose flour
1 package of dry yeast (for sea level use 2 packages)
¼ cup sugar
1 teaspoon salt
1 cup lemon-lime soda
½ cup water
¼ cup (½ stick) butter
1 large egg
3 large egg yolks

TOPPING:
⅔ cup sugar
½ cup finely chopped nuts
2 teaspoons cinnamon
½ cup (1 stick) butter, melted

1. In a large bowl, combine 2 cups of flour, yeast, sugar and salt. Mix well.
2. In a saucepan, heat soda, water and butter until warm (120-130 degrees). Butter does not need to melt.
3. Add to flour mixture. Add egg and egg yolks. Beat for 3 minutes until moistened.
4. By hand, stir in enough flour to make a soft dough. Knead until smooth and elastic, 3-5 minutes.
5. Place dough in a greased bowl, turning to grease all sides. Cover bowl with plastic wrap and foil. Refrigerate 4-24 hours.
6. Mix topping ingredients together.
7. Divide dough in half. Divide each half into 4 parts and each fourth into 6 pieces (24 pieces per loaf). Shape each piece into a ball.
8. Melt butter, and using ¼ cup for each loaf, dip balls and then roll in topping.
9. Place 24 balls in a greased 9-inch by 5-inch bread pan, making roughly 2 layers. Repeat for second loaf. Pour any remaining butter on balls in each pan; divide remaining topping over top of each loaf.
10. Cover and let rise in warm place until doubled, about 30 minutes. Bake at 375 degrees for 30-35 minutes. Cool 10 minutes in pans and then remove.

NOTE: Make this bread up a day ahead and keep tightly wrapped in refrigerator. Place in warm oven for 10-15 minutes before serving. This recipe is adjusted for high altitude. Use 2 packages of yeast for sea level baking.

Yield: 2 loaves

BRECKENRIDGE

How do you imagine a ski area in Breckenridge? You climb Peak 8, mix Cutty Sark with mountain water and dream—just like Trygve Berge and Sigurd Rockne did with Bill Rounds in the late 1950s — and a dream came true. The quaint, nearly deserted mining town of Breckenridge added a small town atmosphere that still lures people here, but now it has paved streets!

THE DERCUMS

Truly remarkable Max and Edna Dercum pioneered two ski areas, Arapahoe Basin and Keystone, and the renowned Ski Tip Lodge. People use words like legendary, irrepressible, industrious, daring, dauntless, awesome, kind and generous to describe them. In the 1940s, they came from Pennsylvania to the rugged west and turned their love of adventure, sport and mountains into a treasured ski legacy.

Pepperoni Pockets

These snacks usually get eaten right away but if there are any left, put some in your pockets for snacking while skiing the next day.

1 package frozen Italian bread, thawed and separated into 30 balls
2-3 sticks pepperoni or salami
1 cup grated cheddar or Monterey jack cheese, optional
1 jalapeno, diced (optional)

1.   Cut pepperoni sticks into 1 inch slices and then into 4 pieces, making 30 pieces.
2.   Wrap balls of dough around pepperoni and if desired add grated cheese and/or jalapenos.
3.   Seal the pockets well; place on cookie sheets and allow to rise, 1 hour.
4.   Preheat oven to 375 degrees.
5.   Bake 20 minutes or until golden brown.

Yield: 30 pieces

Mulled Wine

A cozy mug of this classic hot toddy is perfect for après ski.

2 (750 ml.) bottles of any good dry red wine	16-20 whole cloves
½ cup brandy	6 cinnamon sticks
1⅓ cups sugar or honey	4 teaspoons ground allspice
2 oranges, zested, peeled and sliced	

1.   In a slow cooker or large pot, combine all ingredients.
2.   Warm over low heat for 20-25 minutes; stirring occasionally. Do not allow to boil as alcohol will evaporate.
3.   Leaving seasonings in pot, ladle wine into mugs.

Yield: 10-12 servings

Wild Mushroom and Feta Pâté

The wild mushrooms lend an earthy taste to this meatless pâté.

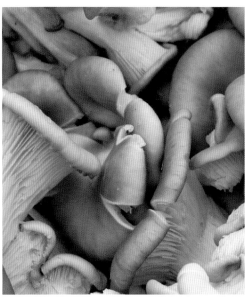

3 tablespoons butter

1 pound assorted wild mushrooms, chopped

2 garlic cloves, chopped

¼ cup chopped shallots

½ cup dry white wine

2 teaspoons chopped fresh or dried thyme

½ teaspoon salt

¼ teaspoon freshly ground black pepper

1 teaspoon white or black truffle infused oil

3 ounces cream cheese, softened

4 ounces crumbled feta cheese

Toasted crostini or crackers

1. Melt butter in large skillet and add mushrooms, garlic and shallots. Sauté until shallots are soft, for 5 minutes.
2. Add wine, thyme, salt and pepper and simmer until most of the liquid has evaporated, about 5-8 minutes.
3. Add truffle oil and cook for 30 seconds.
4. Transfer to blender or food processor and add cheeses; pulse until combined, but do not purée.
5. Adjust seasonings to taste. Refrigerate for 3-4 hours or several days.
6. Serve with crostini or crackers.

Yield: 12-18 servings

Chicken Pesto Bites

For easier preparation, buy a jar of pesto.

CHICKEN:

2 boneless, skinless, chicken breast halves

1 tablespoon black peppercorns

1 bay leaf

1 teaspoon salt

ACCOMPANIMENTS:

Iceberg lettuce

Olives, cucumber slices, baby carrots

PESTO:

1 cup packed fresh basil

¾ cup pine nuts or walnuts

5 garlic cloves

½ cup extra virgin olive oil

½ cup freshly grated Parmesan or
   Romano cheese

¼ cup hot water

CHICKEN:

1. Place chicken breasts in skillet and cover with water.
2. Add peppercorns, bay leaf and salt.
3. Bring to a boil, cover and simmer for 12-15 minutes or until cooked through. Remove from skillet. Discard bay leaf.
4. Chill chicken and cut into ½-1 inch pieces.

PESTO:

1. Combine basil, pine nuts and garlic in bowl of food processor; while processor is running, pour in olive oil in a thin stream.
2. Add cheese as processor is running until mixture is puréed. If thick, thin with hot water.

TO SERVE:

1. In a bowl, mix chicken with 2-3 tablespoons of pesto. Chill.
2. When ready to serve, pile chicken on iceberg lettuce leaves on a platter. Serve with olives, cucumber slices, baby carrots or other vegetables.

SUMMIT WINTER SAMPLER

Take:

Rugged mountains

Snow laden trees

Serene white meadows

Frozen creeks

And fresh tracks

Coat well with gently falling snow

Serve in a bowl, chilled

Yield: 20-30 pieces

COPPPER MOUNTAIN

Not many people can turn a Christmas vacation into the start of a ski area. But Charles Froelicher did just that. In 1968, he set out to find the perfect spot and found Copper Mountain. The US Forest Service praised the area, "If there ever was a mountain that had terrain created for skiing, it would be Copper Mountain."

(*SUMMIT* - Mary Ellen Gilliland)

Tomato Bisque

This soup should be made ahead to enhance the flavors.

¾ cup (1½ sticks) butter	3 cups chicken stock
¼ cup flour	1 teaspoon salt
1 cup chopped onion	½ teaspoon freshly ground black pepper
¾ teaspoon dill seed	¼ cup honey
1 teaspoon oregano	1 cup heavy cream
3-4 cups crushed canned tomatoes	½ cup half-and-half
¼ cup chopped fresh parsley, additional parsley for garnish	

1. Melt butter in stock pot and whisk in flour. Cook over medium heat for 1 minute.
2. Add onion, dill seed and oregano. Sauté until onions are tender.
3. Add tomatoes with liquid, parsley, chicken stock, salt and pepper and bring to a boil; reduce to a simmer for 15 minutes.
4. Add honey, heavy cream and half-and-half and continue to simmer until heated through. Garnish with parsley.

Yield: 6-8 servings

Mixed Green Salad With Fruit

Any prepackaged mixed greens will make this salad easy to fix. Toss and enjoy.

SALAD:
⅓ cup walnut halves or pine nuts
12-14 cups assorted salad greens
2 apples, cored, sliced into wedges
   or oranges sliced into wedges
¼ cup crumbled blue cheese

VINAIGRETTE:
⅔ cup extra virgin olive oil
2 tablespoons balsamic vinegar
¼ cup orange juice
1 tablespoon Dijon-style mustard
1 garlic clove, minced
¼ teaspoon salt
Freshly ground black pepper, to taste

1. Preheat oven to 400 degrees. Bake nuts in pan for about 5 minutes, until lightly toasted, checking often and stirring to avoid burning. Remove from pan and set aside.
2. Combine vinaigrette ingredients in a small bowl and whisk.
3. Fill a large bowl with selected salad greens and when ready to serve, drizzle some vinaigrette over greens and toss lightly. Add more vinaigrette, if needed; reserve remaining vinaigrette in refrigerator for future use.
4. Add apples or oranges, blue cheese and nuts to salad and toss again.
5. Serve at once.

Yield: 6-8 servings

Southwestern Pork Chili

Before hitting the slopes, make this slow cooker dish of pork, vegetables and spices to enjoy later in the day.

CHILI:

1 pound pork tenderloin, cut into 1 inch pieces

1 cup chopped onion

1 green bell pepper, seeded and chopped

1 jalapeno pepper, seeded and minced

2 garlic cloves, minced

1 teaspoon chili powder

1 teaspoon ground cumin

½ teaspoon salt

¼ teaspoon freshly ground black pepper

5 cups reduced-sodium chicken broth

1 (14 ½-ounce) can diced tomatoes, in juice

1 (15-ounce) can pinto or other pink beans, rinsed and drained

GARNISHES:

1 avocado, halved, pitted, scooped out and diced

Chopped cilantro leaves

Lime wedges

1. In a slow cooker, combine pork, onions, bell pepper, jalapeno pepper, garlic, chili powder, cumin, salt and black pepper. Stir to combine.
2. Add broth, tomatoes and beans. Cover and cook on low (6-8 hours) or high (3-4 hours).
3. Ladle soup into bowls and top with choice of garnishes.

Yield: 6 servings

SLOW COOKING AT ALTITUDE

When slow cooking, be sure the temperature is at least 200° F. Do not take the lid off the slow cooker in the first 3 hours to prevent loss of steam and heat.

ULLR FEST

Praising the Norse God of Winter, Ullr Fest hit Breckenridge in 1963 to make below zero tempuratures of January fun. A pretty raucous celebration, Ullr Fest was discontinued for ten years after the 1969 carnival got a little too wild. While more subdued today, the parade retains the original spirit as lively, scantily-clad revelers dare winter elements, blue with cold but wearing playful smiles.

Beef Stew

Freeze this stew and reheat during cocktails for an easy hearty meal.

½ pound bacon slices, coarsely chopped

8 tablespoons extra virgin olive oil

6 pounds trimmed boneless beef sirloin, cut into 1 inch pieces

Salt and freshly ground black pepper

4 leeks, cleaned and coarsely chopped, both white and green parts

6 tablespoons all-purpose flour, divided

1 (750-ml) bottle dry red wine

3 cups low-sodium beef broth

3 (14½-ounce) cans diced tomatoes in juice

3 bay leaves

2 tablespoons chopped fresh thyme or 2 teaspoons dried

2 tablespoons chopped fresh rosemary or 2 teaspoons dried

1 tablespoon paprika

4 large carrots, cut into 1-inch pieces

1 pound small red skin potatoes, halved

1 pound mix of other vegetables (green beans, butternut squash, parsnips, turnips, rutabagas, Brussels sprouts) cut into 1-inch pieces

Salt and freshly ground black pepper to taste

Chopped fresh parsley for garnish, optional

1. In a heavy large pot, cook bacon over medium high heat until brown and crisp, about 8 minutes. Drain on paper towel and transfer to a large bowl.
2. Add 6 tablespoons olive oil to drippings in pot. Increase heat to high.
3. Season beef with salt and pepper and coat with some flour. Working in batches, add beef to pot and sear until brown on all sides, about 4 minutes per batch. Be careful not to crowd the pot with beef or the pieces will not brown. Transfer beef to the bowl with bacon.
4. Add remaining 2 tablespoons oil to pot. Add leeks and sauté until beginning to brown, scraping the brown bits off the bottom of the pan, about 8 minutes.
5. Add 5 tablespoons flour and cook, stirring for 1 minute. Whisk in wine and broth. Add the beef and bacon back to the pot.
6. Add tomatoes with the juice, bay leaves, thyme, rosemary and paprika. Bring to a boil. Reduce heat to medium-low, cover pot and simmer 15 minutes.
7. Add carrots, potatoes and other vegetables (except green beans) and cover and simmer 45 minutes.
8. If using green beans, add now. Uncover and simmer until meat is tender and sauce thickens, stirring occasionally, about 30 minutes.
9. Season stew with salt and pepper to taste. Garnish with parsley.

Yield: 18 servings

Chicken Tagine

Prepare 1-2 days ahead to allow flavors to blend; refrigerate and reheat.

12-16 boneless, skinless chicken breasts, each cut into 6 pieces

2 tablespoons extra virgin olive oil

3 cups chopped onions

6 garlic cloves, minced

2 teaspoons kosher salt

2 teaspoons freshly ground black pepper

2 teaspoons turmeric

½ teaspoon ground ginger

½ teaspoon cayenne pepper

2 cups peeled, seeded, chopped tomatoes

2 cups water

1 tablespoon chopped fresh cilantro

1 tablespoon chopped fresh parsley

⅓ cup halved dried apricots

1⅓ cups golden raisins

2 cups toasted slivered almonds

1. Place chicken in Dutch oven with olive oil, onions, garlic and spices. Toss to evenly coat.
2. Add tomatoes and water and bring to a boil; reduce heat.
3. Cover with lid and simmer 10 minutes.
4. Add cilantro, parsley, apricots and raisins.
5. Remove lid and continue cooking 20-30 minutes.
6. Garnish with toasted almonds.

Yield: 10-12 servings

Corn Spoon Bread

This warm and cheesy side goes well with hearty entrées.

¾ cup cornmeal

1¼ cups all-purpose flour

¼ cup sugar

1 teaspoon baking powder (2 teaspoons at sea level)

½ teaspoon salt

1 (14¾-ounce) can cream style corn

1 cup sour cream

1 cup whole kernel corn (fresh is best)

1½ cups shredded cheddar cheese

6 tablespoons butter, melted

1 (4-ounce) can diced chiles, optional

1 cup milk

1 large egg, beaten

¼ cup canola oil

1. Preheat oven to 400 degrees. Grease a 13-inch by 9-inch baking pan.
2. Blend all dry ingredients together in a large bowl. Stir in the remaining ingredients and stir until well mixed.
3. Pour into prepared pan and bake 30 minutes or until knife inserted into middle comes out clean.
4. May prepare ahead of time; freeze and reheat when ready to serve.

NOTE: This bread is adjusted for high altitude baking. Add 2 teaspoons baking powder at sea level.

Yield: 12-16 servings

IMAGINE: SKIING

Imagine how the early skiers got to the top of mountain bowls. Imagine how they made their way down, floating through untouched powder on long heavy straight pieces of wood with bear trap bindings. Imagine skiing off the top of a deserted miner's shack because you didn't see it coming. Imagination is what drove the skiing industry. And a true love for the sport.

SNOW SCULPTURES

USA Today cites The International Snow Sculpture Championships in Breckenridge as one of the top 10 ways to celebrate winter. In mid-January, teams from around the world apply their proud heritage and creative flair to hand-carve artistic works out of 20-ton blocks of snow. Beyond the experts, everyone gets a vote since there is an award for "People's Choice", "Kid's Choice" and "Artists' Choice".

Double Black Diamond Cake

Black Russian flavoring makes this cake superb with vanilla ice cream.

CAKE:
1 (18½-ounce) yellow cake mix with pudding or moist supreme mix
⅓ cup flour
4 large eggs, lightly beaten
½ cup cold water, plus 2 tablespoons
½ cup vegetable oil
1 tablespoon instant or freeze dried coffee
½ cup vodka
½ cup semi-sweet mini chocolate morsels
½ cup chopped nuts, walnuts and/or pecans

GLAZE:
½ cup (1 stick) butter
¼ cup water
¾ cup sugar
¼ cup vodka
¼ cup Kahlúa liqueur

ICING:
6 (1-ounce) squares unsweetened chocolate, chopped
4½ cups confectioners' sugar
1¾ cups (2½ sticks) unsalted butter, softened
6 tablespoons milk, at room temperature, more if needed
1½ teaspoons vanilla

CAKE:
1. Preheat oven to 325 degrees. Grease and flour a 10 inch tube or Bundt pan.
2. Add cake mix, flour, eggs, water, oil, coffee and vodka to a mixing bowl. Beat vigorously for 2 minutes; then stir in chips and nuts.
3. Pour batter into pan and bake 50-60 minutes or until a toothpick inserted in center comes out clean. Cool, then invert onto plate.

GLAZE:
1. Melt butter in saucepan and stir in water and sugar. Boil for 5 minutes, stirring constantly.
2. Remove from heat and stir in vodka and Kahlúa.
3. Prick top and sides of cake and drizzle glaze evenly over top and sides until glaze is absorbed.

ICING:
1. Place chocolate in a double boiler and heat over simmering water; stir until melted and smooth. Let cool to room temperature.
2. Combine confectioners' sugar, butter, 6 tablespoons milk and vanilla in mixer. Beat on low speed until combined, about 1 minute.
3. Increase mixer speed to medium and beat for 2 minutes.
4. Add melted chocolate and beat on low until combined, then increase the speed to medium and beat for 1 more minute.
5. Add more milk if needed, a teaspoon at a time. Beat icing until creamy but still holds peaks. (Makes 4½ cups icing.)
6. Ice cake. Before icing, cake can be frozen if wrapped tightly.

NOTE: This cake is adjusted for high altitude baking. Omit 2 tablespoons water at sea level.

Yield: 12 servings

Colorado Cookies

This is a simple cookie that includes a favorite food for energy, peanut butter.

½ cup (1 stick) butter, softened

½ cup peanut butter

½ cup sugar

½ cup brown sugar

1 large egg

1¼ cups all-purpose flour

⅓ teaspoon baking soda (use ¾ teaspoon at sea level)

¼ teaspoon salt

¼ teaspoon baking powder (use ½ teaspoon at sea level)

1 (12-ounce) package small peanut butter cups, coarsely chopped

1. Preheat oven to 350 degrees.
2. Cream together butter, peanut butter and both sugars.
3. Add egg and beat until smooth.
4. Mix together flour, baking soda, salt and baking powder and add to creamed mixture. Fold in peanut butter cups.
5. Drop tablespoon-size mounds of dough 2 inches apart onto a lightly greased cookie sheet.
6. Bake for 7-9 minutes or until set but not hard. Allow to cool on a baking rack and store in an airtight container.

NOTE: This recipe is adjusted for high altitude. Use ¾ teaspoon of baking soda and ½ teaspoon of baking powder at sea level.

Yield: 3 dozen cookies

Amen Fudge

This special fudge freezes well and can be made ahead of time for convenience

1¾ cups sugar

1 teaspoon butter

1 (5-ounce) can evaporated milk

1 (12-ounce) package semi-sweet chocolate morsels

3 cups miniature marshmallows, slightly pressed with a cup

1 teaspoon vanilla

1 cup coarsely chopped pecans

1. Spray a 9-inch square glass dish with nonstick spray.
2. Combine sugar, butter and evaporated milk in a heavy 3-4 quart saucepan. Stir over medium high heat until mixture comes to a boil.
3. Turn heat down to create a medium rolling boil and immediately start timing and cook for exactly 5 minutes and 30 seconds (only 5 minutes at sea level). Stir constantly.
4. Remove from heat and quickly stir in chocolate morsels and marshmallows. Mix well and add vanilla and pecans. Pour into prepared dish.
5. Let sit for a few hours before cutting into 64 pieces.
6. Store in air tight container with foil or waxed paper between layers.

Yield: 64 pieces

THE BABES

It just feels good to ski with women friends and to learn together. A program first started in Breckenridge as "Babes on Bumps" by women who believed they could benefit from skiing together. Now it's morphed into wonderful camaraderie. Arapahoe Basin picked up the idea with Legendary Ladies in 2007.

Le Petit Paris

Chef Josh Hall
Proprietor Arielle Lamoure

Pâté de Campagne

Onion Soup

Blanquette de Veau

Crème Brûlée

Molten Chocolate

Le Petite Paris

Bistro ~ Restaurant

You can find a little bit of Paris tucked away in historic Breckenridge on Adams Street at Le Petit Paris Bistro. Once you enter this family run bistro, you feel immediately at home as you are embraced by the gracious hospitality of Arielle Lamoure, hostess and owner.

Pâté de Campagne

PÂTÉ SPICE BLEND

1 tablespoon finely ground bay leaf
1 tablespoon ground cloves
1 tablespoon ground nutmeg
1 tablespoon paprika
1 tablespoon dried thyme
1½ teaspoons dried basil
1½ teaspoons ground cinnamon
1½ teaspoons dried marjoram or oregano,
1½ teaspoons dried sage
1½ teaspoons dried savory
1 teaspoon ground ginger
½ teaspoon ground peppercorns

All spices should be finely ground. Mix together and add ½ tablespoon of fine salt (Sel Melange)

PÂTÉ INGREDIENTS

MiXTURE A
5 pounds pork butt, combination of lean and fatty, cut into large pieces
3 tablespoons salt
½ teaspoon pink salt
¼ teaspoon Pâté spice
Pinch fresh thyme
1¾ teaspoons brandy
½ teaspoon ground black pepper

MIXTURE B
1½ tablespoons finely diced garlic
1 cup finely diced onion
⅓ bunch parsley
¾ pound pork or chicken liver
3 eggs
1½ cups all-purpose flour
5 ounces milk

EGG WASH
1 egg
1 tablespoon water

1. Combine Mixture "A", refrigerate, allow to marinate for one day.
2. Split the mixture into 2 equal parts, coarsely grind each half separately in a food processor or grinder.
3. From Mixture "B", combine the garlic, onions and parsley. Blend until smooth in a food processor.
4. Add the liver and continue to process until well combined.
5. Add the eggs, flour and milk and work until well combined.
6. Combine Mixture "A" to the liver mixture and mix well.
7. Line a pâté mold with caulfat or thinly sliced fatback. Fill the mold with the pâté mixture. Brush the top with an egg wash.
8. Place the pâté in a water bath and cook in a convection oven set at 290 degrees until golden brown.
9. Decrease the temperature to 250 degrees and cook until an internal temperature of 160 degrees is reached.
10. Cool for approximately one day in refrigerator and remove mold.

NOTE: Caulfat is a thin fatty membrane from pigs or sheep and can be ordered from your local butcher.

Yield: 1 Pâté

Onion Soup

5 large onions, peeled and sliced

4 tablespoons (½ stick) butter

1 tablespoon olive oil

2 tablespoons minced garlic

4-5 sprigs of thyme

4-5 sprigs of rosemary

4-5 sprigs parsley

1 cup brandy

6 (12-ounce) cans of beef stock or broth

6 (12-ounce) cans of chicken stock or broth

Salt and pepper to taste

1 baguette

1 garlic clove

1 ½ cups shredded Gruyere or Swiss cheese

1. In a large heavy-bottomed sauce pot, caramelize the onions in butter and olive oil over medium heat. Be sure to stir frequently so the onions will brown and not burn.
2. After the onions are a nice golden brown, add garlic and sauté for 2 minutes.
3. Deglaze the pan with the brandy. Be sure that the heat is off so the brandy does not catch fire!!!
4. Tie herbs with string into a bundle and add to the soup.
5. Add the beef and chicken stock and cook over medium heat until it is reduced by one-fourth. Check seasonings and adjust to taste.
6. Preheat oven to 350 degrees.
7. Slice the baguettes into crostini, approximately ½-inch thick. Brush with olive oil and toast in oven approximately 5 minutes or until golden brown.
8. After the toast has cooled, brush with garlic clove and season with salt and pepper.

TO SERVE:

1. In small oven-safe bowls, place 2 or 3 crostini and add soup. Top with shredded Gruyere or Swiss cheese.
2.. Increase oven temperature to 450 degrees and melt the cheese until it is golden brown.

Yield: 12 servings

Arielle arrived in Breckenridge in 2007 with recipes in hand, and instantly knew the warm and supportive community was the place to start her restaurant. She recruited her sister, Mary Jo Clymo, a trained pastry chef, and niece Carla who add to the friendly atmosphere in this intimate setting.

Sit back, slow down and savor the classic French cuisine that is artfully prepared by Chef Josh Hall. . . and save room for the home made desserts made by Mary Jo.

Blanquette de Veau

4 pounds veal, top-round-cut into bite size pieces

3 tablespoons olive oil

Salt and pepper

2 tablespoons flour

2 onions, chopped into medium dice (¼ inch x ¼ inch)

2 pounds mushrooms

3 garlic cloves minced

¼ cup white wine

6 quarts veal stock

2 cups milk

2 tablespoons butter

5 sprigs of thyme

RICE:

1½ cups white rice

1 tablespoon butter

1 tablespoon extra virgin olive oil

½ white onion, cut into small dice

2 tablespoons white wine

3 cups water

2 bay leaves

1. Preheat oven to 250 degrees.
2. In a large oven-safe heavy bottom pan (10 quarts) heat olive oil.
3. Season the veal with salt and pepper and some of the flour. Sear the veal in the pan with the oil, once browned remove from the pan.
4. Add onions, mushrooms and garlic, cook until tender.
5. Deglaze the pan with white wine.
6. Add veal back to the pan as well as veal stock, milk and thyme.
7. Cover and place in oven for about 3 hours or until veal is fall apart tender.
8. Brown rice in butter and olive oil with onions.
9. Deglaze with white wine. Add water and bay leaves. Bring to a simmer, turn off heat, cover for 15-20 minutes.
10. Uncover and fluff with a fork and adjust seasonings.
11. Serve veal over rice.

Yield: 8 servings

Crème Brûlée

1 quart of heavy cream
1 vanilla bean
9 egg yolks
¾ cup sugar

1. Preheat oven to 300 degrees.
2. In a saucepan, bring heavy cream and vanilla bean to a boil.
3. Remove from heat, discard vanilla bean and let sit for 10 minutes.
4. Whisk together egg yolks and sugar until pale white and sugar is dissolved.
5. Slowly pour the heavy cream mixture into the yolk mixture.
6. Pour the mixtures into small (6-ounce) ramekins and place in a deep roasting pan. Fill pan with hot water three-fourths of the way up the sides of ramekins. Cover with aluminum foil.
7. Bake in oven for 45-60 minutes or until crème is set.
8. Coat the top with sugar and slowly melt with a torch until golden brown.
9. Chill and serve.

Yield: 6 servings

Enjoy a romantic dinner or luscious weekend brunch while absorbing the joie de vivre that vibrates here.

Molten Chocolate

10½ (1-ounce) squares dark chocolate
6⅓ tablespoons butter
⅓ cup sugar
1 tablespoon flour
4 whole eggs
4 egg whites

1. Preheat oven to 350 degrees.
2. In a saucepan, melt chocolate and butter.
3. In a bowl, whisk eggs and egg whites until fluffy, slowly add sugar and flour.
4. Slowly add egg mixture to chocolate mixture.
5. Pour into 6-ounce ramekins and cook 5-10 minutes, checking often.

Yield: 6 servings

Cinco de Mayo

Choose from these flavorful foods to celebrate Cinco de Mayo.

Sangria a la Cesar
Nacho Ordinary Margaritas

Cinco de Mayo Coctel de Salsa
Frijoles con Queso y Tomate
Poblanos Olé
Quiche de Queso

Fiesta Ensalada de Col
Calabacitas
Posole

Sopa De Lima

Camarones con Cilantro y Lima
Enchiladas con Espinacas
Halibut con Salsa

Crema de Frutas Citricas
Torta con Fruta
Tortas de Chocolate

Sangria a la Cesar

If made ahead of time, the flavors will intensify.

1½ liters of red wine
1 tablespoon sugar
1 tablespoon orange juice
2 tablespoons Grand Marnier
1 orange, sliced
1 peach, sliced

1. Mix the wine and sugar in pitcher and stir until dissolved.
2. Add remaining ingredients; stir and chill.
3. Serve sangria in tall glasses over ice and fruit.

Yield: 6 servings

Nacho Ordinary Margaritas

Make these ahead and store in freezer: be sure to serve on the rocks.

1 (12-ounce) can frozen limeade or lemonade
1½ cups tequila
¾ cup Triple Sec
2 (12-ounce) cans Mexican beer
1 lime, cut into wedges

Margarita salt for glass rims, optional
2 lemons, sliced
2 limes, sliced
Green olives for garnish, optional

1. Thaw a can of limeade or lemonade. Pour into pitcher and add tequila and Triple Sec.
2. Add beer and stir. Cover with plastic wrap and freeze.
3. Remove pitcher from freezer and set out for 20 minutes before serving
4. Wipe a wedge of lime around rim of serving glass and then dip into margarita salt.
5. Fill glass with crushed ice and pour margarita mixture into glass.
6. Garnish with lemon and lime slices and green olives.

Yield: 9 servings

DISPEL THE MYTH

A popular myth about Cinco de Mayo is that it celebrates Mexico's independence. Actually, it commemorates Mexico's victory over France at the Battle of Puebla on May 5, 1862. This battle signaled a moral victory for Mexico and proved the country could stand up to powerful foes. Mexico finally won its independence five years later.

Cinco de Mayo Coctel de Salsa

Start with this appealing and nutritious appetizer or first course.

2 medium tomatoes, diced
⅔ cup chopped cilantro, plus sprigs for garnish
3 green onions, chopped
1 garlic clove, minced
1 jalapeno, seeded and minced
1 avocado, halved, pitted, scooped out and diced
1 (15-ounce) can hearts of palm, drained and thinly sliced
2 tablespoons fresh lime juice
¼ teaspoon salt

1. Combine tomatoes, cilantro, green onions, garlic and jalapeno in a bowl. Refrigerate.
2. When ready to serve, add the remaining ingredients and toss gently.
3. Spoon into 6 margarita or martini glasses and garnish with cilantro.

NOTE: This may also be served as a dip with tortilla chips.

Yield: 6 servings or 4 cups

Frijoles con Queso y Tomate

A wonderful dip with black beans, green chiles and tomatoes… ¡Que rico!

2 (15-ounce) cans black beans, drained
½ cup sour cream
1 (8-ounce) package finely shredded Mexican style cheese
1 (4-ounce) can chopped green chiles, drained
½ onion, finely chopped
2 tablespoons salsa, hot variety
1 tomato, chopped, for topping

1. Preheat oven to 350 degrees.
2. Combine beans, sour cream, cheese, chiles, onion and salsa.
3. Place into a 10 inch pie pan or similar size dish.
4. Bake for 45 minutes until bubbly and brown on top.
5. Remove from oven and let cool for 20 minutes to set.
6. Top with chopped tomato and serve with tortilla chips.

Yield: 8-10 servings

WHITEWATER RAFTING

Colorado is known for its excellent whitewater rafting. Rafting companies offer a range of levels, from scenic float trips to heart-stopping challenges for the experienced. May through June offers peak run-offs, but flows vary based on snowpack and weather. Rivers within two hours of Summit county include the Arkansas, Blue, Clear Creek, Colorado and Eagle.

Poblanos Olé

Roasted chiles make this dip an explosion of flavors.

4 medium poblano chiles (sometimes called pasillas)
¼ cup apple cider vinegar
1 tablespoon brown sugar (may use brown sugar blend)
1 tablespoon mustard seed
2 (8-ounce) packages cream cheese, softened

1. Preheat grill to high.
2. Turning as needed, grill peppers until blackened all over. Remove peppers and put in a paper bag; allow to rest for 15-20 minutes.
3. In a saucepan, combine vinegar, sugar and mustard seed. Boil until mixture is reduced in half. Cool.
4. Remove peppers from bag and peel skins, remove stems and seeds (may leave seeds, if desired, for more heat). Finely chop peppers.
5. Combine sauce and peppers; stir in cream cheese. Serve with chips.

Yield: 2 cups

Quiche de Queso

Serve this easy crust-less quiche as an appetizer or as an entrée for brunch or lunch.

4 cups (1 pound) grated Monterey Jack cheese
4 cups (1 pound) grated sharp cheddar cheese
9 large eggs, beaten
1 (5-ounce) can evaporated milk
2-3 jalapeno peppers, seeded and chopped
1 (4-ounce) can chopped green chiles, drained

1. Preheat oven to 350 degrees.
2. Combine all ingredients in a large bowl. Mix well.
3. Pour mixture into a 13-inch by 9-inch greased baking dish.
4. Bake, uncovered for 30-40 minutes or until set.
5. Let stand until cool. For appetizers, cut into 1 inch squares and serve warm or cold. Cut in larger squares for brunch or lunch servings.

Yield: 12 servings

Fiesta Ensalada de Col

Use packaged coleslaw as a time saver.

1 (16-ounce) bag of shredded cabbage
½ cup finely chopped red bell pepper
3 tablespoons sugar, more to taste
½ cup cider vinegar

3-4 pickled jalapenos, finely chopped
2 teaspoons salt
¼ teaspoon crushed red pepper

1. Combine all ingredients.
2. Allow to stand at room temperature for 15 minutes before serving.

Yield: 6 servings

Calabacitas

This squash dish is colorful and tasty for spring-time entertaining.

2 tablespoons extra virgin olive oil
2 tablespoons butter
1 cup finely chopped onion
2 teaspoons minced garlic
2½ cups diced yellow summer squash
2½ cups diced zucchini squash
¾ cup thinly sliced green onions

1 cup (8 ounces) canned sweet corn
1 (7-ounce) can chopped green chiles, drained
Salt to taste
Additional butter, if desired
½ cup shredded Monterey Jack cheese
1 tomato, diced

"Hold out your hands to feel the luxury of the sunbeams."

Helen Keller (author, activist and lecturer, 1880-1968)

1. Heat olive oil and butter in a skillet and sauté onion until softened.
2. Add garlic and sauté for 2 minutes.
3. Add squashes and cook about 5 minutes.
4. Stir in green onions, corn and green chiles and sauté an additional 3 minutes.
5. Season with salt to taste and add additional butter, if desired.
6. Transfer to an 8-inch by 8-inch ovenproof serving dish. Top with cheese and diced tomato. Broil until cheese melts.

Yield: 8 servings

Posole

A perfect dish for those snowy days in May.

2 tablespoons extra virgin olive oil
1 medium-size yellow onion, finely chopped
2 garlic cloves, run through garlic press
1 teaspoon salt
½ pound lean ground beef
½ pound lean ground pork

1 teaspoon dried oregano
2 teaspoons ground cumin
1 cup chopped green chiles
1 (10-ounce) can diced tomatoes
1 (20-ounce) can white hominy with juice

1. Heat oil in large frying pan, sauté onion and garlic until soft.
2. Stir in ground beef and pork; add salt, oregano, cumin, green chili and diced tomatoes. Cook until meat is brown.
3. Add hominy (with liquid) into a large pot. Stir in meat mixture. Cook over low heat for 1-2 hours.

Yield: 8-10 servings

BOEC FUNDRAISER

On Cinco de Mayo, Breckenridge restaurant Mi Casa, hosts a fundraiser to benefit the Breckenridge Outdoor Education Center (BOEC). The Center enables the physically and mentally challenged to enjoy outdoor activity. In winter, participants experience the fun of schussing down slopes in Breckenridge or Keystone. In summer, they join biking, rafting and other wilderness adventures. It's a worthy program dependent on donor support.

Sopa de Lima

A simple chicken soup with plenty of flavor.

1 tablespoon extra virgin olive oil
1 medium onion, finely chopped
8 garlic cloves, minced
4-6 serrano chiles, seeded and thinly sliced
6 cups chicken stock
2 cups cooked, shredded chicken breast
1 large tomato, halved, seeded and diced

4 tablespoons freshly squeezed lime juice, more if desired
6 corn tortillas, cut into thin strips
Vegetable oil to fry tortillas
¼ cup chopped fresh cilantro
1 avocado, halved, pitted, diced, scooped out

1. In a large soup pot, heat oil. Add onions, garlic and chiles and sauté until onions are soft, but not brown.
2. Add stock, chicken, tomatoes and lime juice. Simmer for 15 minutes.
3. Fry tortilla strips in hot oil until crisp. Drain on paper towels.
4. Ladle soup into bowls and top with cilantro, avocado and tortilla strips.

Yield: 4-6 servings

Camarones con Cilantro y Lima

This spicy shrimp entrée is easy to prepare.

MARINADE:
½ cup extra virgin olive oil
3 garlic cloves, pressed
1 teaspoon dried thyme
¼ cup chopped fresh cilantro
½ jalapeno pepper, seeded and minced
1 teaspoon paprika
1 teaspoon kosher salt
1 teaspoon brown sugar
1 teaspoon ground cumin

1 teaspoon Worcestershire sauce
½ teaspoon crushed red pepper
½ teaspoon cayenne pepper
Juice of 2 limes
1½-2 pounds raw, large shrimp, peeled and deveined
1 cup rice, cooked according to package directions
4-6 green onions, chopped
Fresh lime wedges for squeezing

1. Combine all marinade ingredients in a medium bowl.
2. Add shrimp to mixture and marinate in refrigerator for 30 minutes to 1 hour.
3. Place shrimp and marinade in a skillet and cook over medium-high heat until shrimp turn pink, about 5 minutes.
4. Serve shrimp and sauce over rice. Garnish with chopped green onions and lime wedges on the side.

Yield: 4-5 servings

Enchiladas con Espinacas

A distinctive blend of tomatillos and spinach make these enchiladas unique.

ENCHILADAS:

1 teaspoon butter

1 teaspoon extra virgin olive oil

½ large onion, chopped

1 pound mixed mushrooms (cremini, baby bella, white)

1 pound ground meat (optional)

1 (10-ounce) package frozen chopped spinach, thawed, squeezed dry

½ cup bread crumbs

1 teaspoon white pepper

⅛ teaspoon nutmeg

¼ teaspoon chili powder

1 large egg

Kosher salt to taste

2 cups (8 ounces) shredded Mexican blend cheese, divided

12 flour tortillas

SAUCE:

11 ounces fresh tomatillos, husked and quartered

½ cup water

2 serrano chiles, seeded and coarsely chopped

4 garlic cloves, crushed

1 tablespoon extra virgin olive oil

1 small bunch cilantro, chopped

Salt to taste

½ cup heavy cream

THE BEACH AT ARAPAHOE BASIN

Located in the Early Riser parking lot, this stretch of prime real estate is the place to be for spring skiing. Birthday parties and other celebrations are held with crazy costumes and lots of music. Fire up your grill and unfold your beach chairs.

ENCHILADAS:

1. Melt butter and olive oil in a skillet over medium heat. Add onions and mushrooms and sauté until the onions are transparent. Remove from heat and set aside.
2. If using, brown ground meat in a skillet and drain off fat.
3. Place the spinach, bread crumbs, white pepper, nutmeg, chili powder and egg in a food processor and pulse until blended thoroughly; season with salt.
4. In a large bowl, combine onion/mushroom and spinach/bread crumb mixtures, browned meat and 1 cup cheese. Mix well.

SAUCE:

1. Cook tomatillos and water in a saucepan over medium heat, until soft.
2. Combine chiles and garlic in food processor and pulse to chop. Add tomatillos with cooking liquid and process until almost smooth.
3. Heat oil in heavy frying pan and add tomatillo purée. Reduce heat and cook gently, stirring frequently, about 5 minutes, until sauce thickens.
4. Add cilantro and salt. Cook for a few minutes, stirring occasionally.
5. Stir in cream and warm sauce being careful not to boil.

TO ASSEMBLE ENCHILADAS:

1. Preheat oven to 350 degrees.
2. Spoon about ½ cup of filling on one end of each flour tortilla, roll up and place seam side down in a 13-inch by 9-inch baking pan.
3. Pour tomatillo sauce evenly over the enchiladas and sprinkle with the remaining 1 cup of cheese.
4. Bake for 35-40 minutes or until brown and bubbly.

Yield: 4-6 servings

Halibut con Salsa

The glaze makes all the difference and may be used with other white fish.

GLAZE:
6 tablespoons fresh orange juice
6 tablespoons honey
1 medium serrano chile, seeded
¼ teaspoon ground cinnamon

FISH:
6 (5-ounce) halibut fillets, one inch thick, rinsed and dried
Salt and freshly ground black pepper to taste
Cilantro sprigs, optional

SAUCE:
1 large avocado, halved, pitted, scooped out and chopped
2 medium tomatillos, husked and chopped
¼ cup fresh orange juice
¼ teaspoon hot pepper sauce

1. FOR GLAZE: Blend orange juice, honey, serrano chile and cinnamon in blender until smooth. Season with salt and pepper. Can be made a day in advance and refrigerated. Bring to room temperature and stir before using.
2. FOR SAUCE: Combine half of the chopped avocado and half of the tomatillos with the orange juice and hot pepper sauce in blender. Blend until smooth and place in a bowl. Add remaining chopped avocado and tomatillos to the purée. May be prepared 1 hour ahead of time and refrigerated. Bring to room temperature before serving.
3. FOR HALIBUT: May be broiled in oven or grilled on a medium hot grill. If broiling, use lightly greased pan and if grilling, place fish on foil.
4. Make crosswise slits in each fillet about ¾ inches apart and brush with glaze. Season fish with salt and pepper.
5. Place fish under broiler or on grill and cook until fish is opaque but still moist-looking in the center of thickest part, about 8 minutes. Remove and allow to rest 3 minutes.
6. Spoon sauce onto plates and place each fillet on sauce. Garnish with cilantro sprigs.

Yield: 6 servings

Crema de Frutas Cítricas

Serve this lemon and lime pudding in ramekins and top with whipped cream and berries.

2¼ cups whipping cream
¾ cup sugar
3 tablespoons fresh lemon juice
2 tablespoons fresh lime juice

1 teaspoon lemon zest
1 teaspoon lime zest
Whipped cream for serving
Fresh seasonal berries

1. In medium saucepan, combine cream and sugar. Stir until sugar dissolves. Bring to a boil over medium high heat; boil 3 minutes stirring constantly.
2. Remove from heat and stir in lemon and lime juices. Cool 10 minutes.
3. Stir in lemon and lime zests.
4. Divide mixture among six 6-ounce ramekins. Cover with plastic wrap and chill 4-5 hours until set. Best made 1 day ahead.
5. Top with whipped cream and berries.

Yield: 6 servings

CATCH AND RELEASE

Fly fishing in Summit County engages all your senses whether on the Blue, up the Snake or high on a mountain lake. The game begins with the pick of the fly and a great cast. The trout rises to examine the fly; "takes a sip". The alert fisherman sets the hook and makes the catch. Then a gentle toss releases the fish to frustrate the next hopeful fisherman.

Torta con Fruta

Make two cakes and freeze one for future entertaining.

CAKE:
2 cups sugar
2 cups all-purpose flour
2 teaspoons baking soda
2 large eggs
1 (20-ounce) can crushed pineapple
   with juice
6 ounces pecans, chopped

FROSTING:
2 cups confectioners' sugar
1 (8-ounce) package cream cheese,
   softened
½ cup (1 stick) butter, softened
1 teaspoon vanilla
3 ounces chopped pecans for topping

BAKING CAKES AT ALTITUDE

Generously grease and flour cake pans because cakes have a tendency to stick at high altitude.

1. Preheat oven to 350 degrees.
2. Grease and flour a 13-inch by 9-inch pan. If desired, may use two 8-inch by 8-inch pans.
3. Mix sugar, flour, baking soda and eggs. Stir in pineapple and pecans.
4. Bake in oven for 45 minutes or until center tests done.
5. Frosting: Cream sugar, cream cheese, butter and vanilla until smooth.
6. Frost cake fresh out of the oven. Sprinkle with chopped nuts.

NOTE: No altitude adjustments needed.

Yield: 15 servings in 1 large or 2 small cakes

Tortas de Chocolate

Rich little cakes that are full of chocolate flavor.

6 (1-ounce) squares bittersweet chocolate
2 (1-ounce) squares semisweet chocolate
⅝ cup (1¼ sticks) unsalted butter
½ cup all-purpose flour
1½ cups confectioners' sugar

3 large eggs
3 egg yolks
1 teaspoon vanilla
Additional confectioners' sugar for dusting.

1. Preheat oven to 435 degrees.
2. Butter six (6-ounce) custard cups.
3. Melt the chocolates and butter in the microwave or in double boiler.
4. Add the flour and sugar to the chocolate mixture.
5. Stir in the eggs and yolks until smooth.
6. Stir in the vanilla.
7. Divide the batter evenly among the custard cups. Place custard cups on a baking sheet and bake for 14-15 minutes.
8. Using a fine-meshed sieve, dust confectioners' sugar over cakes.

Yield: 12 servings

Food Hedz World Café

Proprietor and Chef David Welch
Proprietor Patti Welch

Fresh Sushi Tuna
Wasabi Soy Vinaigrette

Asian Gaucomole
Homemade Chips

Crab and Lobster Cakes

Chocolate Decadence
Sour Cream Cheesecake

food hedz
world cafe

Executive Chef and proprietor David Welch came to Summit County in 1978 and fell in love with cooking. He worked his way up the ranks as an informal apprentice, learning the discipline of making everything from scratch. Chef Welch rotated among high-scale restaurants in Summit and Eagle counties, and finally landed back at Keystone – this time at The Keystone Ranch, where he was executive chef for nine years and earned Zagat's No.1 rating, three years in a row.

Fresh Sushi Tuna

1 pound of fresh tuna loin, cut into four 4 ounce pieces
1 tablespoon oil

1. Pan sear in oil for 2 minutes on each side. Rare inside.
2. Slice and place over your favorite lettuce mixture that has been tossed in Wasabi Soy Vinaigrette.

Yield: 4 servings

Wasabi Soy Vinaigrette

1 cup light soy sauce
½ cup rice wine vinegar
1 teaspoon chopped garlic
2 ounces chopped fresh ginger
2 limes, freshly squeezed
½ cup sugar
⅛ cup 80/20 oil, or oil on hand
¼ cup sesame oil
¼ cup wasabi powder

1. Combine soy and vinegar in large bowl.
2. Add the garlic, ginger and lime juice.
3. Add remaining ingredients and mix until sugar is dissolved.
4. Let stand for 1 hour before serving.

Yield: 3 cups

Asian Guacamole

3 avocados
½ yellow onion, diced
1 Roma tomato, remove seeds, dice
2 garlic cloves, chopped
1 tablespoon chopped cilantro
2 tablespoons sour cream
¼ teaspoon crushed red chili flakes
1 lime, freshly squeezed
2 tablespoons sesame oil
Pinch black sesame seeds
Pinch white sesame seeds, toasted
To taste salt and pepper

1. Remove avocado flesh from its shell and mash.
2. Add remaining ingredients to avocado and mash till mixed together.

Yield: 4 servings

Homemade Chips

6 corn tortillas cut into triangles
Vegetable oil for frying
To taste salt and pepper

1. Fry in oil at 375 degrees until crisp.
2. Season with salt and pepper. Let cool.

Yield: 6 servings

After decades of cooking behind double doors, David and his wife Patti decided to start Food Hedz World Café, located at 842 N Summit Boulevard in Frisco. He placed himself in an open kitchen, where his customers can tell him exactly how they want their entrées prepared.

Welch serves fresh, high quality cuisine in a casual setting at value prices. The Colorado Hotel and Lodging Association and Colorado Mountain College Culinary School voted him State Chef of the Year.

Crab and Lobster Cakes

1½ yellow onions – diced fine
2 stalks celery – diced fine
¼ each green, red, and yellow bell peppers – diced fine
⅛ cup diced garlic
¼ cup diced ginger
1 carrot – diced fine
80/20 oil (available in grocery stores) or oil on hand
1 cup bread crumbs
5 eggs
1 lemon, freshly squeezed
1 lime, freshly squeezed
¾ cup mayonnaise
1½ tablespoons dry mustard
1½ tablespoons Dijon-style mustard
¾ tablespoon curry powder
¾ tablespoon turmeric powder
½ tablespoon chopped fresh dill weed
½ tablespoon cayenne pepper
1 bunch cilantro, chopped
2½ pounds Dungeness crab
2½ pounds lobster meat
2 tablespoons 80/20 oil (available in grocery stores) or oil on hand

1. Sauté onions, celery, bell peppers, garlic, ginger and carrot in oil until translucent. Set aside.
2. Combine remaining ingredients except crab and lobster.
3. When cool, add cooked vegetables to bread crumb mixture. Gently fold in the lobster and crab. Form into patties.
4. Lightly sauté for 3 minutes on either side. Serve on bread with tartar sauce.

Yield: 20 (4 ounce) cakes

Chocolate Decadence

17 eggs
2 cups sugar
2½ cups cocoa powder
10 ounces chocolate
10 ounces butter

1. Melt chocolate and butter together in microwave, then cool.
2. Whip eggs on high for 3 minutes.
3. Add sugar, mix one minute then scrape.
4. Add cocoa, mix one minute then scrape.
5. Add chocolate, mix 2 minutes and scrape.
6. Pour the batter into a foil lined 8-inch by 8-inch baking pan.
7. Bake in a water bath for 50 minutes at 300 degrees.
8. Cool completely in pan. Carefully take out of pan, foil peeled away. Cut and serve.

Yield: 8 servings

"For me, the key is to see and talk to folks. You need to earn appreciation every single day, all day long," says Chef Welch, so you can be assured that whether taking lunch or dinner at Food Hedz, you'll be impressed. Be sure to say "hi" when you stop by!

Sour Cream Cheesecake

GRAHAM CRACKER CRUST:
¼ pound (1 stick) melted butter
1 pound graham cracker crumbs

1. Melt butter. Add graham cracker crumbs.
2. Press into an 8-inch springform pan.
3. Bake in 350 degree oven for 8 minutes, then cool.

FILLING:
2 pounds cream cheese
1½ cups sugar
6 eggs
1 cup sour cream
1 teaspoon vanilla

1. Using an electric mixer, combine cream cheese and sugar.
2. Add eggs, one at a time, beating well after each addition.
3. Add sour cream and vanilla.
4. Mix until smooth.
5. Pour mixture into prepared crust.
6. Bake at 325 degrees for 1 hour and 15 minutes. Let stand for 30 minutes.
7. Cool for at least 1 hour before serving.

Yield: 1 cake

Bites of Spring

A lovely buffet to celebrate the spring season.

Alpenglow Sunsets

Spinach Mushroom Puffs
Prosciutto Wrapped Scallops with Orange Sauce

Chilled Cucumber Soup

Tomato, Grape and Mozzarella Martini Salad
Chopped Salad in Mustard Sauce

Gratin Dauphinois
Zesty Carrots and Honey
Minty Snap Peas

Pistachio Encrusted Rack of Lamb
Marinated Swordfish

Bow Knots

Apricot Crèpes
Vanilla Panna Cotta with Raspberry Purée
Mud Pie

MOUNTAINS IN SPRING

Come April, there's loads of fun when the sun is warm, the snow is good and the crowds are down. Breckenridge's Spring Massive, a three week festival, and Copper Mountain's Sunsation Weekends offer family fun, mountain competitions, beer and food festivals and music. Arapahoe Basin holds mountain challenges and adventure races. It's time to celebrate the close of the season.

Alpenglow Sunsets

Set the mood for a lavish buffet.

4 cups cranberry cocktail juice
2 cups orange juice
½ cup club soda
¾ cup tequila
Orange slices for garnish

1. Combine juices and club soda in a large pitcher.
2. Stir in tequila and refrigerate until serving.
3. Fill glasses with ice; pour in sunsets and garnish with orange slice.

Yield: 10 servings

Spinach Mushroom Puffs

Irresistible!

1 (10-ounce) package frozen baby spinach, thawed
4 tablespoons butter, divided
4 ounces cremini mushrooms, sliced
Salt and freshly ground black pepper to taste
4 ounces apple smoked Gruyère cheese, grated (can use plain Gruyère)
1 package (17.3-ounce) frozen puff pastry, thawed (2 sheets)
1 egg, beaten
Milk for basting

1. Drain and squeeze moisture from spinach.
2. Melt 2 tablespoons butter and set aside.
3. Melt remaining 2 tablespoons butter in a skillet and sauté mushrooms with salt and pepper to taste. Set aside.
4. Roll out one sheet of pastry squares to a 12-inch by 12-inch square on a lightly floured surface. Cut into sixteen 3-inch squares.
5. Baste melted butter on puff pastry. Sprinkle half of the cheese evenly on pastry squares. Add half of the spinach and mushrooms, leaving a ¼-inch edge.
6. Baste the edge with milk. Fold squares into triangles covering the filling. Crimp and seal edges with a fork. Cut small slits on top to allow steam to escape.
7. Repeat with second pastry sheet and remaining fillings.
8. Place pieces on a lightly greased cookie sheet and refrigerate for one-half to 24 hours.
9. Preheat oven to 425 degrees.
10. Brush top of each pastry with egg. Bake for 18-20 minutes or until the pastry puffs are lightly browned.
11. Cool slightly. Can serve hot or at room temperature.

Yield: 32 pieces

Prosciutto Wrapped Scallops with Orange Sauce

The flavor of orange is a great complement to the dish.

1 pound sea scallops (about 20 large)

5-7 slices prosciutto

1 cup orange juice or tangerine juice

¼ cup balsamic vinegar

1 teaspoon sugar

1 teaspoon grated zest of orange

1. Preheat oven to 450 degrees. Spray baking sheet with cooking spray.
2. Slice the scallops horizontally.
3. Cut prosciutto into strips, ½-inch wide and 4-5 inches long.
4. Wrap each scallop with a strip of prosciutto and place seam side down on baking sheet.
5. Combine juice, vinegar and sugar in a medium saucepan and cook over high heat until thickened, about 15-30 minutes. Add orange peel zest.
6. Place scallops in oven. After 5 minutes, brush scallops with juice mixture. Continue baking until opaque in the center, 2-4 minutes longer.
7. Drizzle scallops with remaining juice mixture.

Yield: 6 servings or 40 pieces

CUCUMBERS

You can't find cucumbers in Cucumber Gulch, but you can find one of the best preserved fens in the area. Fens are unique wetland ecosystems. Thousands of years of accumulated organic material host plant and animal life and act as water filters. Cucumber Gulch, on Peak 8 in Breckenridge, is a lovely area to hike, bird watch, snowshoe and Nordic ski.

Chilled Cucumber Soup

A smooth and creamy chilled soup that looks lovely for spring.

4 large seedless cucumbers, peeled and diced

½ medium onion, chopped

2 ribs celery, chopped

2 tablespoons chopped green bell pepper

3 garlic cloves, chopped

¼ teaspoon freshly ground black pepper

¼ teaspoon seasoned salt

1 teaspoon salt

½ teaspoon dried dill weed

4 tablespoons flour

1 (12-ounce) can evaporated milk, divided

3 cups lowfat (1%) milk

4 tablespoons butter

Chopped dill, chives and ground pepper
   for garnish

1. Place first 9 ingredients in a saucepan and add water to barely cover vegetables.
2. Cover and simmer until celery is tender, about 30 minutes.
3. Purée mixture in a blender until smooth.
4. Combine, in a separate bowl, flour and ¾ cup of evaporated milk. Mix until smooth and set aside.
5. Return puréed mixture to stove and add remaining evaporated milk, milk and butter.
6. Gradually add the reserved flour mixture into the soup and cook, stirring constantly, until thickened.
7. Remove from heat. Cool and chill thoroughly.
8. Garnish with dill, chives and ground pepper.

Yield: 8 servings

Tomato, Grape and Mozzarella Martini Salad

So attractive when served in a martini glass.

1 cup grape tomatoes
¾ cup green seedless grapes
¾ cup red seedless grapes
1 cup kalamata olives, pitted
1 cup mozzarella balls (not marinated)
½ cup extra virgin olive oil
¼ cup dry sherry

Salt and freshly ground black pepper to taste
1 tablespoon minced garlic
Zest of 1 lime
3 tablespoons mint, sliced into thin strips
8 springs mint, for garnish

1. Toss together the tomatoes, grapes, olives and mozzarella balls.
2. In a small bowl, whisk together the olive oil, sherry, salt and pepper. Add minced garlic, lime zest and mint strips.
3. Drizzle vinaigrette over the salad and gently toss.
4. Chill for one to four hours.
5. Serve at room temperature for optimum flavor.
6. Garnish with mint sprigs.

Yield: 8 servings.

SUMMIT SPRING SLUSH

Blend:

Snow melted mountains

Raging rivers

Cloud brushed sky

And lush valleys

Add a generous amount of mud

Serve "Up"

Good for a fever

Chopped Salad with Mustard Sauce

A refreshing combination with a nice crunch.

1 garlic clove
Juice of 1 lemon
1 teaspoon Dijon-style mustard
Extra virgin olive oil
Salt
½ medium sweet or red onion, diced
6 radishes, diced
2 heads Belgian endive, sliced
1 cucumber, peeled, seeded and diced

1 fennel bulb, cored and diced, reserve the fronds for garnish
12-14 cherry tomatoes, cut in half lengthwise
1 avocado, halved, pitted, scooped out and diced
1 head Boston lettuce, leaves separated
Crumbled blue or feta cheese
Freshly ground black pepper

1. Rub garlic clove around bottom of a salad bowl. Squeeze the lemon juice into the bowl; add mustard and enough oil to equal the juice and swirl with a whisk. Season with salt.
2. Toss the next 7 ingredients with the dressing.
3. Serve in individual lettuce cups, garnish with cheese, fennel fronds and pepper.

Yield: 6-8 servings

Gratin Dauphinois

An easy to prepare potato dish that everyone loves.

1 garlic clove, peeled and halved
2 cups whole milk
½ cup heavy cream
2 egg yolks
Salt and freshly ground pepper
2 pounds potatoes, peeled and sliced very thin
4 ounces Gruyère cheese, grated

1. Preheat oven to 375 degrees. Rub the inside of a 13-inch by 9-inch baking dish with garlic clove.
2. In a large bowl, whisk together milk, cream and egg yolks. Season mixture with salt and pepper to taste.
3. Using a large shallow baking dish, layer one third of potatoes, one third of milk and then layer one third of cheese. Press down to flatten. Repeat for second and third layers.
4. Bake in the center of the oven until the potatoes are cooked through and the top is crisp and golden, about 1 hour and 15 minutes.
5. Let rest 5 minutes before serving.

Yield: 4-6 servings

Zesty Carrots and Honey

Cooked carrots never tasted or looked so good.

1 pound carrots, peeling and diagonally sliced into ¼-inch pieces
½ cup orange juice
1 tablespoon lime juice
2 teaspoons butter
½ teaspoon salt
¼ cup water, as needed
⅓ cup honey
1 teaspoon minced ginger
½ teaspoon orange zest
½ teaspoon lime zest

1. Combine carrots, orange juice, lime juice, butter and salt in a 2-quart saucepan. Cook covered over medium heat, stirring often, for 20 minutes until carrots are tender. Add ¼ cup water, if needed, to prevent sticking.
2. Remove from heat and stir in honey, ginger and zests. Mix well and serve warm.

Yield: 4 servings

"You only live once, but if you work it right, once is enough."

Joe E. Lewis (comedian and singer 1902-1971)

IMAGINE: SYLVIA

Sylvia was an 1860s miner's widow who lived in a women's boarding house. Sylvia was a prospector herself, of suitors, not gold. Sadly, she lived out her life alone. Today, the story goes; Sylvia stills resides at the site of the former Breckenridge boarding house, 130 S. Main Street. Local lore suggests she only reveals herself to males, still in hope of finding a mate.

Minty Snap Peas

A quick and easy side dish to serve with lamb.

2 cups (1 pound) snap peas
1 tablespoon extra virgin olive oil
2 cups frozen peas
¼ cup chopped mint leaves
½ teaspoon sugar
½ teaspoon salt

1. In a large skillet over medium heat, sauté snap peas in olive oil. Cook until crisp-tender, about 5-8 minutes.
2. Add frozen peas and cook for 2 minutes.
3. Add mint, sugar, salt and cook for another 2 minutes.
4. Serve immediately.

Yield: 6 servings

Pistachio Encrusted Rack of Lamb

An elegant rite of spring.

2 (8-rib) frenched racks of lamb
1 tablespoon extra virgin olive oil
1 cup panko bread crumbs
1 cup ground pistachios
1 tablespoon minced garlic
1 tablespoon chopped fresh parsley
1 tablespoon chopped fresh thyme
¾ cup Dijon-style mustard
¼ cup crumbled blue cheese

1. Position rack in the middle of the oven and preheat to 425 degrees.
2. Place olive oil in a sauté pan. Add the panko bread crumbs, pistachios, garlic, parsley and thyme. Cook and stir, until crumbs are lightly toasted.
3. Combine mustard and blue cheese in a small bowl and mix well.
4. Spread the racks first with the mustard mixture and then with the crumbs, firmly pressing to adhere.
5. On a baking sheet criss-cross the bones of each rack, meat side up.
6. Roast in preheated oven for 15 minutes or until internal temperature is 145 degrees. Remove from oven, cover with foil and rest for 10 minutes.
7. Carve between each rib and serve two ribs per plate.

Yield: 6-8 servings

Marinated Swordfish

This marinade is quick and easy.

¾ pound swordfish, 1-inch thick

MARINADE:
½ cup soy sauce
2 tablespoons tomato paste
1 tablespoon lime juice
3 garlic cloves, minced

1. Mix marinade in a re-sealable plastic bag.
2. Place swordfish in the bag and coat well. Refrigerate for one hour.
3. When ready to cook, remove swordfish from marinade and discard marinade.
4. Grill fish on a hot grill for 15-20 minutes, turning once.

Yield: 2 servings

"Sit beside a mountain stream—see her waters rise. Listen to the pretty sound of music as she flies."

Mother Nature's Son, Lennon and McCartney

Bow Knots

Pretty and tasty. Serve leftovers (if any!) for breakfast the next day.

TOPPING:
⅔ cup all-purpose flour
⅔ cup dark brown sugar
2 teaspoons cinnamon
¼ cup (½ stick) butter

DOUGH:
3¾ to 4¼ cups flour, divided
½ cup sugar
2 teaspoons salt
1 package (2¼ teaspoons) yeast; (at sea
   level, use 2 packages yeast)
¾ cup milk
½ cup water
½ cup (1 stick) butter, plus additional for
   brushing
1 large egg

1. Mix topping ingredients together until crumbly and set aside.
2. In a large bowl, mix 1½ cups of flour, sugar, salt and yeast.
3. Combine milk, water and butter in a saucepan and warm over low heat to 120-130
   degrees; butter does not need to melt.
4. Gradually add liquid to half of dry ingredients and beat 2 minutes. Add egg and more flour.
   Beat for 2 minutes. Add enough flour to make a stiff dough. Cover bowl tightly with plastic
   wrap and aluminum foil and refrigerate for 2-24 hours.
5. Turn the dough onto a lightly floured surface and divide dough in half. Roll each half into
   a 15-inch by 8-inch rectangle. Along 15-inch side, cut crosswise into strips 1-inch wide and
   8-inches long.
6. Loosely tie each strip into a loose knot. Place on greased baking sheet, brush with melted
   butter and sprinkle on topping. Let rise covered until doubled in size (about 1 hour).
7. Bake in preheated 350 degrees oven for about 12-15 minutes until light brown. Remove
   from baking sheet and cool on wire rack.

NOTE: This recipe is adjusted for high altitude baking. Use 2 packages yeast at sea level baking.

Yield: 30 rolls

SPECIAL THANKS

When the concept of a cookbook was first conceived, Erin McGinnis, of McGraphix Creative, and her team immediately began designing the format. Since then, they have devoted countless hours to the production of this quality book that highlights life in Summit County. Erin's knowledge of our community and her extensive work for the Breckenridge Music Festival have been invaluable to this project.

Apricot Crèpes

Elegant dessert with Grand Marnier.

CRÈPES:

1 cup half-and-half cream
1 cup club soda
4 large eggs
¼ teaspoon salt
1 tablespoon superfine sugar
1 cup sifted all-purpose flour
3 tablespoons butter, melted
½ teaspoon vanilla, almond or
   lemon extract

FILLING:

8 ounces cream cheese, softened
¼ cup (½ stick) butter, softened
2 tablespoons sugar
1 teaspoon vanilla extract
1 teaspoon lemon zest

APRICOT SAUCE:

1 (10-ounce) jar apricot preserves
⅔ cup orange juice
1 tablespoon lemon juice
1½ teaspoons lemon zest
2 tablespoons butter
2 tablespoons Grand Marnier

CRÈPES:

1. In a blender, add cream, club soda, eggs, salt, sugar, flour and melted butter. Blend at top speed for 30 seconds. Scrape down sides and mix again for a few seconds.
2. Cover and refrigerate for at least 2 hours. Stir in vanilla just before cooking. Batter should be a very light cream. If too thick, stir in 1 tablespoon of water to reach desired consistency.
3. Brush omelet or crèpe pan lightly with butter. Set over moderately high heat until pan is just beginning to smoke.
4. Remove pan from heat, pour a scant ¼ cup batter into middle of pan and tilt so batter covers bottom of pan. Return pan to heat and cook for about 1 minute.
5. Turn crèpe over and brown other side, about 30 seconds. This side does not brown evenly; use as the inside of the cèpe.

PREPARE CRÈPES:

1. Preheat oven to 350 degrees. Butter a 13-inch by 9-inch baking pan.
2. In a bowl, blend cream cheese, butter, sugar, vanilla and lemon zest. Spread 1 to 2 tablespoons on each crèpe and fold into quarters.
3. Place crèpes in baking pan and heat in oven for 10 minutes.
4. Remove and serve with apricot sauce.

APRICOT SAUCE:

1. Prepare sauce while crèpes are baking. In a small saucepan, combine preserves, juices, zest and butter. Simmer for 5 minutes. Add Grand Marnier and stir to blend.
2. Spoon warm sauce over the crèpes and serve.

Yield: 8 servings

Vanilla Panna Cotta with Raspberry Purée

A highlight to any special occasion.

PANNA COTTA:
2¾ teaspoons gelatin
½ cup whole milk
3 cups heavy cream
½ cup sugar, to taste
Pinch salt
2 teaspoons vanilla
½ cup sour cream

PURÉE:
2 pints fresh raspberries or 2 bags frozen,
    unsweetened raspberries
½ cup sugar
Lemon juice, to taste
1 teaspoon cornstarch, dissolved in
    1 tablespoon cold water

SPRING THAW

Melting snow rushes to rivers and creeks, and mountain slopes turn to mud. Locals call it Mud Season, a time to get away. But for those who stay, the spring thaw is a reprieve from the flurry of visitors and full schedules. It's time to take a breath and watch the frozen ground give way to a new season.

1. Sprinkle gelatin over cold milk and let stand for 5 minutes.
2. In a saucepan, heat cream, sugar, salt and vanilla. Do not allow to boil. Stir in dissolved gelatin and milk. Set aside to cool for a few minutes.
3. Stir sour cream in a bowl until smooth. Gently whisk cream mixture into sour cream.
4. Rinse eight (6 ounce) ramekins or wine glasses with cold water, shaking out any excess water. Fill each container three-fourths full with the custard mixture. Cover with plastic wrap and refrigerate until firm, at least 4 hours.
5. To make purée, combine raspberries, sugar and lemon juice in a saucepan. Bring to a boil, reduce heat to a simmer and cook until raspberries are very soft.
6. Strain through a fine sieve to remove seeds.
7. Return sauce to the saucepan and cook over medium heat.
8. Dissolve cornstarch in cold water and stir into raspberry sauce.
9. Bring sauce to a boil and cook until slightly thickened, stirring occasionally. Cool in an ice bath.
10. Remove from bath and refrigerate. Top chilled custard with cooled purée. May return to refrigerator until ready to serve.

Yield: 8 servings

Mud Pie

Coffee ice cream can be substituted in this sinfully delicious pie.

1 (6-ounce) chocolate cookie crumb crust; frozen
1 (16-ounce) jar of fudge sauce
1 quart Jamocha Almond Fudge ice cream, softened
1 pint whipping cream, whipped, sweetened with confectioners' sugar
Chocolate shavings, optional

1. Using frozen crust, pour a thin layer of fudge sauce over crust and freeze until hard.
2. Fill frozen crust with softened ice cream. Refreeze until hard.
3. Top with remaining fudge sauce and freeze until ready to serve.
4. Just before serving, top with whipped cream and chocolate shavings.

Yield: 6-8 servings

Nineteenth Hole

After 18 holes, golfers look forward to these fairway favorites and bragging about their scores.

Margaritas Jalapenos

Jalapeno Hotties with Crab
Cheddar Shrimp Nachos
Quandary Quesadillas

Putter's Salad
Grilled Caesar Salad
Gold Run Pasta Salad

Sweet Potato Fries

Keystone Wings
Teriyaki Sliders
The Bogey

Chewy Brownies
Champions' Cheesecake

ATTITUDE

Take your game to new heights on any of Summit County's five impressive golf courses: Breckenridge Golf Club, Keystone Ranch Golf Course, Keystone River Course, Copper Creek Golf Club and Raven Golf Club at Three Peaks. These courses, sculpted into mountains and valleys, offer scenery and views so remarkable that a golfer can enjoy even a bad day off the tees.

Margaritas Jalapenos

Don't hold back on the jalapenos; they make these margaritas special.

2 cups water
1 cup sugar
20 fresh limes, squeezed into large pitcher (about 1¾ cups)
1¾ cups tequila
2 jalapeno peppers, seeded and sliced
Bunch of cilantro, chopped

1. Boil water and sugar for 5 minutes to make a simple syrup. Cool.
2. Mix syrup, lime juice and tequila in a large pitcher. Add 6 slices of jalapenos and a half cup of chopped cilantro.
3. Using a mortar and pestle or a plastic bag and rolling pin, crush remaining jalapenos and cilantro.
4. Salt glasses if desired. Put a tablespoon of crushed ingredients into each glass. Fill with margarita mixture.

Yield: 6 servings

Jalapeno Hotties with Crab

Sweet corn and grilling take the "heat" out of these peppers.

20 - 24 large jalapenos
1 cup lump crabmeat
4 ounces goat cheese, softened
6 ounces cream cheese, softened
1 cup frozen corn kernels, thawed

½ cup chopped green onions, reserve some for garnish
Juice of one lime
Salt to taste
¼ cup tortilla chips, finely crushed
¼ teaspoon chili powder

1. Slice the peppers lengthwise, tip to stem, removing the top third of each. Using a small spoon, scoop out the ribs and seeds. Be sure to wear protective gloves.
2. Combine crab, goat cheese, cream cheese, corn, green onions, lime juice and salt in a bowl.
3. Depending on the size of the jalapeno, generously stuff each with 1-3 tablespoons of mixture.
4. Mix the chips and chili powder and sprinkle on the jalapenos.
5. If desired, may prepare several hours in advance and chill prior to grilling.
6. Preheat grill to medium low and when ready, carefully place peppers side by side.
7. Cook for 10-15 minutes or until slightly charred and firm. Garnish with chopped green onions.

Yield: 12 servings

Cheddar Shrimp Nachos

As the scores are being tallied, serve these warm appetizers.

5 ounces shrimp, peeled, deveined, cooked
 and coarsely chopped
¾ cup shredded cheddar cheese (may use
 Mexican cheese blend)
1 (4-ounce) can green chiles, drained
 and chopped

3 green onions, finely chopped
2 tablespoons coarsely chopped
 ripe olives
3 tablespoons mayonnaise
⅛ teaspoon ground cumin
Corn chips, large scoops

1. Preheat oven to 375 degrees.
2. Combine shrimp, cheese, chiles, onions and olives.
3. Add mayonnaise and cumin and toss to coat.
4. Place a tablespoon of shrimp mixture into each corn chip scoop and place
    on baking sheet.
5. Bake in oven for 5-10 minutes or until cheese melts.
6. Serve warm.

NOTE: Recipe can be halved for smaller groups.

Yield: 30-40 servings

BRECKENRIDGE PUBLIC GOLF COURSE

Breckenridge Public Golf Course is the only municipally owned Jack Nicklaus designed 27-hole golf course in the world. The Bear, Beaver and Elk offer great variety and challenge. With the highest tee box at 9,445 feet above sea level and a club house at 9,324 feet, the course commands spectacular views as players chase their balls up and down 121 feet of elevation change.

Quandary Quesadillas

Frosty glasses of cold Mexican beer go well with these grilled appetizers.

PICO de GALLO:
4 green onions, chopped
1 medium red onion, chopped
3-6 serrano chiles, seeded and minced
5 tomatoes, seeded and diced
Juice of 1 lime
⅓ cup chopped fresh cilantro

QUESADILLAS:
1 (10-ounce) package pork chorizo sausage
1 (7-ounce) can chopped green chiles,
 drained
2 jalapenos, chopped
1 (8-ounce) package shredded Monterey
 Jack cheese
½ cup chopped cilantro
8 (9-inch) flour tortillas
Extra virgin olive oil for brushing

1. In a bowl, combine all ingredients for pico de gallo and mix well. Refrigerate until ready to serve.
2. Cook sausage in a large skillet, stirring occasionally, until meat crumbles and is no longer pink.
3. Prepare grill to medium heat. Lightly brush oil on one side of 8 tortillas.
4. Place 4 tortillas, oil side down, on baking sheet. Distribute crumbed sausage, green chiles,
    jalapenos, cheese and cilantro equally among tortillas. Top with remaining 4 tortillas, oiled
    side up.
5. Grill quesadillas on grill grate until heated through and golden brown, about 3 minutes
    per side.
6. Cut into wedges and serve immediately with sour cream, salsa or pico de gallo.

Yield: 4 servings

Putter's Salad

Ripe tomatoes should always be stored at room temperature.

DRESSING:
1 tablespoon plus ½ cup extra virgin olive oil
¼ cup red wine vinegar
1 tablespoon Dijon-style mustard
½ teaspoon salt
½ teaspoon freshly ground black pepper
1 garlic clove, minced
4 ounces crumbled blue cheese

SALAD:
1 large head red leaf lettuce, torn into bite-size pieces
6 large tomatoes, cut into wedges
18 fresh basil leaves, snipped
8 slices bacon, cooked until crisp and crumbled

1. Whisk 1 tablespoon olive oil, vinegar, mustard, salt, pepper and garlic in a small bowl. Whisk in remaining ½ cup of olive oil. Stir in blue cheese.
2. Combine lettuce, tomatoes and basil in a large salad bowl.
3. Toss with dressing and sprinkle with bacon crumbles.

Yield: 8 servings

Grilled Caesar Salad

Grilling the romaine enhances flavor and tames bitterness.

¼ cup low-fat mayonnaise
Zest of 1 lemon and ¼ cup fresh lemon juice
1 large shallot, roughly chopped
2 garlic cloves
1 tablespoon Dijon-style mustard
1 teaspoon Worcestershire sauce
Dash of hot pepper sauce

½ cup extra virgin olive oil, plus 2 tablespoons
Salt and freshly ground black pepper
10 hearts of romaine, halved lengthwise
3 ounces Parmigiano-Reggiano cheese, shaved

1. In a blender or food processor blend mayonnaise, zest, juice, shallot, garlic, mustard, Worcestershire and hot pepper sauce. With the machine on, gradually add ½ cup olive oil until the dressing is creamy. Season with salt and pepper, cover and refrigerate.
2. Prepare grill to moderately high heat.
3. Lightly brush romaine halves with remaining olive oil and season with salt and pepper.
4. Grill romaine halves, turning once or twice, until lightly charred but still crisp, about 3 minutes.
5. Spread half of the Caesar dressing on a large platter. Arrange the grilled hearts of romaine on top and brush with the remaining dressing. Garnish with the cheese shavings.

Yield: 10 servings

Gold Run Pasta Salad

Fruit pasta can be found at local farmers' markets.

¾ pound small fruit pasta shells, cooked
½ cup raisins
½ cup slivered almonds
½ cup minced celery
½ cup chopped green onions
¾ teaspoon curry powder

¼ teaspoon turmeric
1 cup mayonnaise (or ½ cup each
   mayonnaise and sour cream)
Red bell pepper strips, optional
Blanched broccoli, cut into florets,
   optional

1. In a large bowl, combine all ingredients. Chill before serving.
2. Serve with optional pepper strips and broccoli florets for color.

Yield: 4-6 servings

KEYSTONE GOLF

Two 18-hole championship golf courses, Keystone Ranch Golf Course and the Keystone River Course, sit in the White River National Forest. The Keystone Ranch course, designed by Robert Trent Jones, Jr., combines legendary links style golf with a traditional mountain valley lay out. The River Course follows the path of the Snake River and looks out over distant Lake Dillon.

Sweet Potato Fries

Dip these super easy appetizers in garlic mayo.

5 sweet potatoes, unpeeled, cut into ¼-inch
   wide strips
3 tablespoons extra virgin olive oil
2 tablespoons chopped fresh basil
Coarse salt to taste

½ teaspoon freshly ground
   black pepper
¾ cup mayonnaise
1 garlic clove, minced
1 teaspoon lemon juice

1. Preheat oven to 400 degrees.
2. Place fries on a foil-covered baking sheet; toss with oil.
3. Bake 45 minutes until golden.
4. Combine basil, salt and pepper in a small bowl. Set aside.
5. Combine mayonnaise, garlic and lemon juice in another bowl for dip.
6. Remove fries from oven and sprinkle with basil salt. Serve with dip.

Yield: 6-8 servings

Keystone Wings

These are sure to appeal to the "chicken wing" connoisseur

6 tablespoons chili sauce
3 tablespoons apple cider vinegar
2 tablespoons light molasses
2 teaspoons chili powder

1 teaspoon minced chipotle in adobo
2 garlic cloves, minced
1½ pounds chicken wings
¼ teaspoon salt

1. Combine chili sauce, vinegar, molasses, chili powder, chipotle and garlic in a small saucepan. Bring to a boil. Reduce the heat to low and simmer, stirring, about 3-5 minutes. Remove pan from heat.
2. Preheat grill to medium heat. Spray grate with nonstick spray.
3. Sprinkle chicken with salt and grill, turning occasionally, until browned, about 15 minutes.
4. Brush with barbeque sauce. Continue grilling, turning frequently, until the chicken is deeply glazed and cooked through, 5-10 minutes longer. Remove from grill and wrap in foil to rest 10 minutes.

Yield: 6 servings

ALTITUDE

Some players swear by the laws of physics arguing that golf balls travel farther at high elevations. Thin air imparts less resistance and allows the ball to fly for greater distances. Other players are still waiting for this miracle to occur.

Teriyaki Sliders

Choose spicy mustard or horseradish sauce for your slider.

½ cup vegetable oil	½ garlic clove, minced
⅛ cup honey	1½ pounds flank steak
1 tablespoon chopped green onion	Slider rolls of choice
¾ teaspoon powdered ginger	Spicy mustard, optional
⅛ cup soy sauce	Horseradish sauce, optional
1 tablespoon red wine vinegar	

1. Combine first 7 ingredients in a large re-sealable bag.
2. Place steak in bag and coat well. Refrigerate overnight.
3. Prepare hot grill. Remove steak from marinade and discard marinade. Grill steak 7 minutes per side for medium rare. Remove and let rest 5 minutes.
4. Thinly slice meat on the diagonal across the grain; serve with rolls and choice of condiments.

Yield: 4-6 servings

The Bogey

Here is a twist on the usual BLT that everyone will devour.

12 thick-sliced bacon strips	Salt and freshly ground black
12 slices (½-inch thick) ciabatta bread or	pepper to taste
other bread	Smoked salmon, sliced
Tartar sauce	2 avocados, pitted, scooped out
2 large tomatoes, sliced	and sliced
Lettuce leaves	1 red onion, sliced

1. Fry bacon until crisp and drain on paper towels.
2. On each of 4 slices of bread, spread tartar sauce on 1 side. Top with bacon slices, 2 slices of tomato, lettuce leaves and season to taste with salt and pepper.
3. Spread 4 more slices of bread with tartar sauce and stack on top of lettuce leaves.
4. Make the second layer with salmon slices, avocado slices and red onion slices. Spread remaining bread slices with tartar sauce and place, sauce side down, on top of red onions.
5. Cut sandwich into quarters and use a decorative toothpick to hold together.

Yield: 4 servings

Chewy Brownies

This heavenly dessert is for those people who like fudgy brownies.

¼ cup (½ stick) butter; additional for
    buttering pan
1 cup sugar
2 (1-ounce) squares unsweetened
    chocolate, melted
1 large egg

½ cup flour
½ teaspoon salt
1 teaspoon vanilla
½ cup semi-sweet chocolate morsels
½ cup chopped pecans
Confectioners' sugar

1. Preheat oven to 325 degrees. Butter an 8-inch square baking dish.
2. Cream butter and sugar. Add melted chocolate, egg, flour, salt and vanilla. Stir in chocolate morsels and nuts. Place in baking dish.
3. Bake for 27 minutes. Do not over bake. Remove from oven and sprinkle with confectioners' sugar.
4. Cool and cut.

NOTE: If you double recipe, cook in two 8-inch square baking dishes, not in a 19-inch by 13-inch dish.

Yield: 12 servings

Champions' Cheesecake

Add your personal touch to this impressive dessert with a cherry, blueberry or chocolate sauce.

CRUST:
1½ cups (5 ounces) finely ground
    vanilla wafers
⅓ cup sugar
⅛ teaspoon salt
⅛ teaspoon cinnamon
5 tablespoons unsalted butter, melted

FILLING:
4 large eggs, at room temperature
1½ cups sugar
4 tablespoons flour
¾ teaspoon salt
3 tablespoons lemon juice
¾ teaspoon vanilla
2 pounds cream cheese, room temperature
1 cup light cream (table cream)
Confectioners' sugar

ENVIRONMENTALLY SENSITIVE GOLF

The design of golf courses in Summit County takes ecology to heart. Wetland and natural habitat areas are respected, so while you might lose a lot of golf balls, it's not uncommon to spot wildlife during your round. Beaver, deer and elk, an occasional moose, bear or coyote, and abundant red fox and red tail hawks add game to your game.

1. Mix ground vanilla wafers, sugar, salt, cinnamon and melted butter. Press onto the bottom and one inch up side of a buttered 9-inch spring form pan. Chill crust up to 2 hours.
2. Preheat oven to 325 degrees.
3. In a mixing bowl, beat eggs with mixer for at least 6 minutes, adding sugar slowly. Add flour, salt, lemon juice and vanilla and mix well.
4. In a second large bowl, beat cream cheese with mixer, slowly adding light cream until smooth.
5. Add contents of the first bowl to the second bowl and beat for at least 6 minutes.
6. Pour mixture over chilled crust and bake for 1 hour.
7. Turn off oven, open oven door and leave cheesecake in oven until cool or overnight.
8. Refrigerate at least 8 hours before serving. Sprinkle confectioners' sugar, on top, before serving. May be made up to 2 days ahead. Keep refrigerated.

Yield: 10 servings

Ember

Proprietor and Chef Scott Boshaw

Crab Tamales

Avocado Fondue

Mango Salsa

NEW TO TOWN

The newest restaurant in town, Ember, is housed in a 1914 historic Breckenridge home on Adams Street. You enter a tasteful décor, accented by post modern, contemporary art, to enjoy international fare that is presented by Chef Owner, Scott Boshaw.

Crab Tamales

Enjoy these three Ember delights together.

2 cups masa
½ cup vegetable shortening
1 teaspoon salt
Water, warmed
1 cup crab
4–6 corn husks, soaked in hot water
   for 30 minutes, drain and pat dry

1. In a bowl, mix masa, shortening and salt.
2. Add water until dough feels like wet sand.
3. Massage until smooth.
4. Spread corn husks on counter and leaving 2 inches at the top, spread a 1/8-inch thick layer of masa over center and one side of the husk. Fold the side covered with masa over the center, and then fold the other side over to enclose. Fold down the top flap. Wrap tamale in foil.
5. Steam about 20 minutes in a steamer or pot fitted with a rack.
6. Cut open, add 2 tablespoons of crab per tamale and munch.

Yield: 4–6 servings

Avocado Fondue

1 cup white wine
1 tablespoon lime juice, freshly squeezed
1 tablespoon tequila
1 tablespoon orange juice
4 cups grated cheddar cheese
2 tablespoons cornstarch
3 avocados, peeled, pitted, scooped out and mashed
Salt and pepper

1. In a large saucepan, bring all liquids to a boil.
2. Dust cheese with cornstarch.
3. Add cheese to saucepan and stir to melt. Purée cheese into liquid.
4. Purée avocado into fondue.
5. Season.

The diner is treated to different styles of cuisine from a globally inspired menu. Fish is flown in overnight from around the world to ensure freshness. And two certified sommeliers help you select from a fine list of wines for a remarkable dining experience.

The eclectic atmosphere encourages après ski at the unique bar, a casual dinner with friends or a romantic evening for two.

Mango Salsa

1 tomato, diced
1 mango, diced
1 red onion, diced
½ cup pumpkin seeds
½ bunch fresh cilantro, chopped
1 tablespoon minced garlic
1 tablespoon lime juice, freshly squeezed
Salt and pepper

1. Combine salsa ingredients.
2. Place fondue on plate.
3. Lay tamale atop fondue.
4. Sprinkle salsa over.
5. Crack open Corona.
6. Swing in hammock

Thank You!

We wish to thank the following people for sharing their time-tested recipes, for evaluating the hundreds of recipes we received and for entertaining us in their homes.

RECIPE CONTRIBUTORS:

Leslie Aaholm	Jerry Eaton	Diana Knapp	Crista Povar
Rae Allie	Terri Eaton	Peggy Kornreich	Violeta Powell
Rich Allie	Linda Ebright	Mike Koscso*	Leslie Reardon
Kathy Allitto	Becky Elcan	Georgia Kraatz	Joan Reid
Judy Anderson	Harriet Ellis	Jan Kreis	Rylee Rose
Barb Behmre	Mary Espinosa	Karen Kullby	Jude Rudder
Paige Beville	Amy Evans	Debbie Kullby	Gary Runkle
Susan Biggs	Jan Fahrney	Sandy Kuschnerus	Mary Runkle
Helen Blackburn*	Eileen Finkel	Pat Larson	Jeff Rush
Maria Blong	Charlene Freeman	Evie Lau	John Rynes
Jackie Boroff	Annette Fricke	Maureen Lawer	Caroline Salbaing
Susie Bradley	Jane Gansmann	Jean Lawson	Dianne Sample
Peg Brown	Marge Gavenda	Fran Lazarus	Nancy Sawvell
Abbey Browne	Linda Gibb	Andy Lewis	Barbara Schiller
Chris Browning	Linda Ginsberg	Sally Lewis	Kathleen Schnobrich
Sandy Bruns	Leigh Girvin	Arthur Lock	Andy Searls
Patty Burnett	Judy Goebel	Diane Lock	Jo Ann Shepherd
Valerie Butler	Robert Gordman	Lyn Costello	Spotswood Shotton
Sharon Buzzell	Carol Gosnell	Nancy Macey	Carol Simpson
Sherrie Calderini	Judy Green	Carole Mack	Marte Singerman
Barbara Calvin	Gabrielle Gregory	Joanne Masica	Louise Slater
Claudia Carbone	Martha Griffin	Pauline Masuhr	Ann Smith
Sue Carver	Susie Grossman	Martine Matzke	Grant Soyka
Patti Casey	Linda Hague	Mary Grace McAlister	Gene Sosville
Anne Marie Chapin	Pati Hammer	Mike McCord	Judy Spinney
Vito Ciccone*	Connie Haseloh	Diane McDonald	Evey Statz
Diane Cohen	Mitzie Hawkins	Erin McGinnis	Helga Stone
Jan Coles	Joan Heinle	Annette McGrew	Mickey Sullivan
Karyn Contino	Jo Ann Hess	Josann McKenna	Pat Thomas
Sal Contino	Becky Himpler	Rosalinda Means	Janey Trowbridge
Marsha Cooper	Bill Hirsch	Linda Mirro	Elly Tyler
Barb Corwin	Lynda Hodgson	Lois Montague	Carly Watson
Carolyn Costanza	Pat Hoogheem	Sandra Mortensen	Pam Whitaker
Carolyn Deal	Mary Lou Johns	Judy Mullin	Karen White
Pat DeCarli	Gale Johnson	Judy Murphy	Mary Louise White-
Diana Dettmering	Margorie Julian	Myra Musso	Petteruti
Betty Dixon	Angelique Justich	Sue Nelson	Elizabeth Wickert
Betsy Dobbs	Nancy Karklins	Margery Nemura	Linda Williams
Marilyn Dobbs	Dave Karoly	Pam O'Neil	Ann Wilson
Marie Dodgion	Margie Katz	Elizabeth Packard	Sue Woolley
Maggie Ducayet	Marcia Kaufmann*	Sandi Perlstein	Joyce Yob
Laura Dziedzic	Bonnie Kirschenbaum	Noreen Peschke	*deNOTEs BMF staff or orchestra member*

RECIPE REVIEW COMMITTEE:

Kathy Allitto
Judy Bottomley
Laura Dziedzic
Terri Eaton
Amy Evans
Nancy Karklins
Pam O'Neil
Kathleen Schnobrich
Janet Ulrey
Elizabeth Wickert

RECIPE TESTERS:

CATEGORY HEADS:
Susie Bradley
  Sides
Carolyn Deal
  Entrées
Maggie Ducayet
  Breads
Terri Eaton
  Appetizers
Pati Hammer
  Entrées
Jo Ann Hess
  Soups and Salads
Diane Lock
  Soups and Salads
Kathleen Schnobrich
  Desserts
Evey Statz
  Appetizers

TESTERS AND PARTY SERVERS:

Kathy Allitto
Becky Andrews
Paige Beville
Terri Belver
Maria Blong
Judy Bottomley
Peg Brown
Abbey Browne
Lisa Buck
Patty Burnett
Val Butler
Barbara Calvin
Jan Clark
Jo Copeland

Barb Corwin
Carolyn Costanza
Lyn Costello
Betty Dixon
Marilyn Dobbs
Maggie Ducayet
Wally Ducayet
Laura Dziedzic
Linda Ebright
Mary Espinosa
Amy Evans
Martha Fagan
Jan Fahrney
Gary Galllagher
Marge Gavenda
Judy Goebel
Sheri Goff
Carol Gosnell
Judy Green
Pati Hammer
Jo Ann Hess
Tom Hess
Connie Haseloh
Carol Hjort
Doreen Hofbauer
Pat Hoogheem
Nancy Karklins
Sandy Kuschnerus
Suzanne Lanuza
Jean Lawson
Sally Lewis
Gayle Mayson
Hardy McAlister
Mary Grace McAlister
Joey McKenna
Sue Nelson
Diane Nordstrom
Pam O'Neil
Sandi Perlstein
Kaylon Phillips
Leslie Reardon
Jude Rudder
Mary Runkle
Jeff Rush
Jon Sawvell
Nancy Sawvell
Barbara Schiller
John Schnobrich
Kathleen Schnobrich
Phyllis Shults

Marte Singerman
Gene Sosville
Jay Spencer
Don Sullivan
Mickey Sullivan
Pat Thomas
Janet Ulrey
Nancy Wackman
Carly Watson
Ruby Wendling
Barbara Weis
Liz Wickert
Sue Woolley

LUNCHEON HOSTESSES:

Judy Bottomley
Dareth Newley Bristow
Terri Eaton

DEMONSTRATION CHEFS:

Carolyn Deal
Sandy Kuschnerus

BRIAR ROSE BRUNCH:

Chris Galceran
Ken Nelson
Todd Nelson

TAILGATE HOSTS:

Greg Abernathy
Kim Abernathy
Chuck Calderini
Sherrie Calderini
Douglas Dobbs
Marilyn Dobbs
Dave Karoly
Hardy McAlister
Mary Grace McAlister
Erin McGinnis
Jon Sawvell
Nancy Sawvell

WINE PAIRING HOSTS:

Gene and Dick Sosville

EDITORIAL/SIDEBAR COMMITTEE:

Paige Beville
Doug Brown
Peg Brown
Jerry Dziedzic
Laura Dziedzic
Linda Ebright
Nancy Karklins
Diane Lock
Linda Kay Peterson

SALES COMMITTEE:

Lisa Buck
Barbara Coffey
Jan Fahrney
Nancy Karklins

EDITING/PROOFING:

Paige Beville
Jim Buzzell
Sharon Buzzell
Vera Dawson
Pat DeCarli
Marilyn Dobbs
Maggie Ducayet
Laura Dziedzic
Terri Eaton
Bob French
Judy Green
Nancy Karklins
Sandy Kuschnerus
Sally Lewis
Rob Matzke
Annette McGrew
Nils Nelson
Sue Nelson
Gene Sosville
Mickey Sullivan
Joyce Yob

Index

PHOTO CREDITS
Photography copyright © 2010 by Winsett Photography, Bob Winsett appear on pages: Cover, 18, 19, 22, 26, 27,38, 39, 40, 41, 42, 43, 54, 55, 56, 57, 58, 59, 69, 72, 75, 80, 81, 82, 83, 84, 85, 86, 87, 89, 91, 95, 96, 97, 98, 99, 100, 102, 103, 107, 109, 112, 115, 116, 119, 120, 122, 124, 125, 126, 127, 128, 129, 131, 133, 135, 138, 139, 140, 141, 142, 143, 145, 146, 155, 156, 160, 162, 165, 167, 168, 169, 170, 171, 172, 173, 174, 177, 181, 182, 184, 185, 186, 187, 188, 189, 193, 200, 203, 205, 206, 208, 209, 210, 211; Photography copyright © 2010 by Creative Peaks Photography, John and Linda Mirro appear on pages: 13, 20, 21, 23, 24, 25, 28, 30, 36, 44, 45, 46, 47, 48, 49, 51, 52, 53, 63, 68, 71, 76, 77, 79, 88, 92, 93, 104, 108, 110, 113, 123, 132, 134, 136, 137, 144, 147, 148, 150, 152, 158, 159, 161, 163, 175, 179, 183, 190, 191, 194, 196, 197, 199; Photography copyright © 2010 by Carl Scofield Photography appear on the following pages: 4, 8, 10, 11, 12, 14, 15, 60, 62, 64, 67, Back Cover; Photography copyright © 2010 by Willie Gibson appears on page 16; Photography copyright © 2010 by Joe Kusumoto Photography appears on page: 149; Photography copyright © 2010 by Matt Krane Photography appears on page: 65; Photography courtesy of Summit Huts Association appears on page: 130; Photography courtesy Liam Doran, Firecracker Fifty, appears on page: 29; Photography courtesy Colorado Mountain College, by Ed Kosmicki appears on page: 101; Photography courtesy of Summit Medical Center Health Foundation appears on page: 198; Photography courtesy Breckenridge Golf Club, Head Pro Erroll Miller appears on pages 200, 201, 203; Photography courtesy of the Applause! Cookbook committee appears on pages: 19, 21, 31, 32, 34, 50, 61, 105, 153, 154, 166 .

Live, Love, Laugh, Eat!
ENTERTAINING!
SUMMIT STYLE

Breckenridge Music Festival
Cookbook
P.O. Box 1254
Breckenridge, CO 80424

Phone: (970) 453 9142
Fax: (970) 453 9143
www.breckenridgemusicfestival.com

- If order is sold in Summit County, add 8.275%.

- If order is shipped within the State of Colorado, add 2.9%

- Call with other tax questions.

ORDER FORM:	QTY:	TOTAL:
Entertaining! Summit Style! @ 24.95 per book		$
Colorado Residents add sales tax*		$
Shipping and handling at $5.50 for first book		$
Each additional book shipped to same address is $3.00		$
TOTAL:		$

METHOD OF PAYMENT: ○ MasterCard   ○ VISA

○ Check made payable to Applause!/BMF

Account Number_____ Exp. Date_____

Signature_____

SOLD TO:

Name _____

Address _____

City_____ State _____ Zip _____

Daytime Phone _____ Evening Phone_____

Fax_____ Email _____

SHIP TO: (attach additional addresses)

Name_____

Address _____

City_____ State _____ Zip _____

Thank you for your support!

APPLAUSE!
SUPPORTING THE BRECKENRIDGE MUSIC FESTIVAL